AMERICAN SPACE, JEWISH TIME

AMERICAN SPACE, JEWISH TIME

Stephen J. Whitfield

Archon Books 1988

First published 1988 as an Archon Book,
an imprint of The Shoe String Press, Inc.,
Hamden, Connecticut 06514

Printed in the United States of America

The paper used in this publication meets the minimum requirements
of American National Standard for Information Sciences-Permanence
of Paper for Printed Library Materials, ANSI Z39.48-1984.♾

Library of Congress Cataloging-in-Publication Data

Whitfield, Stephen J., 1942–
 American space, Jewish time.

 Includes index.
 1. Jews—United States—Civilization. 2. United
States—Civilization—Jewish influences. 3. Jews—
United States—Politics and government. 4. United
States—Ethnic relations. I. Title.
E184.J5W49 1988   973'.04924   88-19241
ISBN 0-208-02184-1 (alk. paper)

For Kim and Andrea,
with love

CONTENTS

ACKNOWLEDGMENTS

Every historian dreams of a review akin to that accorded to *Yosippon*, a tenth-century chronicle, written in Hebrew, of the Second Temple period. Tam Ibn Yahia noted that "all the words of this book are righteousness and truth, and there is no wrong within it." The reviewer added, a bit defensively, that "although it is characteristic of historical works to exaggerate things that never were . . . [and] to invent things that never existed, this book, although it is part of the same genre, is nevertheless completely distinct from them . . ."

If there is any truth and righteousness seeping from this book, the criticism and example of estimable colleagues, associates, and friends are in large measure responsible. Those who have helped me, whether by their conversation, their own research and writings, or their gleeful pouncing upon my errors and my misinterpretations, are too numerous to mention. To list all of them would tax the patience of the reader a little too early; my apologies are therefore added to my gratitude. But a special salute must be accorded to Albert S. Axelrad, Richard H. King, Richard S. Tedlow, and Cary D. Yales, for having taught me so much. Some of the chapters have been criticized and commented upon in earlier versions by Steven M. Cohen, Benny Kraut, Howard Marblestone, Alexander Orbach, Jonathan D. Sarna, Marc Lee Raphael, Benjamin Ravid, and Robert S. Wistrich. Though all of these readers are expert in various facets of Jewish studies, they never posted in front of a professor of American

x   Acknowledgments

studies any forbidding signs that warned: "Authorized Personnel Only." The author alone is of course accountable for those errors which remain.

For granting me permission to draw upon those portions of this book that have appeared earlier in different form, I am grateful to the following: the Anti-Defamation League of B'nai B'rith, which published *Jewish Life in America: Fulfilling the American Dream* (1983), for chapter 1; *Modern Judaism* (vol. 6, October 1986), for chapter 4; *Virginia Quarterly Review* (vol. 62, Winter 1986), for chapter 5; *Forum: On the Jewish People, Zionism and Israel* (vol. 56, Summer 1985), for chapter 6; Oxford University Press, which published *Studies in Contemporary Jewry: An Annual, Vol. III: Jews and Other Ethnic Groups in a Multi-Ethnic World* edited by Ezra Mendelsohn (1987), for chapter 7; *American Jewish History* (vol. 75, March 1986) for chapter 8; and the Zalman Shazar Center of Israel, which published *Religion, Ideology and Nationalism in Europe and America: Essays Presented in Honor of Yehoshua Arieli* (1986), for chapter 9.

I am especially thankful to Donald Altschiller for his lore, knowledge, and relentless prodding, and to Hayim Goldgraber for the friendly demonstration of similar attributes. Extra credit is due Steve Antler, whose friendship and technical virtuosity enormously facilitated this work. Typists of the skill and scrupulousness of Heather Hastings, Shirley Meymaris, Grace Short, and Angelina Simeone have set standards worthy of emulation. James Thorpe of Archon Books has been wonderfully receptive to my thoughts on the topic of American Jewry, which he has helped to stimulate; he has made this book possible. Brandeis University has provided a unique vantage point from which to write it, and its scholarly environment remains especially congenial to the composition of a volume of this kind. Special thanks are extended in particular to two colleagues: Lawrence H. Fuchs and Jacob Cohen. The title of this book was graciously provided by Leonard Fein, who has been indulgent with my larcenous habits with his ideas as well.

I continue to cherish a deep sense of indebtedness to my mother and to my late father, for the ideals of Judaism and of learning that they sought to instill. Bernard and Dorothy Cone had nothing directly to do with the composition of this book, with the design of its argument, or with the sifting of its evidence. But I wish to record a certain pride in my status as their son-in-law. My wife Lee has not only offered the encouragement and support that come naturally to a former co-captain of our high school's cheerleading squad. More importantly she has enriched our home with love. In the spirit of the Jewish people and (it so happens) of this book, she deserves to be included among those whom the Prophet Zechariah (9:12) called "prisoners of hope."

1

INTRODUCTION

"The history of the Jews must for ever be interesting," James Madison remarked in a private letter in 1820. "The modern part of it is at the same time so little generally known, that every ray of light on the subject has its value."[1] Ever since the former president made that observation, so much has been written about modern Jewish experience that, even if confined to its American locale, the acquisitions librarians can barely keep up with the pace. So crammed are the shelves of books about the Jews—including their American branch—that perhaps the sin of adding ever so slightly to that literature cannot be palliated. In this case, however, the sense of wonder that I have tried to satisfy must be honored. They are more than a religious group, for it has included those who accept none of its doctrines, observe none of its rituals. Birth alone has sometimes sufficed for membership; therefore, Jewish memories are relevant. They are more than an ethnic group, for it has included those of every race and color and ancestry. Conversion alone has sometimes sufficed for membership; therefore, Jewish beliefs matter too. Such complications guarantee the enduring aptness of Madison's sense of the awesomeness, the poignancy, and the granular oddity of the history of the Jews.

From the grandeur of their scriptures and the boldness of their idea of a deity came the only great universal religions that the world has ever known, Christianity and Islam. Yet the Jews were also deprived for two millennia of their own land, of a government that could be defined as exclusively their own, of the means of physical self-defense, of laws that could be enforced in support of their own values or against their enemies, of a common language apart from that of prayer. It could therefore be assumed that the Jews have lacked the means by which nations are formed and peoples are kept alive. They were indeed often anxious for their own survival.

But they have preserved their rituals and kept their memories evergreen, praying for rain for the crops of Palestine when neither crops nor Jewish settlements were in place there, awaiting the moment of deliverance while keeping intact a sense of themselves as a historical unit. When the nation-states of the West were formed and the cohesive forces of patriotism took hold, the Jews continued to persist as a minority group. As nationalism rose, the power of religion went into eclipse; and modernity has come to mean the end of moral absolutism. All of us came to realize that we would no longer be given a true-false test but instead a multiple choice, especially as Western societies became more tolerant and open. But Judaism itself did not vanish. Even when the terrain shifted from the struggle for the right to be equal to the assertion of the right to be different, the Jews have prevailed. They have remained a puzzle which the historian must often despair of deciphering.

Ever since Abraham left Ur of the Chaldees, no spot on earth has attracted more of his descendants than the United States. Almost six million Jews currently reside here, making 42% of world Jewry of American nationality. And yet they are a statistically insignificant minority within the nation, constituting under 2.5% of its population. If the impression that they have made on the public institutions, the economic foundations, and the democratic culture of the United States is nevertheless so much greater than a glance at their numbers would warrant, that may be due to the more ancient and tenacious heritage which American Jews are both perpetuating and transforming.

That process is the subject of the chapters that follow, which are devoted to the distinctiveness of the Jewish subculture that has been created in the United States. I have not tried to be comprehensive, however; for the aim of this book is to illustrate a theme, not to exhaust it. There are occasions when readers would rather have an author address topics that he knows something about than watch him struggling helplessly to surmount an Everest of material merely out of a sense of duty—because it's there. It is recommended that readers consider this volume one of those occasions.

Those who wish to learn more about the demographic profile of American Jewry, about its family and occupational structure, about its residential patterns are urged to scour elsewhere in the stacks. Readers who are curious about its inner world of organizations, so honeycombed with federations and councils and defense agencies and philanthropies, as well as those readers interested in the spiritual condition of American Jewry, in the renascence of piety and observance among some of the young are similarly advised. These phenomena are undeniably worthy of scrutiny. But I have been frustrated by the effort to write something fresh about them, and can at least take comfort in the availability of many other works on these subjects—and in the eagerness of other scholars to plug the holes in the literature that still remain. Contrary to the fashion in history and the social sciences, numbers and data have been kept to a minimum in this book, largely because their use should be confined to imitators of Al Smith, who could, one of whose staffers claimed, "make statistics sit up, beg, roll over and bark."[2] I would hope nevertheless that the portrait of American Jewry that is presented here is recognizable and novel, plausible and vivid.

Its condition would scarcely be familiar to the forebears of the community even of a few generations ago; and yet it has not entirely been folded into the undifferentiated history of the rest of America, which itself has come to appear increasingly heterogeneous both in the past and the present. But even after allowances are made for the effects of acculturation and assimilation—and for the romantic exaggerations of an allegedly cohesive Ashkenazic Jewry prior to Emancipation—it remains intriguing how continuous the Jewish people has remained in so hospitable and congenial a nation as the United States. The case for that persistence is formulated in the following chapters, which are based on the assumption that the perspectives of both American and Jewish history are necessary to appreciate that distinctiveness. As Americans, Jews have responded differently from other minority groups in their native land; as Jews, Americans are unusual among the communities of the Diaspora. The full case for these twin features of "American Jewish exceptionalism"[3] would require wheeling all the guns of the comparative method into action, utilizing all relevant evidence from both Jewish history and the American experiment. Since our ground time here will be brief, this book is intended only to suggest promising and relevant lines of inquiry.

The record of the American encounter with self-government has continued to justify the belief that here, unlike elsewhere in the Diaspora, minority rights and individual liberties would be secure. The hope that America would be different has been strikingly confirmed. If anything, the past couple of decades in particular have proven how receptive the political system has been to the extension of civil rights and to the incessant quest for a more just society. Although nearly all Americans are Christians, Judaism has been frequently honored as one of the three great faiths; and adherence to it has not only been accepted but also publicly celebrated by both Protestants and Catholics as indigenous to American pluralism. Rabbis are expected to join ministers and priests in blessing or dignifying the rites of popular sovereignty. Earlier fears associated with the specter of "bloc voting" have also evaporated so completely that aspirants to national office require skullcaps for their ethnic rallies almost as much as make-up for their television appearances, and causes such as the defense of Israel and the emigration rights of Soviet Jews are by now almost as uncontroversial as farm subsidies and veterans' benefits.

The Constitutional prohibition against a religious test for public office has permitted Jews to participate in the nation's service to so complete an extent that, if constituents have sometimes had trouble seeing their officials, it may be because Friday the senator left early. Politicians of Jewish birth have held, in one recent legislative session, as many as eight seats in the United States Senate and four times that number in the House of Representatives. In the past two decades or so, Jews have chaired the Council of Economic Advisors, the Federal Reserve Board, and the National Security Council, and headed the Department of Defense as well as the American delegation to the United Nations. They have run the post office and the Department of Transportation, and quarterbacked the negotiating team on arms control with the Soviet Union. Were it not for a scandal involving Abe Fortas, who had a knack for collecting checks the way other citizens collect stamps, a Jew would have become chief justice of the United States in 1968.

Note the contrast from half a century ago, when the Roosevelt administration could elicit so much loyalty from American Jewry without bestowing any equivalent offices or positions upon any of its members, apart from Secretary of the Treasury Henry Morgenthau. A low profile was, it seems, the stance that many Jews preferred anyway. The report that Roosevelt intended to appoint Professor

Felix Frankfurter to the Supreme Court provoked a delegation of distinguished and wealthy Jews to scurry to Washington to urge the president against the nomination in 1939, out of the fear that it would intensify anti-Semitism.[4] That Jewish birth has now become so politically irrelevant is one sign of how fully the American promise of equal opportunity has been fulfilled. Special mention should be made here of Henry Kissinger, whose spectacular career as national security advisor and then secretary of state under Richard Nixon and Gerald Ford seemed to eclipse the reputations of the two presidents who served under him. That a foreign-born Jewish intellectual was designated to represent the United States in negotiations with Chairmen Mao and Brezhnev was unusual enough. But Kissinger captured not only a Nobel Peace Prize but popular sentiment as well; and at one foreign policy breakfast meeting in Chicago, the menu featured the cereal Special K, as though confirming his status in 1972 as the single most admired American, according to the Gallup Poll, ahead even of the president, ahead even of Billy Graham. The contestants for Miss Universe in 1974 even voted Kissinger "the greatest person in the world today."[5]

In only one respect did public policy seem to abrogate the promise of equal rights. The principle of affirmative action, by which no citizen could suffer discrimination on account of race, national origin, or sex, was sometimes implemented in a way that was indistinguishable from the establishment of quotas. Such implementation seemed to violate standards of fairness in the assessment of individual promise and performance. Many Jewish organizations and communal leaders opposed what they considered a distortion of the aim of ensuring justice in a pluralistic society. But whatever the extent of such preferential hiring practices, most Jews have favored affirmative action as such—70% in 1984, for example, well ahead of the rest of the population. Indeed, almost a fourth of the American population even supported job quotas for minorities as a way of levelling the playing field.[6] In any event, the general status of Jews in American society so far appears to have been unaffected. Impressionistic evidence suggests that Jews may even have indirectly benefited, since so many Jewish women have been poised to take advantage of academic and professional opportunities that the assault on sexual discrimination has widened.

The openness of the public culture to the aspirations of individual Jews and to the practice of Judaism is astonishing enough, in contrast to the melancholy history of earlier Diaspora communities. The extent to which civil rights and liberties have been enlarged in recent decades has elicited pride as well as gratitude. To an unprecedented degree, Jews have been able to move freely within the larger society, and the opportunity to pursue individual happiness has beckoned as never before. Yet despite the abolition of public discrimination and the Constitutional guarantee of freedom of association, about two-thirds of American Jews still form their closest friendships with other Jews.[7] The process of acculturation may have blurred distinctions between Jews and their gentile neighbors, but a sense of peoplehood has not been entirely suppressed.

For what binds many Jews to their ancestors and to their co-religionists overseas has not disappeared; the threads of continuity may be frayed, but they have not snapped. Even when the God of their fathers has been abandoned, the cooking of their mothers has been remembered. Even when the cooking of their mothers has been forsaken, Jews in the United States have invented alternatives, like lox and bagels—a treat which has become so supremely American that the billboards of Eastern Airlines proclaim that bagels are integral to the "power breakfasts" served on its flights. Even when ancient harvest festivals like *Succot* and *Shavuot* are minimized and the commemoration of the destruction of the Temple in Jerusalem ignored, eight out of every ten American Jews still participate in some sort of Passover *seder*.[8] Most Jews still assume that the identity of other Jews matters, that they share what the Germans call a *Schicksalsgemeinschaft*—a "community of fate." However delicately and indefinably, connections can still be made and felt, as Kissinger himself discovered during negotiations in Israel after the Yom Kippur War. At least according to apocrypha, he informed Golda Meir: "You've got to understand that first I'm an American, then I'm a Secretary of State, and only then am I a Jew." "We understand," Mrs. Meir is supposed to have responded, "but you should know that here we read from right to left."

If Jews tend to form such close bonds with other Jews, that may be because, though the American populace has increasingly located itself in urban areas, the Jews are in this respect even more American. Over 95% of American Jewry reside in a city or its immediate surroundings, and four Jews out of every five live in only ten population centers. One out of every three Jews still lives in the New York area, but Los Angeles has replaced Chicago as the second largest concentration of Jews in the United States.[9] In fact, since more Jews prefer to live in Los Angeles than in Tel Aviv (despite the similarities which satirists

have observed), the California city has become the second largest
Jewish community in the world. Newer Sun Belt communities have
also been established in places like Palm Springs, of which the comedian Mort Sahl remarked back in the 1950s: "You've got to admire
those people, carving out a nation in the desert." By the 1990 census,
it is likely that Miami will top Philadelphia as a center of Jewish
population; and the shift to the Southeast and Southwest is likely to
affect the character of Jewish life in ways that are not easy to foresee.

Though Americans live about as comfortably as any people on the
planet, the Jews are even more fortunate in their escape from the
poverty that pervaded the life of the *shtetl* in Eastern Europe. Their
ascent in such numbers into the upper tax brackets is another sign of
their conspicuousness within the class structure of the United States.
At the dawn of the twentieth century, according to one government
report, the typical Jewish immigrant from Eastern Europe landed
with $9.[10] Not all of these refugees from autocracy and misery were
abjectly and abysmally poor, but, as one of their folk sayings had it,
they only ate chicken if they were sick, or the chicken was. But even
when most Jews belonged to the working class, they tended to encourage middle-class ambitions among their children. With parents cher-
ishing the hope that their children "won't have to work in a shop,"
even in the garment trade unions Jews have been more likely to
remain among their leaders than their members. In Boston, for
example, the rate of upward mobility among Jews was double that of
other ethnic and racial groups.[11]

The children and grandchildren of the immigrants had become so
firmly entrenched in the middle class, and often the upper middle
class, that Jews now rank near or above certain Asian-American
groups in affluence. Average Jewish incomes exceed those of the
Episcopalians and Congregationalists who founded most of the New
World colonies over three centuries ago, and is 72% above the national
average. Even more oddly, even when compared to others of similar
social characteristics such as years of education, Jewish families still
earn more.[12] Even in families with no one working, Jewish families
earn more. In recent estimations of the richest millionaires, there are
a few Italian-Americans, one black, no Hispanic; but about a quarter
are Jews, who are almost entirely self-made, in contrast to the many
Protestants who made the list through inheritance.[13] Yet for all the
economic rewards bestowed upon the Jews, deprivation persists; and
its presence is at regular intervals rediscovered. According to 1973
and 1981 surveys, about 15% of New York's Jews were living at or

near the poverty level; and figures elsewhere are comparable. The rapidity of the ascent is nevertheless what is so dramatic about the condition of Jewry in the United States. The executive director of the American Israel Public Affairs Committee, Tom Dine, has wondered aloud what his grandmother would think of a situation in which Senator Jay Rockefeller comes to these grandchildren of penniless immigrants in order to raise funds. As the Brazilians say, money whitens.

How does social science account for such spectacular upward mobility? One theory which should not be immediately discounted is that Jews are simply more talented than other peoples. Their gifts could flourish especially after the walls of medieval ghettos tumbled, after the isolation of the *shtetlach* was punctured, as centuries of frustrated energies were suddenly left behind and formidable powers of adaptation to modernity were revealed within a couple of generations. The belief in the superiority of the Jewish "race" can be found not only in the grandiose pronouncements of Benjamin Disraeli, but also among nineteenth-century writers less susceptible to romanticism. Nietzsche, for instance, acknowledged the Jews' "energy and higher intelligence, their accumulated capital of spirit and will, gathered from generation to generation through a long school in suffering." Thus Nietzsche explained their preponderance in modern society. Mark Twain was impressed by the "marvellous fight in this world" that the Jew had made, "with his hands tied behind him." Even at the dusk of the nineteenth century, the Jew was "exhibiting no decadence, no infirmities of age, no weakening of his parts, no slowing of his energies, no dulling of his alert and aggressive mind." Exceptional accomplishment was therefore the predicate of exceptional talent, and anti-Semitism the consequence of envy aroused by "racial" superiority. "To hear some people talk these days," Milton Himmelfarb of the American Jewish Committee wrote in 1969, "one would think that the merit principle is a Jewish conspiracy."[14]

But whatever tribute the testimony of Nietzsche and Twain pays to Jewish self-esteem, it leaves unexplained why Jewish influence is more pronounced in some fields rather than others, why Jews gravitate toward some occupations and leave others untouched. Even if all forms of ethnic and racial discrimination in the United States were to be miraculously obliterated, the nation's occupational structure would probably not reveal a random distribution of minorities. Their experiences and values are hardly identical, and therefore their predispositions and interests can in the aggregate be expected to diverge. A ubiquitous bumper sticker in Boston proclaims that God invented whiskey to prevent the Irish from ruling the world. Neither talent nor intelligence can be summoned at random, to be enlisted and developed whenever a barrier of discrimination is battered down.

The precondition of status and prosperity, many Americans have believed, is education—an article of faith to which the Jews have subscribed even more ardently. The nation's schools have long been noted for their efforts to accommodate the masses. But it would scarcely be possible for more Jews to be attending college than at present, since over six out of every seven of them of college age can currently be found on campus.[15] Even though the distinguished psychologist Henry Goddard had, as a result of testing immigrants at Ellis Island, declared 83% of the Jews to be "feeble-minded,"[16] Jews seem to have become more cerebral. They are more likely than their gentile neighbors to hold advanced degrees, and to have entered the professions—one of which is education itself. By 1970, the proportion of Jews serving on university faculties was over three times their percentage of the general population. And the better the reputation of the university, the more likely Jews were teaching there; in the most prestigious institutions of higher learning, 30% of the faculty is Jewish.[17]

The transformation of the Ivy League into the "oi-vey league" deserves to be put into historical perspective. In 1936 the director of admissions at Yale College reported to its president, James R. Angell, that over a third of the 10.9% of Jewish students came from New Haven, Bridgeport, and Hartford. "It seems quite clear," President Angell replied, "that if we could have an Armenian massacre confined to the New Haven district with occasional incursions into Bridgeport and Hartford, we might protect our Nordic stock almost completely." A Yale dean of the era complained that "a few years ago every single scholarship of any value was won by a Jew. . . . We could not allow that to go on. We must put a ban on the Jews." He therefore peppered the director of admissions with a query about an incoming freshman class: "How many Jews among them? And are there any coons?" Early in the 1930s one of those undergraduates, a commuter named Eugene Victor Rostow, had considerable justification for publishing an article denouncing this "ancient prejudice" at Yale, though the institution was hardly the worst offender among the elite private colleges.[18] Over two decades later, Rostow had become dean of the Yale Law School. Within the past generation, Jews have become presidents of several Ivy League colleges and of other distinguished universities, and they have remained disproportionately represented in the nation's scientific elite.

Even as Americans have continued to dominate the international competition for Nobel Prizes, Jews have become laureates with astonishing frequency. It is odd that the feverish anti-Semitic imagination had not located the center of the international Jewish conspiracy in Stockholm. Or perhaps it ought to be located at the Bronx High School of Science, which has produced more Nobel laureates in physics than entire countries like Italy or France or Japan—to say nothing of smaller nations. Among them is Steven Weinberg, who has taught elementary particle physics at Harvard and has organized physics seminars at the Hebrew University of Jerusalem. When the University of Texas was still gushing with oil revenues, it felt the urge to staff its Department of Physics with a Nobel laureate of Professor Weinberg's eminence. To lure him down from Boston to Austin, it allowed him to fill three tenure-track positions. It is only a little surprising that the University of Texas also reputedly offered him a salary roughly commensurate with the university president's. But what is truly mind-boggling is that the university reportedly made him an offer within striking distance of the salary of the varsity football coach.[19] Other Jews have continued to receive honors in the sciences and medicine, and have won almost half the total number of Memorial Prizes that Americans have earned in economics. The last three American Nobel laureates in literature have been Saul Bellow (1976), Isaac Bashevis Singer (1978), and Joseph Brodsky (1987). Since the Second World War the saga of cultural and intellectual life in America would scarcely be intelligible without acknowledging the contributions of Jews in virtually all the arts and perhaps most branches of learning.

Because of the speed with which talented Jews injected themselves into the general society, a sensation akin to being shot from cannons, American Jewish culture could never be far from its own demotic origins. One of the peculiar charms of the world of the *shtetl* was that lowly occupations did not prohibit its progeny from harboring intense religious, spiritual, intellectual, and aesthetic aspirations. It is startling to realize that Zachar Segal, the humble father of Marc Chagall, made a living by packing herring. Equivalents could be found in the New World as well. The father of the Canadian novelist Mordecai Richler sold scrap, the father of Philip Roth sold insurance in black neighborhoods, the immigrant father of Leonard Bernstein sold beauty-shop supplies—and continued to doubt that music was an avenue of financial security, at least compared to beauty-shop supplies. Samuel Bernstein, who really knew only of the itinerant *klezmer* musicians who played at weddings and *bar mitzvahs*, therefore kept a place open in the business for Lenny even after he had become his country's embodiment of musical genius.[20] The grandfather of the art critic Harold Rosenberg was a ritual circumciser (*mohel*), which does not account for the brilliance of Rosenberg's analysis of modern sculpture. When Aaron Copland told his immigrant parents on Washington Street in Brooklyn that he wanted to become a composer of classical music, his father, who worked in a department store, asked: "Where did you get such a strange idea?"[21] Such examples could be easily multiplied. They help explain why artists of Jewish origin could have negotiated their way so successfully through popular forms, and have continued to exert a considerable influence on the national imagination through their roles as entertainers and entrepreneurs in popular culture.

A noticeable change has occurred in recent decades, however. The fresh appreciation of ethnic differences that began in the mid–1960s has included the celebration of Jewish identity in many best-selling novels, in serious analyses of *Yiddishkeit* (Jewishness) such as Irving Howe's *World of our Fathers* (1976), in musicals like *Fiddler on the Roof* (1964), and in other cultural artifacts too numerous to mention. No longer would most Jews wish to emulate the comedian who admitted to have "cut off my nose to spite my race." Indeed, the exotic appeal that ethnicity offered to the participants in mass culture has sometimes even seemed to put the dominant groups in the society on the defensive. Nelson Rockefeller found it advantageous to ventilate hints of his admittedly distant Jewish ancestry; Caroline Kennedy marched down the aisle (of a church) with a Jew; a character in the film *Pete 'n' Tillie* (1972) emphasizes his one-fourth Jewish ancestry because "I'm a social climber." John Updike even wrote a couple of novels skillfully impersonating a Jewish literary celebrity named Henry Bech. Dr. Spielvogel's most notorious patient also notices the historic transformation in the status of the Jews. "For every Eddie [Fisher] yearning for a Debbie [Reynolds]," Alexander Portnoy realizes, "there is a Debbie yearning for an Eddie—a Marilyn Monroe yearning for her Arthur Miller—even an Alice Faye yearning for Phil Harris. Even Jayne Mansfield was about to marry one, remember, when she was suddenly killed in a car crash?" And even the child star of *National Velvet*, "this stupendous purple-eyed girl who had the supreme *goyische* gift of all, the courage and know-how to get up and ride around on a horse," married Mike Todd (né Goldbogen).[22] The pop singer Linda Ronstadt, growing up in Arizona, has recalled the effect of reading Herman Wouk's *Marjorie Morningstar* (1955) as a teenager: "It screwed me up about love and romance and everything. But I loved it then, and it made me wish I was Jewish."[23] By the mid-twentieth century in the most rambunctious society on earth, the Jew was no longer alone in the corner eating the dip.

Such signs of inclusion and affirmation were all the more exhilarating, amusing, and strange because of the radical insecurity that had dogged the history of the Diaspora. The earlier generations who dreamed of an open society also feared arousing the adversaries of freedom; and the children and even grandchildren of immigrants hoped that homogenization would bring placidity, if not security. An extreme instance of the anxieties of the "Diaspora mentality" can be found in the career of the German refugee scientist Karl Landsteiner, who discovered the A, B, AB, and O blood groups and therefore won a Nobel Prize in 1930. He filed an injunction against the editors of *Who's Who in American Jewry*. They had dared to mention his Jewish extraction, which might, he feared, "cause . . . mental anguish, pain or suffering to . . . members of my family." Were his nineteen-year-old son, kept ignorant of his Jewish antecedents, to see his father's name in the forthcoming edition, "it would be a shock to him and might subject him to humiliation."[24] But in the benign American climate since then, punctuated by the social and military achievements of the state of Israel, Jewishness has ceased to be a source of shame. One could almost say—were it not a delicacy that Jews are supposedly forbidden to eat—that the world has been their oyster.

The ease of American Jewry in the decades after the Second World War coincided with the moral and psychic burden that the irreparable losses of the Holocaust imposed. For nostalgia and sentimentality were not the only responses that the Jewish past evoked; and the memory of the most desolate chapter in all of Jewish experience has come explicitly to the surface only within the past couple of decades or so. When the 1960s began, the term "Holocaust" was barely, if at all, in circulation; and the catastrophe to which it referred was only infrequently mentioned. It was as though a numbing had been inflicted too painful for American Jewry to acknowledge, a wound too deep for language itself to start to heal. But even then that reaction to the murder of most of the Jews of Europe was beginning to be replaced by a more direct grappling with the nightmare of the

Holocaust, and within the past generation a confrontation with the ineffable has begun to occur that has hardly run its course.

Here books were probably decisive. At the beginning of the 1960s, the memoir of a survivor of Auschwitz and Buchenwald was translated from the French; and beginning with *Night*, Elie Wiesel became the best-known and undoubtedly most articulate witness to attempt to impose his memories and visions of the horror that American Jews had been lucky enough to escape. It was one index of his impact that he later became chairman of a government-sponsored Holocaust memorial council—and one sign of Jewish self-assurance that, a few feet away from the president of the United States, Wiesel publicly rebuked Ronald Reagan in 1985 for honoring the memory of the S.S. men buried in Bitburg cemetery.[25] In 1961 Raul Hilberg's *The Destruction of the European Jews* became the first major work in English to take scholarly account of the disaster. The memoirs, histories, films, television programs, plays, poetry, and fiction that have been published thereafter defy tabulation. They also challenge the capacity of ordinary, decent, common-sensical readers and audiences to absorb their message.

But writers were not alone in haunting the consciousness of American Jewry. In 1960 Israeli agents captured Adolf Eichmann in Argentina. The following year he was put on trial in Jerusalem, and in 1962 a hangman executed the former S. S. lieutenant-colonel who had been responsible for transporting the Jews of Nazi-occupied Europe to their deaths. The judicial procedures and revelations not only seared Israeli society but also helped make it possible for the Holocaust to haunt the agenda and the idiom of organized Jewry in the United States. Whether in the curriculum of Jewish education, whether in observance of *Yom Ha-Shoah* (Holocaust Remembrance Day), whether in forums and symposia and speeches reverberating through the institutional life of American Jewry, the recollection of how over one-third of world Jewry—including a million children—was extinguished has become an inextricable part of the Jewish mentality in the United States.

How deeply this sense of cataclysm had become embedded was revealed in 1967. Early in June the threat that Arab encirclement posed to Israel seemed to call into question once more the capacity of the Jewish people to survive, and the Six-Day War tapped fears that once again American Jewry would be unable to help beleaguered brethren to avert a Holocaust. That war was probably a turning point in modern Jewish history, primarily because the stunning victory of the Israel Defense Forces made it possible for Jerusalem to be reunited under Jewish sovereignty, and because the West Bank and Gaza fell under an occupation that still defies a political solution. The war also disclosed how central the welfare of Israel had become to the destiny of the Diaspora.

To be sure, the levels of American *aliyah*—immigration to Israel—have remained persistently low, so subterranean in fact that far more Jewish bodies that are going permanently from New York to Israel have been dead than alive. According to the most recent figures (1985), more New York Jews have been sent for burial in *eretz yisroel* (387), mostly on the Mount of Olives in Jerusalem, than have gone to live in the Holy Land (76).[26] Such preferences are an extraordinary rebuke to classical Zionist ideology. But they do not mean that Jewish hearts beat no differently than anyone else's in the United States. During and after the 1967 war, Jews discovered—perhaps more poignantly than they had realized—how devoted they were to the perpetuation and security of the state of Israel. Abraham Joshua Heschel of the Jewish Theological Seminary felt that during the crisis immediately before that war, as well as during it, "all of Jewish history was at stake. . . . The anxiety was grueling, the isolation was dreadful . . ." The preeminent Jewish spiritual thinker then added these astonishing words: "I had not known how deeply Jewish I was." Rabbi Richard Rubenstein also felt "surprise over the depth of my own feelings. There are unconscious depths to the phenomenon of Jewishness which even those of us who have spent our lives in its study cannot fathom."[27] No wonder then that support for Israel has remained the most urgent cause around which American Jewry, for all its disparate tendencies, has rallied.

The Six-Day War also inaugurated an outpouring of philanthropic support that was unprecedented in the annals of American Jewish generosity. Sustaining that level of philanthropy has remained the formidable challenge of the fund-raising agencies—and the envy of other American charities. But that challenge has generally been met. The annual budget of the United Jewish Appeal, for example, is one-third the budget of the national United Way (to which Jews of course also contribute). In 1981 the UJA raised $543 million, and in 1982 received pledges of $567 million. Such figures need to be placed in comparative perspective. The United Jewish Appeal raises more money per year than the combined efforts of the American Cancer Society, the American Heart Association, the Muscular Dystrophy Association, the March of Dimes, and the National Easter Seal Society.

The reasons for such generosity are too complex to be recorded here, but solicitors who work through the primary agencies of Jewish philanthropy, the federations from the 227 communities that constitute the Council of Jewish Federations and Welfare Funds, attribute pride in Israeli accomplishments as an important motivation. American Jewry also freely elects to tax itself to support the young and old, the ill and the needy, under the auspices of social welfare institutions throughout the United States. Many contributors have also expressed their conviction that only viable Jewish institutions can combat unfavorable sentiments in the United States, and that since the terrible ordeal of the Second World War American Jewry could not be dormant while brethren were in danger.[28]

Another effect of the Six-Day War was to arouse sentiments of Jewish nationalism within the USSR. At the beginning of the 1960s, the fate of Soviet Jewry seemed sealed, and was absent as an item on the American Jewish agenda. But in the aftermath of the Israeli victory, some Soviet Jews wished to dramatize their plight by attempting to "hijack" a plane from Leningrad. They were captured, tried, and convicted in 1970; but they stirred the admiration of other Soviet Jews and troubled the conscience of many of their American co-religionists. Pressures within and outside the Soviet Union led its government to relax its grip on Jews seeking to emigrate to Israel and to the West. Since 1970 over a quarter of a million Soviet Jews have managed to emigrate, although that grip tightened again early in the 1980s and only with *glasnost* was somewhat relaxed. The march that attracted over 200,000 American Jews to Washington immediately before the Gorbachev-Reagan summit conference in December 1987 was far in excess of any of the anti-Nazi rallies held in the 1930s and 1940s, and a measure of how taut the bonds with Jews overseas have remained.

To varying degrees most American Jewish institutions have taken an interest in the struggle of Russian co-religionists to emancipate themselves. That interest resonated within the American government itself, when the Jackson-Vanik amendment of 1973–74 and the Helsinki agreement of 1975 linked the bestowal of most-favored nation status on the Soviet Union to the relaxation of emigration restrictions. Although American Jewish activists have widely regarded Soviet compliance as unsatisfactory, such efforts reflected the political effectiveness of a tiny minority whose own position in the United States was so secure that it could devote itself to the assistance of Jewry abroad. Another instance of the capacity of American Jews to communicate their concern was the swap of prisoners in 1979, which demonstrated the commitment of the Carter administration to human rights. The FBI had arrested two Soviet spies operating on American soil. The spies were exchanged not for Americans in Soviet custody but for five Soviet nationals who were political prisoners, including two Jews convicted in the Leningrad trial nine years earlier. For American diplomacy to consider the lives of non-American citizens so precious was a pointed contrast to its failures before and during the Holocaust. The episode was nevertheless an inspiring breakthrough for the human rights movement, in which the influence of American Jews has been decisive. Memory and hope thus conspired to spur the struggle for *pidyon shevuyim* (the release of captives), and the combination of bitter recollections and idealistic moralism is probably the most succinct description of the distinctive political impetus of American Jewry.

Its dedication to liberalism has also incorporated feminism, surely one of the most pervasive and important of the social and political causes to have erupted in the United States within the past generation. If any one book was responsible for igniting the revival of feminism, it has been *The Feminine Mystique* (1963) by Betty Friedan (née Goldstein), who remembers her own upbringing in terms of the advice: "You were supposed to marry the doctor, not *be* one."[29] Other women of Jewish birth have been prominent in both the moderate and radical wings of the movement, and have made an incalculable impact upon the very texture of national life. The Jewish world has also been affected. The Reconstructionist seminary accepted women ever since its founding in 1968, and the Reform movement ordained rabbis beginning with Sally Priesand in 1972. Amy Eilberg became the first Conservative rabbi when the Jewish Theological Seminary ordained her in 1985. Women have won increased responsibilities in all the religious movements, including Orthodoxy. Organizations dominated by female volunteers have continued to affect Jewish life; Hadassah, for example, has been the largest women's voluntary organization in the United States, period.[30] Sexism has nevertheless long been embedded in Judaic culture, not only within its religious doctrines and observances but also within its historic traditions, for the assumption of hierarchical sex roles has also been woven into the fabric of the societies in which Jews participated. "When the hen starts to act like the rooster, it's time to call for the *shochet* [the ritual slaughterer]," goes one piece of Yiddish marital and family counseling. In the transformation of such attitudes, Israel has helped as well in the promotion of egalitarianism. The contributions of women to its *kibbutzim* and to its defense forces were part of its international image, and one popular American feminist poster showed a photograph of Prime Minister Meir above the caption: "But can she type?"

The liberality and progressivism of so much of American Jewry have given it a singular political subculture. And yet it has become evident that exercising the freedom to be different has not irritated bigots, who have remained on the discredited perimeters of the social order. In the era after the Second World War, and in the wake of the Holocaust, anti-Semitism has enjoyed no respectable constituency, and has been widely understood to be both undemocratic and un-American. Vandals nevertheless still perpetrated synagogue and cemetery desecrations, and demagogues have publicly uttered epithets and canards. Such bigotry has been disreputable; and even the contemporary political figure who has done the most to revive it, the Reverend Jesse Jackson, would certainly not want a phrase like "He Warned America Against the Jewish Conspiracy" inscribed on his tombstone. But even though civil rights groups and defense agencies have learned to assume that their victories may not be permanent, even though many Jews still surmise that familiar expressions of anti-Semitism are not confined to the remote past, the very limited scope of such prejudice has been a noteworthy—and praiseworthy—facet of the American scene.

Public opinion polls have also consistently shown a large reservoir of good will among gentile Americans towards the state of Israel. Since President Anwar Sadat's visit to Jerusalem in 1977, Egypt has been the sole Arab state to galvanize comparable expressions of benevolence and trust. The sharp criticism of Israel voiced in international forums, particularly the United Nations, has nevertheless vexed and angered so many American Jews that anti-Zionism has appeared a greater menace than traditional versions of anti-Semitism. Indeed, since pro-Israel sentiments are so integral to the political and psychological orientation of American Jewry, anti-Zionism increasingly came to be defined as anti-Semitism. This definition is one clue to the importance that American Jews have continued to attach to the legitimacy and security of the only member of the community of nations whose existence has seemed open to debate. The political attacks upon its sovereignty and viability could not be easily separated from the history of earlier forms of hostility to Jewry, and the most important of Diaspora communities has therefore felt a special intimacy and concern for the fate of Israel.[31] If anything, American Jews

have historically been far better attuned to the problems of persecution overseas than to the challenge that their own special identity
might pose at home.

But even the most benign account of their recent past must be
tempered by recognition of a demographic danger. Looming large in
the history of the Jewish people, its American component is nevertheless faced with possible depletion of its human resources; and ever
since the early 1960s, omens about the survival of the community
itself have been sounded.

Three factors have commanded attention. American Jewish history
could be told in terms of the waves of immigration that have not only
washed across the nation itself but have also replenished the life of
this particular community. Only about two thousand Sephardim lived
here during the Revolution; and the second wave of German Jews was
large enough to check some of the effects of assimilation, even as the
far more massive wave of Eastern Europeans performed the same
function by the turn of the century. Immigrants from the Soviet
Union, Israel, and Latin America also arrived here in the 1960s and
1970s, but they have registered a less significant impact than their
predecessors. The Holocaust devastated the source of further immigration and obliterated precisely those communities where Jewish
religious and cultural life was most creative and radiant. American
Jewry will therefore be required to perpetuate itself.[32] Of course the
consulates have not shut the gates. From Montreal and Teheran and
Buenos Aires, some Jews have still been coming. Even Guy de Rothschild landed here in 1982, when the Mitterand government national-
ized his bank. The baron, who may have been down to his last $30
million (apart from his homes, his art collection, his vineyards, and
his stud farm), arrived alongside the boat people in quest of economic
opportunity and security.[33] Such colorful cases should not be mistaken for revitalization. From now on, American Jewry cannot expect
to be nourished, as in the past, by other Diaspora communities, where
the forces of secularization and assimilation might have been more
retarded than here.

The second factor is the birth rate. Jews have been admired for
many attributes—their industriousness and their intelligence, their
economic skills and their ethical curiosity. Planned parenthood organizations should also honor them for achieving what amounts to
zero population growth in the past couple of decades. Jewish families
may not be philoprogenitive enough to hit the standard replacement
level of 2.1. However exemplary the practice of limiting children once

was in accelerating the ascent from poverty, however similar this practice has been among other families in the urbanized and educated middle classes, the Jews' efficiency in methods of birth control has instilled fears about group survival itself.[34]

The third factor is the most uncertain, the most problematic, the least susceptible to a policy consensus within the community itself: intermarriage. An increasing tendency toward exogamy has characterized all significant ethnic and religious minorities as succeeding generations have come to maturity in the United States. Nevertheless, according to one sociologist, Jews "do out-marry somewhat less frequently than other major white ethnic groups (such as Italian or Irish Catholics) in similar generational, social class, and residential circumstances."[35] Only in the last two decades has the increase in intermarriage rates been so dramatic that panic buttons have been pressed. In a few major cities in the Sun Belt, more Jews marry gentiles than marry other Jews; and the current national rate seems to be hovering between one-fourth and one-third.[36] Such rates demonstrate the degree to which Jews have become integrated within the host society, the extent to which accidents of birth have not hampered the national promises of self-fulfillment, the pursuit of happiness, and romantic love. Like Jay Gatsby, Jews too have wanted to pick out the green light at the end of the dock. From such patterns may be inferred the disappearance of distinctive traits separating Jews from their neighbors—or the opposite, since Jewish partners may be valued in the marriage market because of a reputation for stability and sobriety, for being good providers and good homemakers. But whatever the reasons, many rabbis and other communal leaders have warned that the pool of Jews from which gentiles can select eligible mates may be fated to suffer serious depletion.

Rabbi Alexander Schindler of the Reform movement has therefore urged his fellow Jews to reconsider their traditional reluctance to proselytize. It is no longer a capital crime, as it was in the Roman Empire under Constantine and his successors, to convert a gentile to Judaism. It is no longer hard to be a Jew, despite the folk wisdom of Diaspora history, at least in the United States; and many "Jews by choice" have come to savor the pleasures of that identity and try to meet the challenges of its faith. So much vigor has often been injected into Jewish religious life as a result that Milton Himmelfarb has quoted the generalization of one rabbi who has supervised many conversions: "Our imports . . . [are] better than our exports—and, perhaps, better than the average of our domestic market, too."[37] But rates of conversion to Judaism have not been high enough to spike fears that the Jewish community is dangerously shrinking. Rabbi Arthur Hertzberg has argued that the erosion of Jewish life in the United States has been checked only by renewed immigration, or by outbursts of anti-Semitism. The unlikelihood of either instigation to remain Jewish has led Hertzberg to answer the question of American Jewish survival in the negative: "History, sociology, and the emptiness of contemporary Jewish religion all point in the same direction."[38]

But not all the precincts have reported; all the evidence that needs to be sifted has not been gathered. The demographic profile may set certain limits, but it cannot determine with any precision how American Jews invigorate their heritage or exploit their resources or activate their ideals. History is not only a combat zone in which abstract forces struggle remorselessly and impersonally; it is also subject to the vicissitudes of collective will, to the power of human agency. It is not a trajectory that can easily be extrapolated from data, for history is nothing more than the incomplete and barely legible minutes of the last meeting—not a mandate that binds the future. It is therefore reassuring that some of the most astute analysts of American Jewish life do not need to invoke the mystique of a chosen or eternal people. Several of their most nimble sociologists and demographers and historians manage to appeal to the evidence of a resilient and persevering people; such scholars do not give the impression that they are participating in any deathwatch. For those who do not believe that a nation without Jews would be a better one, some comfort can be gained from the exemplary self-abnegation of Casey Stengel: "I never make predictions, especially about the future."

Whatever its destiny, this minority has already left its skid marks. For American Jews have exerted an extraordinary impact upon the character of the United States, and have achieved a synthesis of their citizenship and their peoplehood that must fascinate the student of Jewish history as well. The political history of other nations is pock-marked by rulers with sobriquets like Ivan the Terrible and Pedro the Cruel and Vlad the Impaler. American schoolchildren by contrast are supposed to revere such early leaders as George Washington, who promised the members of the Newport, Rhode Island synagogue that the new government would offer "to bigotry no sanction, to persecution no assistance,"[39] and James Madison, the father of the Constitution, who studied Hebrew on his own, and who helped erect a wall of separation between church and state that has been such a blessing—and not only to Jews.

No reader needs to be reminded that the past is burdened with ample enough evidence of pain and waste, of the needless suffering and blasted hopes that have proven to be the fate of our entire species. But human struggles and aspirations have sometimes been rewarded too, and here the American experience is relevant. For it also suggests that promises can be at least partially fulfilled, injustices can be combated, some human betterment need not be restricted to the imagination of a world to come. That is why history need not be a source of despair but can also be its antidote.

2

THE PAST AS PROLOGUE

Just before midnight on July 3/4, 1976, a team of Israeli commandos stormed Entebbe airport in Uganda to rescue 83 Israelis, 20 French Jews and the crew of an Air France airliner, all of whom had been hijacked a week earlier by a group of Palestinian and German terrorists. Though the commander of the unit, Lieutenant-Colonel Jonathan Netanyahu, was killed, as were two hostages, the episode was an epiphany. "The story of the raid, of the escape by plane of the surviving hostages and their rescuers, and of the safe return of the whole party . . . to Israel . . . broke as a sensation almost without parallel in the postwar world," wrote the British military historian John Keegan, who compared it to the assassination of President Kennedy. "It came as news which would recall ever after to the hearer the place, time, and circumstances in which he learned it, so complete was its unexpectedness." Keegan added: "But unlike the news from Dallas, and so heightening its impact, was the quality of improbability, mystery, almost fantasy that it carried with it. The world had speculated for a week on the terrorists' intentions, [Idi] Amin's complicity, and the likelihood of a massacre. It had simply not entertained the notion that the Israelis might bring off a rescue. And even after they had done so, the raid continued to seem a piece of wizardry, of mythic legerdemain in the tradition of Ulysses against Cyclops, rather than an act of war."[1]

One element that affected the sensation that the raid generated was also its date—the coincidence that the news broke amid the Bicentennial celebrations that were then punctuating Independence Day in the United States. It must be acknowledged that July 4, 1976 was not a moment to warrant much of a sense of satisfaction—much less complacency—in American history. Only two years earlier an unindicted co-conspirator had been forced to resign the office of the presidency, or face impeachment. Only a year before the Bicentennial, Saigon had become Ho Chi Minh City, highlighting the collapse of an American policy that for over a decade had failed to stop the advance of Communism in Vietnam. Given the attention riveted on Indochina and the national honor that was committed, the horrible and pointless loss of over 55,000 American dead and the wounding of over 300,000 other Americans, and the squandering of well over $200 billion to pay for the war, seemed a bleak disaster that was unprecedented in American history. Unforeseen over the horizon that Bicentennial day was the Iranian hostage crisis and the ignominious failure of an American rescue mission in 1980, its helicopters smashing into one another in the desert. In the aftermath of this nadir of American will, the secretary of state resigned in protest against the *excessive* force with which his government had tried to rescue its citizens. Cyrus Vance had also objected to the sheer impracticality of the operation that President Carter, in a weird euphemism, deemed "an incomplete success."[2]

America resembled a wounded civilization at the very moment in which its destiny seemed so conspicuously intertwined with Israel's. Indeed, Colonel Netanyahu was himself almost as much an American as an Israeli. For he was born and partly raised in the United States, and educated not only in Jerusalem but at Harvard; and even in Israel he was briefly associated with Brandeis University. The fact that his father, an editor of the *Encyclopedia Judaica*, was a professor of Jewish history at Cornell, teaching and exploring the subject to which the son's gallantry was to contribute, is an invitation to consider how both the histories of Americans and Jews have been understood, how their respective pasts have differed, even as those differences illuminate their singular features. Even as their destinies as democracies in a world filled with tyrannies have become increasingly connected, even as the capacity to define and defend their interests in a hostile world remains problematic, even a sketchy examination of how Americans and Jews have penetrated the meaning of history may be instructive.

The complications of this topic are not reduced by acknowledging that the American and Jewish heritages are not entirely separable entities. In fact, they slightly overlap, making comparisons treacherous. Jewish culture in the Diaspora has never been utterly isolated or immune from the influences of host societies. The point need not be belabored, for example, that German Jews after their emancipation came increasingly to resemble other Germans even as they distanced themselves from Eastern European Jews, who differed even more strikingly from, say, Jews living in Arab lands. In the United States it is impossible to exclude some sort of Jewish involvement from any full account of its culture, if only because of the Judaic roots of Christianity itself. Even before barely more than a few Jews immigrated here, the Puritans had identified themselves with the Israelites of the Old Testament; and colonial students at Harvard and Yale were probably more facile in Hebrew than most of the Jewish students enrolled in those institutions today. A developing pluralism has long been receptive to the disproportionate contributions of the Jewish minority of the American population, so that a rigid separation of Jewish and American attitudes toward the past risks oversimplification.

A generalization can nevertheless be proposed that the Jews have lived between memory and messianism, to which it is tempting to juxtapose Americans who have lived between amnesia and nostalgia. It would be more fair to note that Americans have been somewhat deficient in what Nietzsche called the sixth sense—the feel for history. That is why the Jews who live *in* America have sometimes developed complicated responses to the twin legacies that have been bequeathed to them. Such in any case is the argument that is advanced in this chapter.

I know of only one previous attempt at comparison, Daniel Boorstin's essay on "A Dialogue of Two Histories," which was published in *Commentary* in 1949. He eloquently argued for a respect for diversity rather than submission to the trope of homogenization, and was critical of the official stances of defense organizations, which "have seemed more anxious to prove the Jewish title to a share in authentically American culture than to discover how they are qualified to enrich it." Boorstin stressed three key divergences of orientation. One is toward time, of which the Jews have experienced an abundance and which the Americans have compressed. Take only one phase of Jewish history—from, say, the emergence of Hillel to the consolidation of the Babylonian Talmud: it is double the span of all of American history.³ The contrasting brevity of the American past can be suggested by a couple of examples. The commander of Allied forces in the Pacific at the birth of the atomic age was General Douglas MacArthur (1880–1964), whose earliest military memory consisted of marching to the Rio Grande to guard against Geronimo's Apaches. The secretary of war who ushered in the nuclear era was Henry L. Stimson (1867–1950), whose great-grandmother had reminisced with him of her own childhood conversations with George Washington.⁴

Boorstin added that "the characteristic arena of American history has been *nature*, while that of Jewish history has been *society*." Americans have defined their experience in terms of conquering the land, even if such memories were transformed into metaphors like the New Frontier. By contrast, in the hamlets in which Eastern European Jews resided, life was with people, and there in the *shtetlach* "Jewish history . . . revealed . . . potentialities for survival among other men, however different . . . they have been or have thought themselves to be." Finally, Boorstin noticed a difference in orientation toward others. By confronting their enemies directly, Americans have tended toward a sensibility that emphasizes "the simple and measurable[,] . . . stunting . . . the sense of paradox and of that awareness of evil that goes with it." The Jews of the Diaspora have instead lived surrounded by enemies; and feeling besieged forced them to look to God or to themselves, promoting a sensibility of complication and moral exploration. Boorstin did not argue that American Jews were any less American because they were Jews, only that they should "accept a double inheritance . . . [and] the burden of an inner tension."⁵

But scintillating and suggestive as Boorstin's essay is on the topic of how Jewish and American histories differ, he did not consider how Jews and Americans have reflected upon those differences, how their attitudes *toward* history have crystallized.

One effect of Entebbe was to heighten consideration of the oddity of Jewish history. For the raid served as the most spectacular proof of the re-introduction of the Jewish people into historical action, after nearly two millennia as a peculiarity, a moribund aberration. Though the Jews had survived their exile, they seemed bereft of the attributes of peoplehood as nationalist ideology had ordinarily come to define it. Throughout their dispersion, they were an anomaly. The Jews were identifiable enough to suffer persecution, from the pogroms of the Middle Ages to the Holocaust that has come to haunt the contemporary imagination. But in the Diaspora the Jews were not free to establish a polity that could bind them into a people. Though they were often brave enough to accept martyrdom for their faith and were often penalized for believing in their God, they were rarely strong enough to defend themselves against massacres. Though the Talmud codified a ferociously intricate set of laws governing all phases of conduct, enforceable legislation could not necessarily be passed within their own community. Though they revered a single book, they lacked a common vernacular through which national aspirations might be expressed. Any interest in an independent political destiny was frustrated.

With the Roman destruction of the Second Temple, a scholar named Yohanan Ben Zakkai shaped the meaning of exile by establishing an academy at Yavneh. He had escaped from the besieged city of Jerusalem by hiding himself in a coffin; and Diaspora history ever since seemed enclosed in the carapace of death, so devitalized did its external condition appear. That husk of imminent mortality nevertheless concealed an eerie will to endure. But the story of the Jewish exile has been so singular, so replete with helplessness and so devoid of overt political action, that some scholars refused to designate this experience as a field of history at all. A founder of the *Wissenschaft des Judentums*, Leopold Zunz, subscribed to this view, failing to appreciate Jewish resilience as an appropriate historical theme. For with the destruction of the Jewish state, the survivors and their descendants had supposedly performed no acts for historians to record. History, Franz Kafka implied, could be defined as the annals of gentiles. A character in a recent Israeli novel is more talkative on the subject: "We never made our own history; the gentiles always made it for us. Just as they turned out the lights for us and lit the stove for us and milked the cow for us on the Sabbath, so they made history for us the way they wanted; and we took it whether we liked it or not."[6]

This theme was repeated—and then elaborated upon—by Hannah Arendt, who argued that, as a pariah people, the Jews had developed a heightened sense of human fraternity, or *menschlichkeit*—goodness, integrity, decency. But they also paid a price, in "so radical a loss of the world, so fearful an atrophy of all the organs with which we respond to it—starting with the common sense with which we orient ourselves in a world common to ourselves and others . . . that . . . we can speak of real worldlessness." Lacking "a world to win," a field of action, the Jews were subjugated to the will of others, instead of becoming protagonists in the drama of history. They were (perhaps) a chosen people, but not a choosing people.[7] Sir Lewis Namier, who was the pre-eminent historian of eighteenth-century British parlia-

mentary and imperial politics, as well as himself a paradoxical combination of Anglican convert and Zionist activist, once de-legitimated
the very subject of Jewish history. Instead, Namier reductively proclaimed, there was "only a Jewish martyrology."[8] Thus two of the
most original thinkers to have emerged from the Jewish people in this
century devalued the very course of that people's destiny.

In recent years the denial of the existence of the subject has been
replaced, on occasion, by denial of its importance. An example of
indifference is manifest in *History* (1965), a magisterial survey that the
Council of the Humanities of Princeton University commissioned. It
was written by Leonard Krieger, Felix Gilbert, and John Higham,
himself a gentile who has made distinguished contributions to American Jewish history, especially the study of anti-Semitism. Yet this
volume contains nothing about Jews or their past. As Lucy S. Dawidowicz has incisively pointed out, "the authors discuss every kind of
history imaginable—ancient history and urban history, agricultural
history and institutional history, Chinese history, Islamic history,
Latin American history, but not Jewish history." Numerous scholars
are mentioned—but not Salo W. Baron, who taught Jewish history for
thirty-six years as a chaired professor at Columbia University, an
institution that is not exactly remote from Princeton. His mammoth
Social and Religious History of the Jews was also passed over as well,
though its sixteen volumes "not only . . . [make it] a landmark in
Jewish historiography, but also . . . set a standard for erudition and
critical scholarship that few American historians can match."[9] Here
Dawidowicz was, if anything, too cautious in her claim. For which
other historian of U. S. citizenship has published anything comparable to that magnum opus, which forms the centerpiece of a bibliog-
raphy and scholarly career bristling with over five hundred books,
articles, notes, and reviews? Which other American historians can
draw upon archival material in twenty languages?[10]

Baron's stress upon the social and economic history of the Jews, as
opposed to the idealist views of predecessors like Heinrich Graetz,
also happens to have posed an implicit challenge to the theology of
Franz Rosenzweig (1886–1929), who helped perpetrate the familiar
depreciation of the Jewish past. For Rosenzweig as well the Jews were
an ahistorical people, though not for the reason that Zunz had
advanced. Because the Israelites and their descendants sought to
obey the eternal law of God, because they lived in accordance with
the rhythm of religious observance and the cycle of festivals, they
constituted a timeless people. Rosenzweig took seriously the concept

of *am olam*, which radically sundered the Jews from all others, who lived by contrast within history. "We have long ago been robbed of all the things in which the peoples of the world are rooted," he argued in *The Star of Redemption* (1921). "For us, land and language, custom and law, have long left the circle of the living and have been raised to the rung of holiness. But we are still living, and live in eternity. Our life is no longer meshed with anything outside ourselves."[11] Here a certain kind of theology attempts to ignore the historical research that roots the Jews within time, and pretends to outflank all the evidence of a history that has indeed been integrated with the outside world.[12]

A more influential interpretation of the Jewish past, imposing a secular *eschaton* upon it, derived from Zionism, which itself marked a caesura in Jewish tradition. This orientation was first articulated by Moses Hess (1812–1875), who had, it so happens, converted Friedrich Engels to Communism, and helped to convert Karl Marx and Mikhail Bakunin as well. In a prescient Zionist tract, *Rome and Jerusalem* (1862), Hess argued that only the restoration of a national homeland could end the exemption from the turbulence of history that exile had imposed upon the Jews. Nationalism and a re-emergence into history were therefore intimately connected: "The Jewish people, which has not in vain defied for two millennia the storms of world history . . . and from all the ends of the earth has never ceased to look to Jerusalem, belongs unquestionably to the peoples believed dead which in the consciousness of their historical task must assert their national rights."[13] In returning to the land so that the Third Jewish Commonwealth could be established, the builders of Israel were indeed to fulfill this imperative. The "connection between the renascence of the Jewish people and its historical consciousness" struck Gershom Scholem as obvious, triggering "a new awareness of the dynamics and dialectics of Jewish history."[14] For the Zionists broke with the pattern of powerlessness, inaugurated their own version of political action, and in such moments as the ninety minutes at Entebbe rewrote the script of passive victimization that Jews seemed destined to enact in their exile.

But whether Jews were Zionists or not, they were legatees of a religion that differed from Christianity in its sense of the past. The deity of the Hebrews was known not by His attributes—as theologians might have tabulated them—but by His history. In the First Commandment delivered on Mount Sinai, Yahweh introduces Himself as "the Lord thy God, who brought thee out of the land of Egypt, out of the house of bondage" (Exodus 20:2). Such a divinity created the world, but He is also related to a particular people that experiences a history as well. He is the deity of its patriarchs—the God of Abraham, Isaac, and Jacob. That nation's identity was forged in the exodus from Egypt and sealed in the covenant, and thereafter all Jews have been enjoined at the Passover *seder* to put themselves in the original position of the Hebrews who once were slaves and then through God's help won their freedom. What happens on that holiday is therefore an astonishing act of imagination, or what Professor Yosef Hayim Yerushalmi calls "reactualization." For Jews are not expected to think back to what Egyptian slavery was like, or to meditate on how the exodus might have been accomplished. The *Haggadah* asks them to identify with the fate of their ancestors so fully that the distinction between past and present has in effect been obliterated. The dia-chronic sense evaporates in the process of "remembering" what the participants have not themselves experienced. One of the first rituals to be performed at the *seder* is to raise a piece of *matzah* and announce (in the present tense): "This is the bread of affliction which our forefathers ate in the land of Egypt."[15]

Not only the Book of Exodus but much of the rest of the Hebrew Bible can of course be read as a historical work, chronicles of the political and religious destiny of a people. It honors chronology, and it remains an invaluable basis for the researches of modern archeolo-gists, historians, and philologists. But with the Roman destruction of the Jewish state, this historical dimension to the Jewish sensibility largely disappeared. In exile in Rome, Josephus Flavius wrote his *Jewish War* (75–79 c.e.) and then *Jewish Antiquities* (93–94 c.e.). Yet he was, apart from a very few exceptions, the last historian whom the Jewish people would produce for the next fifteen centuries.[16]

In that interregnum the Jews lived with memory, so that redemp-tion might be hastened; but they did not live with history. The rabbis made so little effort to record the history of their own post-Biblical era, saw so little point in commemorating or interpreting the flux of medieval events, that the poet Moses Ibn Ezra observed that "all the other nations have exerted themselves to write their histories and to excel in them." But the Jews who lived before him had "ignored and despised such matters." For fifteen centuries from the fall of Judea to the Renaissance, the commandment to remember was fulfilled—but not by historians, who tended to apologize for the very nature of the enterprise in which they so infrequently engaged. Their vocation was dismissed as a diversion; the status of history on the shelves of Jewish libraries could hardly be described as privileged. Nor were the works of gentile historians regarded with esteem, for the histories of the peoples among whom the Jews dwelled in the Diaspora were known as *sifrey milchamot*—"books of wars." No wonder then that the first post-medieval attempt at a history of the Jews was written by a gentile, a Huguenot who found safety in Holland. "I dare to say," Jacques Basnage announced, "that no historian has appeared among the Jews themselves who has gathered together so many facts concerning their nation."[17]

Historical imagination could grip the Jews only when emancipation had severed the chain of tradition, only when the past could no longer be transmitted according to the internal dynamic of Jewish family and communal life, only when memory ceased to be a dependable vehicle through which a heritage of longing could be reaffirmed. Only when faith and law and observance dissipated under the impact of modernization could Jews turn to other means to wrest meaning from Jewish life and identity. When little else was left, the past could be studied not only for some inspiring examples of moral conduct, but for clues to the mystery of Jewish prevalence. God could no longer be cited as guiding the general destiny of the "children of the covenant." But critical history—using the same methods of interpretation, verification, and reasoning that professional historians were developing to analyze, say, the history of ancient Rome or of the papacy—might fortify a sense of peoplehood, and give pertinence to the need to define what still might be meant by Jewish identity.[18] In a brilliant book, *Zakhor*, Professor Yerushalmi has elucidated the paradox that resulted: "Though Judaism throughout the ages was absorbed with the meaning of history, historiography itself played at best an ancillary role among the Jews, and often no role at all." He adds that even though "memory of the past was always a central component of Jewish experience, the historian was not its primary custodian."[19]

Emancipation meant that Jews had become citizens, with religion alone intended to distinguish them from others. But secularization meant that many Jews no longer had a religion either. And democratization has generally meant the decline—and today in America the virtual disappearance—of the anti-Semitism that Spinoza, for one, believed had largely preserved the Jewish people. What then was left? An increasingly persuasive answer is given in the film *Norma Rae* (1979), when the Southern textile worker (played by Sally Field) asks the New York labor organizer (played by Ron Liebman) what makes

Jews different. "History" is his sole (and gnomic) reply. But what did it mean? A fuller answer—and a rejoinder to Leopold Zunz as well—was offered by Simon Dubnow, who proclaimed that "the Jewish people has at all times and in all countries . . . been the subject, the creator of its own history, not only in the intellectual sphere but also in the general sphere of social life. During the period of its political independence as well as in its stateless period, Jewry stands among the other nations . . . but with the distinctive characteristics of a nation . . ." He added that it "fought always and everywhere for its autonomous existence in the sphere of social life as well as in all other fields of cultural activity."[20]

Dubnow himself deserves more than passing mention in any discussion of the Jewish struggle to unravel the enigma of history. Though his native tongue was Russian, though his political and religious views were liberal (a picture of John Stuart Mill was placed on his desk), Dubnow spoke his last, reverberant words in Yiddish: "*Schreibt un farschreibt!*" (write and record). He was killed by the Nazis, who had already confiscated his library, during a raid on the Riga ghetto in 1941. Except for Baron, who was born in 1895, no scholar after Dubnow could have imagined the possibility of filtering all of Jewish history through one synthesizing intelligence. But even though that task would by now be inconceivable, Dubnow's legacy is nevertheless salient—in its affirmation of the value of the Diaspora, in its soft-pedaling of the primacy of religion and in its exaltation of *k'lal yisroel* (the Jewish community), in its generosity of spirit and its rationalism, and in its struggle to blend the universal and the particular.[21] Dubnow's dying words thus reconciled in a flash the false antinomy that Emerson had established between the party of memory and the party of hope, and his powerful vision of Jewish history activated both passions.

If the Jews are no longer poised between memory and messianism, they can at least find vindication for their peculiar fate not in an unbroken line of transmitted tradition from generation to generation, nor in any genuine expectation of redemption at the end of days, but in a more diffuse sense that they may know who they are by grasping what they have been. By now, as Yerushalmi has insisted, all of Judaica is treated historically; all the versions and varieties of faith and observance and conduct are analyzed in terms of temporality and are subject to critical inquiry. Historians have hardly succeeded to the posts of communal authority which rabbis and sages vacated in the wake of emancipation, but their prestige in the world of scholarship is not entirely negligible and has sometimes stretched beyond it. Professor Baron himself testified at the trial of Adolf Eichmann in Jerusalem, serving as a witness against one exemplar of the unprecedented barbarism that Baron analyzed for the court.

If anyone has personified the awe that modern Jews have accorded to the appreciation of the past, if anyone has crystallized the Jewish cultivation of the sixth sense, it has been Gershom Scholem (1897–1982), whom *Commentary* identified in its obituary notice as simply "the greatest Jewish scholar of the age." Certainly no one else came close to stirring as much interest and fascination among intellectuals, whose own fields rarely if ever overlapped with Scholem's own specialization in the history of Jewish mysticism. Arendt was among the first to recognize the revolutionary impact of Scholem's *Major Trends in Jewish Mysticism* (1941) in revising the comprehension of the Jewish past; and when the *New York Times Book Review* invited the formidably well-read Daniel Bell to name the most important book of the postwar era, he chose *Sabbatai Sevi: The Mystical Messiah* (1973). A leading specialist in Romantic poetry and in literary theory, Yale's Harold Bloom, wrote *Kabbalah and Criticism* under the inspiration of Scholem, whom the literary critic praised for having "made himself indispensable to all rational students of his subject."[22] (Scholem himself was much more guarded about Professor Bloom's expropriation of his research, quipping: "It's a free country.") To George Steiner, himself no slouch, Scholem was "the total scholar" and a "genius."[23]

In boosting the reputation of this historian, others went even further. "There are certain magisterial works of the human mind that alter ordinary comprehension so unpredictably and on so prodigious a scale that culture is set awry," the novelist Cynthia Ozick exclaimed, "and nothing can ever be seen again except in the strange light of that new knowledge[,] . . . an accretion of fundamental insight [that] takes on the power of a natural force. Gershom Scholem's oeuvre has such a force; and its massive keystone, *Sabbatai Sevi*, presses down on the grasping consciousness with the strength not simply of its invulnerable, almost tidal, scholarship, but of its singular instruction in the nature of man." By the time Ozick was done, even Aristotle began to look like an underachiever; even Freud was confined to "a peephole into a dark chamber," while Scholem had become elevated into "a radio telescope monitoring the universe."[24] His scholarship is surely important and invaluable enough to survive such ludicrous overpraise, but what matters here is the manifest pertinence that the research of a historian represented for Jews who themselves were not historians. A century earlier, Scholem himself told one interviewer, his arcane work would have reached no audience whatsoever, regardless of its quality.[25]

From his special slant in the field of mysticism, Scholem underscored what must be regarded as a distinctive feature of Jewish history—its messianism. For he claimed that "Judaism, in all of its forms and manifestations, has always maintained a concept of redemption as an event which takes place publicly, on the stage of history and within the community. It is an occurrence which takes place in the visible world," unlike Christianity, "which conceives of redemption as an event in the spiritual and unseen realm, an event which is reflected in the soul." According to Maimonides, the Jewish idea of redemption is not based directly on human will; and his co-religionists were therefore inclined to choose a "*life lived in deferment*, in which nothing can be done definitively, nothing can be irrevocably accomplished." This incessant postponement Scholem considered the price that the Jews historically paid for their commitment to messianism: "The magnitude of the Messianic idea corresponds to the endless powerlessness in Jewish history during all the centuries of exile, when it was unprepared to come forward onto the plane of world history. There's something preliminary, something provisional about Jewish history." Scholem discerned "something grand about living in hope, but at the same time there is something profoundly unreal about it."[26]

"America was promises" too, the poet Archibald MacLeish exclaimed.[27] But the promises (at least after the erosion of Puritanism) were without eschatological depth, and seemed fully within human reach. Cruel incongruities have nevertheless scarred the American past; and whether in the conquest and slaughter of Indians, or the two very terrible centuries of human bondage, our national past has hardly escaped the labyrinthine darkness that has enveloped human suffering. American history has been tarnished by protracted racism and by episodes of mob violence. And yet much of the turmoil of Europe has not been replicated. The United States has endured one terrible Civil War, but still adheres to one Constitution; has undergone a terrible cycle of depressions, but has still known no revolution after the battle of Yorktown; has been afflicted with an unbroken legacy of racial discrimination and an ugly record of labor violence and oppression, but can also take pride in genuine achievement toward the elusive ideal of equality. All of the pivotal institutions of popular sovereignty were forged by the end of the eighteenth century; none has been created since then. Contrast the experience of Stendhal (1783–1842), who survived ten different regimes and six different constitutions.

In that respect Americans have largely avoided what General Alexander Haig once called a "vortex of cruciality," and their sense of the past was bound to differ from that of Europeans. As C. Vann Woodward has perhaps been most influential in pointing out, only Southerners, with the bitterness of their defeat and the dissipation of their illusions, could lay claim to a historical sense at variance with the American norm of complacent triumphalism. White Americans have generally been spared the evils of tyranny and cruelty that have elsewhere been so normative to human experience. White Americans have generally not had to try to wrest from the coils of the past the instruments of liberation. Though even Southerners in the mid-nineteenth century were exempted from the full force of tragedy, it is no accident that it was Faulkner's Gavin Stevens who countered the national *mentalité* by asserting that "the past is never dead. It's not even past."[28]

It is therefore not only prologue, but present as well, and its very recalcitrance can impede the struggle to comprehend it— and the need sometimes to be emancipated from its constraints. William James liked to quote Kierkegaard's paradox that "we live forwards, but we understand backwards."[29] It is a memorable rationale for the discipline that neither thinker ever practiced, though James (echoing Benjamin Franklin) did make the persuasive argument that any other discipline—including the natural sciences—can be humanized once it is explained in historical terms. It is noteworthy how few important American philosophers ever practiced or even meditated much on history itself, unlike their colleagues in Europe. Voltaire and Hume produced important pioneering works of history; Hegel offered grand meta-historical theory; Nietzsche constructed his anatomy of *The Use and Abuse of History* and speculated more famously on the origins of Greek tragedy; Whitehead was an intellectual historian; and Bertrand Russell wrote a major history of philosophy, plus other works that are informed by acute sensitivity to the past. The versatile Marx, who was only twenty-four years old when Moses Hess hailed him as "the greatest, perhaps the only true philosopher now alive,"[30] injected a historical method into what became the social sciences.

Such thinkers lack American counterparts; neither James nor Charles S. Peirce nor John Dewey did anything comparable. The general omission of historical problems in American thought can perhaps be traced to the influence of Emerson, whose work is, if anything, anti-historical in its implications. Emerson's interest in the past was restricted to biography—to representative lives; and his faith in the formation of a new character type ("the simple genuine self against the whole world") tended to stifle the effort to cultivate the tradition bequeathed from Europe and, more distantly, from the ancient world. Emerson's various injunctions (to "lop off all superfluity and tradition, and fall back on the nature of things," and to "forget historical Christianity") were songs of innocence rather than experience.[31]

Among the important twentieth-century American thinkers, perhaps only two sustained an interest in historical questions. Reinhold Niebuhr cast into high relief what he called the ironic historical destiny of Americans, who found themselves by the mid-twentieth century trapped within their own ideals and illusions; and Niebuhr also managed to put that story in a large international context. The logic of his own deepest beliefs nevertheless compelled Niebuhr to assert the primacy of Christian faith over the imperatives of historical understanding. Sidney Hook wrote *The Hero in History* (1943) under the vestigial influence of Marxism; and it is a discriminating exploration of the problem of free will and individual agency, embedded in a historical context. No other important American philosopher seems to have shared Hook's impassioned interest, though a third theoretician might be added to this very short list—his teacher Morris Raphael Cohen. The City College professor was attracted to historical issues and stuffed his writings with historical illustrations, but his oeuvre is now largely neglected. Perhaps the most famous statement that a philosopher ever uttered on the subject of history is: "Those who cannot remember the past are condemned to repeat it"[32]—a line so apodictic and memorable that everyone who ever came across it, Wilfrid Sheed once quipped, has been condemned to repeat it. But George Santayana (1863–1952) did not write much about the past. Nor in fact did he ever bother to become an American citizen, for he had been born in Spain and chose to spend the last four decades of his life in Europe, mostly in Italy. His American identity is therefore a tangled issue.

The delicate fate of historiography in the United States can be limned in a unique memoir and meditation for which a blues singer named Henry Adams won a posthumous Pulitzer Prize in 1919. The author of *The Education of Henry Adams* (1907) may still rank as the most subtle and interesting historian that this country has ever produced, even though so much about his legacy and his sensibility strikingly collided with the national temperament. As the grandson and great-grandson of presidents who helped establish the republican tradition itself, Adams was strategically placed to calibrate how populism and commercialism had upset the possibilities of order, stability, continuity—the eighteenth-century arrangements to which he felt heir, and which he later pushed back into the high Middle Ages in Europe. The second paragraph of the *Education* conveys how unfit he felt to adapt to modernity. "Had he been born in Jerusalem under the shadow of the Temple and circumcised in the Synagogue by his uncle the high priest, under the name of Israel Cohen," Adams sarcastically conjectured, "he would scarcely have been . . . much more heavily handicapped in the races of the coming century . . ."[33]

Subsequent pages constitute the most articulate expression that an American ever uttered of how irrelevant the past was to his own life. Adams was one of the first academics to apply the positivist research methods developed in German higher education, and he was one of the first presidents of the American Historical Association. But he did not find among his contemporaries an adequate recognition of the energies that the dynamo had unleashed with the eclipse of the Virgin. It must be admitted that self-mockery and irony encased so much of what Adams wrote that it is tempting to suspect him of an irrepressible—and indecent—need to justify his own cynicism. That is why Adams's sense of isolation need not be blamed entirely on his fellow historians, who did not take to heart his cranky notices of impending disaster. Those who instead read his pamphlets at face value were obviously not clever enough to detect the satire on science that Adams may have intended, which also confirmed his melancholy sense of how unappreciated his work was. However deeply he would ponder the grandeur of the medieval cathedrals and monuments during his restless motor-tours of France, the past was simply not usable. Adams was a scholar who tried—and failed—to become a seer; and a book like his *Education*, which is the return ticket of his voyage to the end of night, discounted the value of history even in the very act of recording it.

Works of fiction can be summoned as evidence of an American penchant to disregard the pertinence of the past, to allow the sixth sense to atrophy. In his utopian novel *Walden Two* (1948), the Harvard psychologist B. F. Skinner invents a community in which the subject of history is treated disdainfully, "as entertainment. It isn't taken seriously as food for thought." The author's *raisonneur*, T. E. Frazier, insists that operant conditioning could so revolutionize human motivation that the study of the past would only obscure the grasp of the circumstances in which the communitarians find themselves. "What we give our young people in Walden Two," the protagonist announces, "is a grasp of the *current* forces which a culture must deal with. None of your myths, none of your heroes—no history, no destiny—simply the *Now!* The present is the thing. It's the only thing we can deal with, anyway, in a scientific manner."[34] So brazen an abandonment of the wellsprings of tradition is not treated in an ironic manner, nor has the anti-historicism of the novel prevented its sales from surpassing well over a million copies.

Such fictional voices are the unacknowledged descendants of the archetypal American boy, Huckleberry Finn, whom the widow Douglas dares to attempt to "sivilize" and give Bible lessons. But it gradually dawns on Huck that Moses, for example, "had been dead a considerable long time; so then I didn't care no more about him; because I don't take no stock in dead people." In Vladimir Nabokov's *Lolita* (1955), the cultivated but gloomy European intellectual Humbert Humbert is obsessed by the past. Seeking constantly to re-enact it, Humbert is haunted by the remorselessness of change and the finality of death, even as he dares to hope that only art can dispel the inevitability of oblivion. His compulsive literary allusions place him, for all his repellent eccentricity, securely within a certain aesthetic tradition. By contrast the American teenager who is the title character is represented, apart from her sex life, as typical. She is "the ideal consumer, the subject and object of every foul poster"; and she tells her stepfather and lover near the end of the novel that "the past was the past," a topic of no interest.[35] Such adolescents were about to dance to Chuck Berry's "School Days," a song of innocence that became an anthem of the youth culture of the 1950s: "Hail, hail, rock and roll,/Deliver me from the days of old." They joined in the national disregard for the past as prologue.

Figures of American folk wisdom have concurred. Henry Ford's snap judgment that "history is bunk" was not based on a reflective consideration of the capriciousness of memory upon which so much methodology depends, or the ambiguity of the evidence that scholars are obliged to examine, or the corruption of interpretation due to subjectivity, or the ultimate inscrutability of the past. His dismissal was due not to an open mind but an empty one. When Ford sued the *Chicago Tribune* for libel in 1919, and was put on the witness stand to prove its charge that "the flivver king" was an "ignorant idealist," he

proceeded to identify Benedict Arnold as "a writer" (was Ford thinking of Arnold Bennett?), to draw a blank on the causes of the
American Revolution, to confuse it with the War of 1812, and so
forth.[36] Such embarrassments apparently did not diminish Ford's
legendary status. Or take the case of Will Rogers, who once remarked:
"If every history or books on old things was [sic] thrown in the river
and if everybody had nothing to study but the future, we would be
about two hundred years ahead of what we are now." Such voices of
horse sense constituted odd echoes of Jefferson's far more subtle
dictum that "the earth belongs always to the living generation." When
Jefferson himself was formulating plans for the University of Virginia
in 1818, he made the study of history a rather insignificant feature of
the curriculum. In this final blow that he struck in a lifelong "crusade
against ignorance," Jefferson gave the subject no separate or special—
much less privileged—status, but placed it in a category "interwoven
with Politics and Law."[38]

A century and a half later, the prestige of history has declined
even further. Though never quite exercising hegemony in the social
sciences and humanities, history has failed to elicit widespread and
sustained curiosity; and the number of its students has dipped dramatically. In 1970 44,663 college students were majoring in history.
Nine years later the figure had sunk to 19,301.[39] As a result the gap
in generational experience has become a chasm. A scene in the film
Save the Tiger (1973) reflects a blankness which virtually every history
teacher has found replicated in classroom episodes. The fatigued
businessman played by Jack Lemmon picks up a young hitchhiker to
whom he unwinds his combat memories of Anzio in the Second
World War. But she had not realized that the Italians had been our
enemies in that war. The majority of the young, including those on
college campuses, who voted for Ronald Reagan shared with him
something of that amnesia. Even President Reagan's most enthusiastic
champions never claimed that his beliefs and policies were informed
by historical sensitivity; and the form that damage control took
during the scandal of a visit to the cemetery at Bitburg was not only
to equate the Jewish victims with the S. S. killers buried there, but
also to hope that the past itself might be forgotten. On such an
occasion, the president did not wish to "reawaken the memories" of
the Holocaust;[40] and his aspiration to suppress consideration of such
ineffable experiences can therefore be seen as connected to the
general optimism that was central to his popular appeal.

From the perspective of the discipline, the picture is not entirely bleak, however, even in the White House. In the twentieth century, two of the Reagan's predecessors, Theodore Roosevelt and Woodrow Wilson, were practicing historians, even serving as presidents of the American Historical Association. Though not an academician like Wilson, Roosevelt nevertheless produced nine volumes of history.[41] John F. Kennedy was a life member of the American Historical Association, but—if Herbert Parmet and Garry Wills are correct— received a Pulitzer Prize in biography for a book, *Profiles in Courage* (1956), that he did not actually write. Kennedy nevertheless exhibited a gifted amateur's flair for the subject. "No President since Wilson had such a disciplined interest in historical studies," Arthur Schlesinger, Jr., has asserted, "and . . . no President since Lincoln made history so organic a part of his political perspective."[42] Employing Schlesinger as a White House advisor, Kennedy could drop clever historical allusions and be understood. After he met with Roger Blough of U. S. Steel and forced the company to agree to roll back prices, Schlesinger asked the president how the surrender meeting had gone. Kennedy bragged to the author of "The Causes of the Civil War" (1949): "I told him that his men could keep their horses for the spring plowing."[43] And though Harry Truman was the only president in this century not to attend college, he also claimed to love reading works of history; his childhood favorite had been Plutarch's *Lives*. Only one major party nominee for the presidency has ever earned a doctorate in history, but in that instance even those historians who have nursed especially virulent grievances cannot blame their fellow citizens for their anti-intellectualism. For it is unlikely that George McGovern's spectacular defeat in 1972 was due to his particular field of specialization—or to the quality of his dissertation on the Ludlow, Colorado labor violence of 1913–1914.

If there is an American amnesia, however, it is undoubtedly connected to the national penchant for zippetty-doo-dah optimism, in which few if any glitches appear on the screen. Unlike the Jewish sense of history, with its messianic dimensions, such optimism is rarely religious. The American contrast to the Jewish "life lived in deferment" was the deathbed quip of Thoreau, who was asked by an eager disciple for some wisdom about the imminent afterlife. Thoreau replied: "One world at a time."[44] But a sunny-side-up disposition can also transform itself into the politics of hope. One of the first fellow travelers was Lincoln Steffens, whose famous line about the Bolshevik Revolution—"I have been over into the future, and it works"[45]— encapsulates the national trait of putting faith in the future rather than revering the past. (In making some variant of pragmatism the operative test of the polity, Steffens was also speaking in a distinctly American accent.) The liberal journalist Stuart Chase, challenging the fellow travelers who were so unstinting in their admiration of the "Soviet experiment," once asked: "Why should the Russians have all the fun of remaking a world?"[46] It is tempting to generalize that an American is most likely to ask that sort of question, whereas anyone who is invested with an authentic sense of the past is bound to suspect the Sisyphean futility of the struggle to remake the world.

And yet, even though all the follies of the world cannot and will not be abrogated, America did promise something different. To be sure the rise of another "redeemer nation" did not restore the Garden of Eden. The gates of Paradise remained closed until further notice because, after the initial divine effort to build upon the human estate, this property was condemned. But for the Jews, perhaps more credibly than for any other immigrant group, the United States remained a reasonable facsimile, a Diaspora that was consistently so benign that it did not seem like an exile at all. As a political refugee in Paris, Heinrich Heine called America "a loophole of escape . . . larger than the prison [of Europe] itself."[47] Or so it seemed. Bernard Berenson, a Lithuanian immigrant whose conversion to Episcopalianism helped catapult him to stardom as an art historian and connoisseur, got so carried away that he began referring to "our Puritan forebears"— which provoked Meyer Schapiro to jibe that Berenson must have thought that "rabbis [sailed] on the *Mayflower*."[48] In the midst of a *Partisan Review* piece on Francis Parkman, who chronicled Western expansion and conflict, the critic Alfred Kazin even waxed eloquent about "our forests," as though Kazin were the descendant of intrepid frontiersmen rather than the son of an immigrant house painter in Brooklyn.[49] Such feelings made it increasingly difficult to sustain the traditional suspicion that gentiles evoked, to satisfy the injunction of Deuteronomy 25:17 to "remember what Amalek did to you."

Nevertheless, the love affair with America was so close to being requited that neither the emergence of Zionism nor subsequent pride in Israel could shake it. Such intensified feelings of peoplehood—far from generating conflicting loyalties—were simply another way of being Jewish in America. The result has been some strange and exhilarating mixtures, as the Jews introduced themselves into the culture once established by the Puritans and extended by the Transcendentalists, the Pragmatists and others. In an early Saul Bellow novel, the anti-Semitic persecutor complains that the author of a volume on Emerson and Thoreau is named Lipschitz.[50] That was at the dawn of an era in which such works would be commonplace, when Kazin would take possession of the forests and when perhaps the pre-eminent student of Puritanism would be Sacvan Bercovitch. But in a presidential address to the American Historical Association, Carl Bridenbaugh lamented that "many of the young practitioners of our craft, and those who are still apprentices, are products of lower middle-class or foreign origins, and their emotions not infrequently get in the way of historical reconstructions." Without blaming them for their origins, Professor Bridenbaugh believed that "they find themselves in a very real sense outsiders on our past and feel them-selves shut out. . . . The chasm between them and the Remote Past widens every hour."[51]

It is true that many Jews had begun to chronicle and interpret the American experience, even though they—no more than Brooklyn's gifted historian of antebellum Southern slavery and agrarianism, Eugene Genovese—had never walked behind a plow, or had ever trapped muskrats (to use Professor Bridenbaugh's example of how "the priceless asset of a shared culture" was built). But it could also be inferred from his clumsy remarks that the historiography of the United States, especially after the Second World War, could not be adequately told without tabulating the achievements of historians of Jewish birth. They have represented no school or movement, and indeed have located themselves virtually everywhere on the political spectrum (from Communist to arch-conservative). Except for Oscar Handlin, none has contributed significantly to the history of the Jews as such, either here or abroad. But post-World War II American historiography would have been impoverished without the work of Boorstin, Handlin, Daniel Aaron, Bernard Bailyn, Stanley Elkins, Eric Foner, Eric Goldman, Herbert Gutman, Louis Hartz, Richard Hofstadter, Gerda Lerner, Leonard Levy, and far too many others to mention. The quality and influence of their writings may not be dependent upon their own ethnic and religious background, but at least that heritage did not seem to blunt their comprehension of the American past, did not apparently lead them to see any advantages to amnesia; and some creative tension may well have animated their work.

Another American of Jewish birth, though a non-historian, once offered so distinctive and inspiring a defense of the historical enter-prise that she deserves the last word in this chapter—in the form of an enjoinder to cultivate the sixth sense. Gertrude Stein (1874–1946) was born in Allegheny, Pennsylvania, and had lived in Oakland, in Cambridge, and in Baltimore, before spending the final four decades of her life—even under the German occupation—in France. The exile imposed upon so many Jews was a fate that she freely adopted. Even as an expatriate, Stein cherished her native land as much as other American Jews; and unlike most Americans, she was absorbed in the epic of its development. Untrained as a historian, she was acutely conscious of the ambiguous entangling of past and present, whether defining the United States as "the oldest country in the world" (because it "created the twentieth century"), or labeling the young writers who visited her salon "a lost generation." One passage in *The Making of Americans* (1925), here transposed into free verse, vibrates with the force of the historian's hunger to endow with meaning the human record in all its commonality and variety, in all its availability and interest:

There are many that I know and they know it.
They are all of them repeating and I hear it. I love it
and I tell it. I love it and now I will write it.
This is now a history of my love of it. I hear it
and I love it and I write it. They repeat it.
They live it and I see it and I hear it. They live it
and I hear it and I see it and I love it
and now and always I will write it.
There are many kinds of men and women
and I know it. They repeat it and I hear it
and I love it. This is now a history of the way they do it.
This is now a history of the way I love it.[52]

3

CULTURE

"We have listened too long to the courtly muses of Europe," Emerson proclaimed in "The American Scholar" in 1837. For "our day of dependence, our long apprenticeship to the learning of other lands, draws to a close. The millions that around us are rushing into life, cannot always be fed on the sere remains of foreign harvests."[1] Despite this declaration of intellectual independence, Emerson assumed and understood that the formulation and development of "high culture" has been primarily European, evolving from the classical heritage of Greece and Rome, preserved and extended through the Church, then broadened and secularized from the Renaissance through the Enlightenment. It has become the stuff of survey courses, a set of standards of thought and expression that dignified and ennobled human existence itself. American culture could not help defining itself against a certain recognizable tradition, and appraising itself according to standards that were indebted to Europe.

What qualified and modulated the version of high culture on native grounds were "those millions . . . rushing into life" around Emerson's American scholar and artist. Forced to operate almost entirely within a democratic marketplace, without the vestiges of monarchical or aristocratic privilege, the creators and custodians of American culture have been peculiarly sensitive to the limitations and imperatives of a mass society. They have long been closer to the popular taste of their fellow citizens than their European counterparts were required to be. The result has not only been greater caution and subordination to mass taste, but also some degree of insecurity as to the precise frontiers that in Europe presumably separated the folk arts from the innovativeness and subversiveness of the most consequential figures in European cultural history. Emerson's quip that Walt Whitman represented a "remarkable mixture of the *Bhagvat-Geeta* and the *New York Herald*"[2] is one sign of this formlessness, or rather of spilling over boundaries that in Europe were more likely to separate the serious artist from the masses. American culture has been making things up as it goes along, and the categories and definitions that might have been imported from abroad have not completely fettered its development.

The result has been a continual uncertainty about the precise character and achievements of American culture, especially when viewed in the light of transatlantic heritage from which it has stemmed. Despite Emerson's Phi Beta Kappa address, the national struggle for cultural distinctiveness—and distinction—sometimes took more than a century to succeed. The British publisher Penguin Books did not transfer its volume on Hawthorne from the English Men of Letters Series to its newly created Penguin American Classics until 1982, and at last report the University of Exeter still teaches American literature under the category of Commonwealth literature. Despite the power that the United States has exerted in the world, Oxford University only recently established a chair in American history;[3] and perhaps its most distinguished historian, A. J. P. Taylor, has never even been to the United States. American democratic culture itself has sometimes appeared to fall short, when weighed against the elite standards formulated overseas; and certain nearly ineradicable prejudices have sometimes magnified such disdain. When an interviewer once asked the reactionary English satirist Evelyn Waugh whether he had found "illuminating or helpful" professional criticism from, for example, Edmund Wilson, Waugh asked: "Is he an American?" (The extraordinarily learned and cultivated critic had praised Waugh as "the only first-rate comic genius that has appeared in England since Bernard Shaw.") When the interviewer replied in the affirmative, Waugh cackled: "I don't think what they have to say is of much interest, do you?"[4]

Interesting ideas have nevertheless emerged within the democratic marketplace; and its requirements and sensibilities have had to be taken into account, if not always honored. When those requirements have been debased and those sensibilities dulled, the expressions of mass culture have indeed looked paltry and vulgar. But it was also possible to draw upon the resources of high culture to create something different, something fresh and vibrant and compelling. That, I think, has been the special service that many creative Jewish Americans have performed.

More than any other definable group, the Jews could be expected, as they adjusted to and helped construct American popular culture, to be aware of the legacy of a deeper, more ancient tradition that had congealed in Europe, if not as far back as biblical Palestine. Even those American Jews who have appealed to mass audiences have sometimes been haunted by the shadows of high culture. In the unstable mixture of mass entertainment touched by high culture, the dynamics of a specific American Jewish expression are most likely to be located. It constitutes an effort to bridge the chasm between the fashionable and the transcendent, the ephemeral and the exalted. It is a hybrid, composed both of some high cultural memories and pretensions and of the commercial necessities and ambitions of popular culture. Those who went about "making it" in so flamboyant a fashion might have been well aware of the success of other Jews in storming the heights of high culture, or might well have been sensitive to the nature of high culture itself. The result has been a mixture, something that is neither *milchik* nor *flaychik*, neither dairy nor meat. Jay Cantor, the young author of the widely-acclaimed first novel, *The Death of Che Guevara* (1983), promised to make that juxtaposition the subject of his second work of fiction. Popular culture had formed him, but it "was only one of my parents. The other was our 'high' culture. My book is about the tension in the family."[5]

That is the disjunction that is addressed in this chapter, for I wish to argue that American Jewish culture cannot be found at its most impressive in the perpetuation or rejuvenation of the Judaic heritage of biblical Israel or of the Old World. Instead that culture yields its most formidable images in those expressions of Jewish sensibility that can be located in the arts of the wider society. The proper way to grope toward a definition of American Jewish culture is to ask the following questions: What are the special features of the works of those Jews who have been creative figures within American culture? What do creative Jews do that differentiates them from other creative Americans? What kinds of cultural expression are representative of American Jews, so that it becomes proper to speak of a Jewish sensibility? The most resourceful, the most original, the most gifted

American Jews have generally attempted to burst the constraints of whatever has passed for a normative Jewish ambience, have instead breathed life into American culture generally. That is why the student of American Jewish culture cannot explore only how American Jews have addressed Jewish issues, or how they have attempted to situate themselves within the boundaries of Jewish history or sought to realize their own Jewishness. In order to assess American Jewry at its most creative, it is necessary for scholars to venture past the gates of academic *Judengassen*, to examine the work of Jews in the popular arts as well as in the pulpit and in the philanthropies. It is not the slightest disparagement of the perpetuation of Judaic learning and thought in the United States to suggest that, in terms of assessing the creativity of American Jewry, such scholarship and resourcefulness have generally been marginal. Because of the velocity of assimilation and acceptance, they have constituted a sideshow, compared to what has been going on under the main tent.

At least initially, a historical orientation is necessary, for the problems of culture in a mass society certainly emerge in the nineteenth century. In her seminal study of *American Humor* (1931), Constance Rourke observed that, in the formation of folklore and in the rudiments of mass entertainment in the previous century, Americans drew upon three different stereotypes, assumed three different masks, to reveal something about themselves in the development of a national character. One was the Yankee—shrewd, clever, thrifty. Another was the frontiersman—boisterous, strong, domineering. The third was the black—affable yet with an undertone of melancholy, richly emotional, musical.

This third mask was preferred by those Jews who felt that they could not address the mass audience as themselves, drawing upon their own culture and heritage, fathoming the depths of their own religion and history. But they could assume a mask that allowed the deepest emotions to be expressed, to convey their joy and their sorrow, their *shmaltz* and their pain, a spirit that soared and plunged outside the range of Anglo-Saxon gentility. In the evolution of American mass culture, the most representative and talented Jews made little conscious effort to resolve the antinomies of Jewish identity, or to promote a separate destiny for their people. Instead they sought to address a mass audience, to dissolve into general Americana. They were sometimes able to exploit and adopt the givens that had been established in the nineteenth century; and the black image was the most available and alluring, the richest in possibilities of soulful energy.

Thus Irving Berlin achieved the first of his many hits with "Alexander's Ragtime Band" (1911); and a host of pluggers seemed to follow the injunction of Berlin's song: "Yiddle on Your Fiddle, Play Some Ragtime." Other Jews applied burnt cork to their faces to become "mammy singers," beginning with Al Jolson and Eddie Cantor; and the show business careers of Sophie Tucker and Fanny Brice began as "coon callers."[6] An all-black revue called *Blackbirds of 1928*, which included the hit "I Can't Give You Anything But Love, Baby," was co-written by lyricist Dorothy Fields, who was the daughter of Lew Fields of Weber and Fields.[7] George Gershwin wrote "Rhapsody in Blue" and *Porgy and Bess* and a one-act piece about Harlem called "Blue Monday Blues" (later "135th Street"). Jerome Kern and Oscar Hammerstein II wrote a black show-stopper called "Ol' Man River" for *Show Boat* (1927). The son of a cantor, Harold Arlen, was a leading composer of songs rooted in the blues, such as "Stormy Weather" and "Blues in the Night." The process by which Kurt Weill found an American idiom culminated in his last Broadway work, *Lost in the Stars* (1949), which showed how fully he was inspired to realize the ideal of opera in blackface. Indeed, Todd Duncan, who played and sang the leading role in this "musical tragedy," had the honor of having been Gershwin's original Porgy well over a decade earlier.[8] Such composers as Gershwin, Arlen, and Weill were thus fulfilling the 1893 prediction of Antonin Dvořák, just as he was finishing the last movement of his symphony *From the New World* in New York, that "the future of music in this country must be founded upon what are called the Negro melodies."[9]

The completeness of the Jewish identification with the plight of an even more vulnerable and despised people can be seen in the remarkable autobiography of a jazz saxophonist and clarinetist, Milton Mezzrow's *Really the Blues* (1946). He adopted the argot, the manner, and above all the music of ghetto blacks: "They were my kind of people. . . . I was going to be a musician, a Negro musician," he decided early in life, "hipping the world about the blues the way only Negroes can." Mezzrow married a black woman, and seemed actually to believe that he had in fact turned black. He insisted: "I became a Negro," and he managed to "pass" as black among both whites and blacks. If his autobiography is to be believed, "mezz" became a Harlem slang term for the best marijuana available.[10] Another Jewish experiment in putting on blackface was Gertrude Stein's "Melanctha," in *Three Lives* (1909). I am not entitled to pass judgment on the authenticity of its idiom and cadences. But consider the response of Richard Wright, who called it "the first long serious literary treatment of Negro life in the United States." The novelist recalled:

> As I read it my ears were opened for the first time to the magic of the spoken word. I began to hear the speech of my grandmother, who spoke a deep, pure Negro dialect and with whom I had lived for many years. All of my life I had been only half hearing, but Miss Stein's struggling words made the speech of the people around me vivid. . . . [Later] I gathered a group of semi-literate Negro stockyard workers . . . into a Black belt basement and read "Melanctha" aloud to them. They understood every word. Enthralled, they slapped their thighs, howled, laughed, stomped, and interrupted me constantly to comment upon the characters. My fondness of Steinian prose never deserted me after that.[11]

These were the musical and literary equivalents of the role that the Spingarns were to play in the operation of the NAACP, that Melville Herskovits was to play in the discovery of a viable African past,[12] that other scholars of Jewish birth were to achieve in reconstructing Afro-American history.

The tables were turned in an odd way in 1938, according to songwriter Sammy Cahn, who claimed in his autobiography that he heard two black performers in the Apollo Theatre in Harlem singing a new song entirely in Yiddish. The audience seemed to love it. Cahn bought the sheet music, written by Sholom Secunda and Joe Jacobs, and stirred the interest of three white Gentiles, the Andrews Sisters, who recorded it when Cahn met the condition of Decca to translate the words into English. It became the most popular song of the year, and "Bei Mir Bist Du Schoen" earned $3 million for Decca.[13] The popularity of that kind of tune came to an end in 1954, when a Cleveland disc jockey named Alan Freed brought to a certain culmination this Jewish penchant to wear the black mask. Freed introduced white teenagers listening to his radio program to the music that he named "rock and roll." Among the hits from the 1950s were by black groups such as The Coasters, whose writers were Jews named Jerry Leiber and Mike Stoller. They even wrote a quintessential "black" song like "Hound Dog," which Willie Mae "Big Mama" Thornton first recorded. The point is not that Elvis Presley's version made it famous but that, according to one music critic, "'Hound Dog' is unthinkable outside the impulses of black music, and probably a rewrite of an old piece of juke joint fury."[14] The rest, to coin a phrase, is history.

Perhaps the last major attempt for Jews at some level to imagine themselves into a black world that could then be showcased to the greater American audience itself was *Carmen Jones*. Oscar Hammerstein II wrote the lyrics; and since the composer, Georges Bizet, had himself been a Jew, the circle was closed. Billy Rose presented *Carmen Jones* as a Broadway revue in 1943 with an all-black cast. In 1954 it was made into a film by Otto Preminger, the Austrian-born producer-director who was to do the film version of *Porgy and Bess* five years later. Preminger was proud of having smashed the unwritten rule that "pictures with black actors won't make money." Hammerstein himself personified the operations of popular art under the shadow of high culture. For the grand opera that his grandfather staged was embedded in his childhood memories, but was poignantly associated from his own family's experiences with financial failure.[15]

Even when ethnic assertiveness and openness became common, beginning a decade or so after Alan Freed's audacious experiment, even when black consciousness beginning in the 1960s produced not white imitators but the hunger of Jews and other minorities to explore their own heritage and identity, a common theme or subject matter that binds American Jewish culture remains elusive. Directly ethnic subjects in mass culture are still too recent a phenomenon to be used as the basis for generalizations applicable to the past century, nor can the essence of American Jewish culture be found merely in penetrating the masks that creative Jews have often worn.

For I do not believe that that essence has a content, or can be found in particular thematic patterns. For most of the twentieth century, Jewishness as an explicit subject was mostly concealed. When not disguised in blackface, it sometimes took the form of a general interest in how impediments to love and understanding, those barriers created by race, religion, and ethnicity, might be scaled. This theme can be found in *Show Boat* (Edna Ferber; Kern and Hammerstein), in *The King and I*, the subplot to *South Pacific* (Hammerstein and Richard Rodgers), with its defense agency slogan that "You've got to be taught to hate"; and especially in the remake of *Romeo and Juliet* called *West Side Story* (Jerome Robbins's conception; Leonard Bernstein and Stephen Sondheim). It took the form of a special interest in intermarriage, or in the special allure of the *shickse*, as in American Jewish novels and films too numerous to mention in this context.

But such an emphasis on common themes and subject matter would exclude too much to bear the weight of any generalizations, and cannot specify the particular forms that talent can take. In the realm of theory, one size doesn't fit all. That is why a distinctive Jewish expression in American culture is likely to be found in its form, in a special approach that several representative Jews in popular culture have adopted. Unlike most black artists themselves, unlike gentiles generally, some Jewish contributors to American culture have addressed the mass audience without completely losing sight of the rarified expressions of American and Western culture. Operating so closely within the groove of the marketplace, such Jews have offered a distinctive perspective, even as they have helped to shape a notably democratic culture. The evidence to sustain this hypothesis is necessarily impressionistic, but it is ample enough to be worth proposing.

Musical composition and performance have been perhaps the most striking case of the Jewish penchant to breach the gap between high culture and popular or folk art. Perhaps that is because music has never entirely severed itself from the common impulse to enjoy—if not necessarily make—melody, and serious composers have long drawn from the pool of popular song. Perhaps more than any of the other arts, music has become the most hospitable to the blurring of the lines that would separate, say, the world of opera and the symphony orchestra from demotic musical expression.

George Gershwin (1898–1937) is undoubtedly the most celebrated and exemplary case of a popular composer aspiring to a higher realm. His own family was not musical, and did not own a piano until he was twelve, though he had a little classical training. By his mid-teens, however, he was already swept into the whirlwind of popular song.[16] From Tin Pan Alley to Broadway was not too terribly far a distance, but with the success of "Rhapsody in Blue" (1924) came the possibility of ascent into serious music. The Metropolitan Opera approached him to write an opera, but the road to that particular "Heav'nly Lan'" was rather sinuous. Interestingly enough, he had even considered writing an opera inspired by Ansky's Yiddish play, *The Dybbuk*. Instead Gershwin decided to make an opera about Charleston's Catfish Row, which meant that he had to fight for the property to DuBose Heyward's book with a cantor's son, Al Jolson, who had been so indelibly associated with Gershwin's song, "Swanee." Jolson wanted Jerome Kern and Oscar Hammerstein II to make it into a blackface musical, and they indeed had once been interested in bidding for the property before deciding to abandon Catfish Row to Gershwin.

The composer's shocking death of a tumor at the age of 39 makes conjecture on his eventual professional direction idle; but it should be noted that Gershwin's willingness to follow his muse outside of his expected range, his refusal to define himself exhaustively in the genre of the musical, was an immediate commercial failure. His "American folk opera" ran only 124 performances on Broadway in 1935. The critic and composer Virgil Thomson dismissed it as "crooked folklore and half-way opera," and the $10,000 that the composer earned on royalties were spent paying the copyists. *Porgy and Bess* finally reached the Met in 1985, well after it had been the first American opera to be mounted at La Scala.[17] Gershwin had achieved immortality by disregarding the rigidities of hierarchy, by breaking the rules. But then, if there were rules for geniuses, we could all be geniuses. One critic, Wilfrid Sheed, considers the question pointless whether Gershwin was "a serious composer manqué or just a pushy songwriter. . . . Ask any European whether he'd rather hear an evening of Gershwin or Aaron Copland, and you'll see that George made the right choice artistically."[18]

That is not fair to Copland (1900–   ), himself an imposing figure whose work Europeans have indeed appreciated and who made "serious" music accessible to his fellow citizens as has no other twentieth-century American composer. Copland's vocation has been the honorable search for a "musical vernacular," whether writing patriotic ballets or a serial "Piano Fantasy," aiming at some sort of thematic reconciliation between the individual and the community. Though his work is commonly viewed as distinctly American, he told one interviewer: "I think of my music as Jewish, because it's dramatic, it's intense, it has a certain passionate lyricism in it. I can't imagine it written by a *goy*." Copland wrote film scores in Hollywood too, an experience that once caused him to complain to Groucho Marx: "I have a split personality." "It's okay," the comedian replied, "so long as you split it with Mr. Goldwyn."[19] A psychologically more complicated case was Oscar Levant (1906–1972), who had classical training as a pianist but played with dance bands in the 1920s and wrote popular hits. In the 1930s he studied composition with Arnold Schoenberg in Los Angeles, while socializing with Harpo Marx. Levant also won acclaim as a concert pianist for his interpretations of Gershwin's Concerto in F and "Rhapsody in Blue," before he succeeded in new careers on a radio quiz show and on television talk shows. Even before self-destructing into drug addiction and neurotic self-loathing, Levant discovered that his worlds sometimes collided. He once found himself at a dinner party at which the only other guests were Harpo, Schoenberg, Beatrice Lillie, and Fanny Brice, who kept trying to persuade the inventor of atonal music to demonstrate his genius: "C'mon, professor, play us a tune."[20]

The leading composers of Hollywood film scores often straddled the two worlds of serious music and popular culture. The fullest exemplar of these twin tastes has undoubtedly been André Previn, who wrote more than fifty film scores, of which four won Oscars (for, among others, *Porgy and Bess*). Previn studied conducting under Pierre Monteux, whom he later succeeded as conductor of the London Symphony Orchestra. But by the age of fifteen, he was already arranging film scores at M-G-M. Previn was also a jazz pianist whose records are still available. In part because of his responsibilities as music director of both the Royal Philharmonic Orchestra in London and the Los Angeles Philharmonic, one journalist has described Previn's talk as "a blend of English locutions, hipster slang, literary allusions and show biz familiarity." And it is also said that Previn "can play Gershwin better than anyone who conducts him better, and he can conduct him better than anyone who plays him better."[21]

Previn's role model has been Leonard Bernstein (1918–   ), whose education and training (Harvard, Curtis School of Music) differentiate him from the Jews in popular culture who kept looking behind and above their shoulders. Bernstein is of course fundamentally a product of the world of serious music. But no one in American musical history has moved so easily or so spectacularly into other genres, and it may be no accident that Bernstein is the first important conductor to have been entirely American-trained as well as American-born. For purposes of the thesis of this chapter, the familiar outline of his career can only invoke cries of *dayenu*. Had he only composed symphonies and a ballet and an opera without also winning an Oscar for the score of *On the Waterfront* . . . Had he only conducted the New York Philharmonic and virtually every other major orchestra, without also working on Tin Pan Alley (under the name of Lenny Amber—the English translation of *bernstein*) . . . Had he not done more than any other American to explain, glamorize, and popularize classical music without also writing Broadway shows . . .[22] The recent Deutsche Grammophon recording of *West Side Story*, in which he conducts his complete score for the first time, is the most impressive evidence of a facility to operate successfully in a hybrid form. Bernstein denies that his recording of *West Side Story* is an opera (though "it's on its way to becoming one"), but it has been cast with opera singers who make convincing the musical aspirations within which the original Broadway production were only latent.[23]

Although it is a supremely popular form, the Broadway musical, with its origins in the European operetta, has long attracted educated and cultivated composers and lyricists. With the striking exception of the blue-blooded Cole Porter, it has also overwhelmingly attracted Jews, which means that almost any generalization about this genre—as an expression of distinctive Jewish talent—has wings. Broadway is nevertheless an especially convincing instance of this blending of "high" and "low" cultures. Its current presiding figure, whose career began as the lyricist of *West Side Story*, is an emblematic figure in this respect. Stephen Sondheim (1930–   ) has emerged largely out of the tradition of the musical. When he was fifteen, his Pennsylvania neighbor, Oscar Hammerstein II, spent an afternoon criticizing the musical Sondheim had written—his first—in prep school, giving him a crash course in how to write lyrics for Broadway shows, showing him the pitfalls a few easy lessons could avoid. Sondheim went on, of course, to write music as well as lyrics, and studied composition formally with Milton Babbitt after graduating as a music major from Williams College. His versatility is remarkable, for in a fourteen-show career, he has drawn upon Japanese music (*Pacific Overtures* in 1976), the opera (the 1979 *Sweeney Todd*—which has indeed been staged at the New York City Opera), the waltz (*A Little Night Music* in 1973), as well as the tradition of the Broadway musical itself (*Follies* in 1971—done in a sold-out concert version in Lincoln Center in 1985, played by the New York Philharmonic). *Follies* was a commercial flop, losing its entire original $800,000 investment, but it was a *succès d'estime*, winning seven Tony Awards; and its record producer called it "almost the first truly adult musical. It's about complicated people who may or may not be speaking their minds. There's a surfeit of sub-text." His musical based on an impressionist painting, *Sunday in the Park with George*, won a Pulitzer Prize in 1985. Though Sondheim prefers "to write in dark colors about gut feelings," he could echo the madam who sings the song he wrote for the movie, *The Seven Per Cent Solution*: "I Never Do Anything Twice."

At least among American-born Broadway composers, Sondheim's formal training in serious musical composition does make him an anomaly. But it is worth observing how neatly his work fits the pattern that other Jews have exhibited in popular forms. For his musicals reveal in a resplendent way a seriousness, a virtuosity, an experimental effort to transcend the popularly established limitations, to break conventions for the sake of a sophistication drawn from other (or higher) realms that other creative Jews have also demonstrated. Despite his dominance of the contemporary Broadway musical, Sondheim himself tends to listen only to "serious" rather than popular music, preferring late nineteenth- and early twentieth-century composers such as Ravel and Rachmaninoff. "What makes him so contemporary," one historian of the musical theatre observed, "is that he doesn't say, "S Wonderful,' like Gershwin, but 'I *think* it's wonderful.'" (Sondheim's favorite American musical, incidentally, is *Porgy and Bess*, that hybrid of opera, theater, and folk art.) And his pertinent, wry, literate, acidulous, often gloomy lyrics and dazzlingly complex and intricate musical inventiveness thus greased the exit of ditties like "Tea for Two."[24]

Sondheim might well be sympathetic toward the motto of Kurt Weill (1900–1950): "I have never acknowledged the difference between 'serious' music and 'light' music. There is only good music and bad music." Long before Weill got to the United States, the career of this cantor's son from Dessau confirmed a willingness to obliterate the distinction. While in his twenties, Weill had already written synagogue music, a string quartet, and a violin concerto; but his adaptation of American jazz led to his most sensational hybrid, *The Threepenny Opera* (1928). Formally trained in advanced composition under Ferruccio Busoni, Weill immigrated to the United States in time to collaborate with Max Reinhardt on *The Eternal Road* (1937), an ambitious pageant of Jewish history first staged at the Manhattan Opera House. Weill managed to write successful Broadway show music thereafter, from *Knickerbocker Holiday* (1938) to *Lady in the Dark* (1941) to *Lost in the Stars*. But even then he was reaching for something more, writing to the music critic of the *New York Times* after the last show that the audience "accepted a lot of very serious, tragic, quite un-Broadwayish music of operatic dimensions."[25] He may well have been on the verge of synthesizing the opposites that marked his career when he died of a heart attack at the age of fifty. A later music critic of that newspaper judged Weill in 1987 as "perhaps the most important precursor of the worldwide movement today that hopes to revitalize opera by infusions of energy from the popular musical theater." Marc Blitzstein's *The Cradle Will Rock* (1937) was an early sign of Weill's influence.[26]

Perhaps the only other European-born and trained composer to triumph on Broadway was Frederick Loewe (1901–1988). His father had created the role of Prince Danilo in the Berlin production of *The Merry Widow*, and he himself was also a pupil of Busoni's. As a pianist Loewe made his debut with the Berlin Philharmonic at the age of fourteen. Two year later he won the Amsterdam Medal as the best young concert pianist on the continent of Europe. Such talents came in handy when he collaborated with Alan Jay Lerner (1918–1986) on *Brigadoon* (1947), *Paint Your Wagon* (1951), *My Fair Lady* (1956), and *Camelot* (1960). As evidence of facility in moving in different strata, the Harvard-educated Lerner wrote material for Victor Borge before he joined up with Loewe; and before he transformed *Pygmalion*, among the masterpieces of the century's premier British playwright, Lerner was working on a musical adaptation of Al Capp's *Li'l Abner*. It is a sign of the increased blurring of distinctions that in 1986 the New York City Opera staged, with its own singers, Lerner and Loewe's *Brigadoon*, after the musical had already enjoyed at least seven New York revivals since its first run. The general director of the opera company, Beverly Sills, emphatically denied that "we're doing *Brigadoon* to get people to go to *Mefistofele* or *La Bohème*."[27]

Among jazz musicians, there was something unique about Benny Goodman in the proximity of his connection to classical music. Though he was too poor to take music lessons anywhere other than in his Chicago *shul* and at Hull House, Goodman managed to combine a second career in "serious" music with his jazz, especially when the era of the big bands largely came to an end by the 1940s. His classical recording career began in fact as early as 1938, when he recorded the Mozart Clarinet Quintet with the Budapest String Quartet. His album, *Private Collection*, includes performances of the Brahms Clarinet Quintet and Trio in A Minor, Beethoven's Op. 11 Trio for Piano, Clarinet and Cello, and Weber's Clarinet Quintet. Goodman also taught at Juilliard and at Boston University, and commissioned a clarinet concerto from the most successful of all American composers of "serious" music, Aaron Copland. Both are kinsmen of Jacob, the grandfather in Clifford Odets's Depression drama, *Awake and Sing*. Though Jacob lacks a formal education and lives at the edge of economic desperation, he adores opera; and his fragile spiritual world is shattered when his beloved Caruso record is smashed.

Consider as well the paradoxical stature and taste of the most successful female vocalist in American history. Though she cannot read music, Barbra Streisand has made thirty-eight albums. But even more oddly, she admits that she "really can't stand listening to pop music, although I know I should. Most of the time I don't listen to any music. When I do, it's classical. My favorite piece is Mahler's [unfinished] Tenth Symphony, and I also love Bartók's Second Violin Concerto and Maria Callas singing Puccini." It is also hard to decide which of Streisand's actions was more *chutzpahdik*: cutting a classical album, in which she learned *Lieder* by listening to their recorded versions, or persuading Stephen Sondheim to rewrite three of his presumably flawless songs (including "Send in the Clowns"—which originally took him only one evening to write anyway) for her *Broadway Album*.[28] Sondheim incidentally praised "not just her voice but her intensity, her passion and control. She has the meticulous attention to detail that makes a good artist."[29] And the late Canadian pianist Glenn Gould, reviewing *Classical Barbra* for *High Fidelity* magazine in 1976, announced: "I'm a Streisand freak and make no bones about it. With the possible exception of Elisabeth Schwarzkopf, no vocalist has brought me greater pleasure or more insight into the interpreter's art. . . . The Streisand voice is one of the natural wonders of the age, an instrument of infinite diversity and timbral resource."[30]

It would be counter-intuitive to expect that Donna Summer or Aretha Franklin would express preferences for Mahler and Bartók. They were not the composers that Diana Ross had in mind when the Supremes sang "I Hear a Symphony." For the black contribution to American popular music has been quite different—and far more iconoclastic. The black attitude was probably most cogently formulated by Chuck Berry, who hailed rock 'n' roll without any of the anxiety of influence and who urged Beethoven just to "Roll over . . . and tell Tchaikovsky the news!" That is another way of indicating the singularity of the role of many Jews in American culture, who differ from other ethnic groups in the extent of the cues that they still take from the courtly muses of Europe.

Equally noteworthy is the skill with which some Jews took familiar forms and then enlarged them to the scale of their own expressive ambitions. This is not a matter of serious composers enhancing the idiom of musical expression, but of popular songwriters drawing upon avant-garde music to break the bounds of a popular genre. Perhaps the strongest case for this extension of boundaries is Burt Bacharach, a product of—among other finishing schools—the entertainment crucible of the Catskills. But Bacharach has also studied privately under two of the most eminent composers of "serious" music, Henry Cowell and Darius Milhaud, from whom Bacharach seems to have learned the value of changing harmonies and rhythms.

With lyricist Hal David and vocalist Dionne Warwick, Bacharach has, according to one music critic, "succeeded in drawing the popular song away from the dreary, old 32–bar format and away from the verse-and-chorus tradition."

Perhaps an even more striking case of a popular songwriter breaking previous boundaries by drawing upon the advances and resources of high culture has been Bob Dylan. Abandoning the early influence of Woody Guthrie, Dylan refused to be limited by the constraints of folk music. He made its vocabulary far larger, its syntax far more complex, its range so wide that after a while his work could no longer be labeled folk music at all—a classification Dylan himself resisted and repudiated as fully as any other category to which his music has been consigned. Dylan became the first singer-composer to smash the barrier of the three-minute track suitable for AM radio play, because what he wanted to say could not be shackled to those three minutes; and the density of his vocabulary, which Allen Ginsberg heavily influenced, often seemed to overwhelm the musical carapace within which it was enclosed. Dylan's verbal virtuosity and complexity generally exceeded his musical gifts—which made him a mutant in the traditions of folk music and conventional rock 'n' roll, whose pious simplicities may account for the rarity of Jews in the field.[31]

But though entirely self-trained, no American has exerted a more powerful influence on folk and rock musicians from the 1960s, at least until fairly recently. Dylan managed to draw upon the cryptic imperatives of the modern literary imagination, and upon gnomic references that established him as a seer in a genre whose verbal resources stressed accessibility and immediacy, a field largely barren of such arabesques. One of the few other Jews in the folk and protest music of the 1960s, Phil Ochs, claimed of Dylan that, "from the moment I met him, I thought he was great, a genius . . . I had an increasing lot of secret fear: 'Oh, my God, what can he do next? He can't possibly top that one.'" When Ochs played *Highway 61 Revisited* (1965) for the first time, he "just laughed and said it's so ridiculous. It's impossibly good. . . . How can a human mind do this? The writing was so rich I just couldn't believe it." With that album, Ochs concluded, Dylan had "done it. He's done something that's left the whole field ridiculously in back of him. He's in his own world now."[32] Dylan flew through the end of the envelope because, though a drop-out from the University of Minnesota (honorary degree, Princeton University), he has been so receptive to the complex possibilities of serious contemporary poetry.

Other talented Jews stretched the dimensions that they inherited as well; the supporting evidence need not be confined to music. Another college drop-out, Jules Feiffer, a product of the shlock comic book houses of Will Eisner et al., gave the comic strip penetrating psychological and political sophistication when his work began appearing in the *Village Voice* in the 1950s. Such psychological nuance, such satiric force had no precedent in the comic strip. It was a striking instance of a popular artist (the critic Leslie Fiedler unfairly called him "a vulgarian") making a popular form intricate by giving it the stamp of an adult individual talent receptive to advanced currents of thought. Feiffer's later career as a playwright is not relevant in this context, but it does disclose a cultural ambitiousness that could hardly be found among the comic strip writers and cartoonists with whom he apprenticed. A very different sort of cartoonist has been Art Spiegelman, the creator of *Maus: A Survivor's Tale* (1986), drawn from his own family's experience as Polish Jews sent to Auschwitz. In this book, nominated for a National Book Critics Circle award, the Jews are depicted as mice (the metaphor that Kafka uses for them in his 1924 parable, "Josephine the Singer, or the Mouse Folk"), the S. S. tormenters as cats. Though this work invokes what may be the worst horror of the century, Spiegelman claims that *Maus* could exist in no genre other than a comic book: "It's my voice. It's the way I speak and understand things. . . . I'm trying to write epic poetry in telegram form. What's exciting to me is forcing this medium to express those subtleties. It's not an impoverished language, just a difficult one." Feiffer himself has praised *Maus* for revealing "a new way to express a unique and personal view of life."[33]

Saul Steinberg (1914–   ) fits perfectly into this thesis of rearranging and ignoring cultural hierarchies as well. Though most celebrated for his cartoons for the *New Yorker* magazine, his oeuvre has been exhibited at the Whitney Museum of American Art. For he is, according to Harold Rosenberg, "a frontiersman of genres, an artist who cannot be confined to a category. . . . One may think of Steinberg as a kind of writer, though there is only one of his kind." In presenting his eerie modern parables of urban civilization and its discontents, "Steinberg's compositions cross the borders between art and caricature, illustration, children's art, *art brut*, satire, while conveying reminiscences of styles from Greek and Oriental to Cubist and Constructivist." Rosenberg concluded that the cartoonist "tantalizes those who wish to separate high art from the mass media." The artist himself has also wondered how he ought to classify himself, sometimes calling himself "a journalist," at other times defining himself as "a writer who draws," elsewhere (and least helpfully) considering himself a sort of "novelist." The result is an anomaly, in which "a Steinberg" is, in one critic's estimation, "virtually a genre in itself."[34]

Just as a few Jews have made comics and cartoons more grown-up, others have made the children's book more serious. Its premier contemporary writer/artist is undoubtedly Maurice Sendak, the Brooklyn-born son of Polish immigrants. His "American childhood [was] composed of disparate elements strangely concocted, a childhood colored with the memories—never lived by me—of *shtetl* life in Europe . . . a conglomerate fantasy life perhaps of many first-generation children in America." Yet he has also recalled "being bombarded with the full intoxicating gush of America in that convulsed decade called the thirties," especially from the atelier of Walt Disney. Sendak was to transform a genre that has rarely offered a full-time challenge to the most acute intelligences; and while acknowledging the influence of William Blake as well as Disney, Sendak wrote out of personal obsessions rather than formulas. In books like *Where the Wild Things Are* (1963), *In the Night Kitchen* (1970), and *Outside Over There* (1981), Sendak has endowed this genre with an imaginative density and power that resemble what can be accomplished in more prestigious and exalted forms. The final volume of his trilogy was marketed for adults as well as children. British composers have transformed both *Where the Wild Things Are* and *Outside Over There* into operas; for the latter Sendak did the sets, costumes, and libretto as well. The American premiere was played by the St. Paul Chamber Orchestra, conducted by Pinchas Zukerman. Sendak has also designed the sets for productions of Prokofiev's *The Love for Three Oranges* and of *The Magic Flute* ("I love Mozart. . . . I think some of the most touching moments in *The Magic Flute* have to do with children.") A friend recalled a ride in which Sendak "sang all of *Fidelio* in German, using different voices for the various parts. But Maurice also has a real interest in, and hunger for, popular culture. He's a TV enthusiast who watches news programs, soap operas, drama and talk shows." Such tastes have blended into work that has won truly international acclaim, though winning the leading award in his field led him to quip that its name should be changed to Hans Jewish Andersen Medal.[35]

A capacity to swing both ways may account for why Edmund Wilson himself wrote "An Open Letter to Mike Nichols" (1968), urging the former comedian, whose grandmother had written the libretto for Richard Strauss's opera *Salome*, to direct classic American dramas. It was an inadvertent vindication of the democratic view that an immigrant from Danzig, who had stepped off the *Bremen* right before World War II, noticed a delicatessen sign in Hebrew and wondered, "Is that allowed here?," would be eminently capable of grasping and mounting works that derived from a different cultural tradition.[36] Such blurring may explain the lavish praise that Robert Brustein, then a professor of dramatic literature at Columbia University, heaped upon Zero Mostel, a rabbi's son best known for introducing theater audiences to Tevye in *Fiddler on the Roof*—but a star of Eugène Ionesco's absurdist political satire, *Rhinoceros*, as well. "In a just world and a healthy culture," Brustein insisted, "this powerful talent," the nation's "most versatile actor . . . would undoubtedly be playing all the great theatrical roles: Falstaff, Dogberry, and Toby Belch, Tartuffe and M. Jourdain, [Brecht's] Azdak and Herr Puntilla."[37] That Mostel was already squandering his great gifts was a fear that is beyond the scope of this chapter to consider. But another rabbi's son has also illustrated the ease with which cultural frontiers can be crossed. Erich Segal is a classical scholar who formerly taught at Yale, an authority on the masters of Roman comedy such as Plautus (the source for *A Funny Thing Happened on the Way to the Forum*), a scenarist who collaborated on the screenplay for the Beatles' full-length cartoon, *Yellow Submarine*, and a pop novelist who wrote *Love Story* and other best-sellers that have been as hot as a blast of geothermal steam.

If this emphasis upon the bifocal vision of so many Jews in the popular arts is plausible, then a solution has been found to what might otherwise elude any scholar on the prowl for a common denominator to American Jewish culture. If such a case makes some sense, then it becomes easier to confront the challenge that is posed by Jewish history. For from that perspective, perhaps the *least* impressive feature of this Diaspora community is its contribution to Jewish culture itself. To be sure, many of the forms of Judaic culture that were invented or emphasized elsewhere have been preserved in the United States. The various versions of Jewish faith have been adapted to American conditions, often with much skill and energy, tenacity and inventiveness. The achievements of this Diaspora community in organizational life, in philanthropy, in political security and impact, and in the reduction of discrimination have, however, dwarfed whatever influential and dynamic contributions it has made to the mainstream of Jewish cultural history itself.

Many of the most significant figures in American Jewish thought and literature have not been native-born Americans at all, but immigrants from a richer, fuller *Yiddishkeit*, like Heschel, Wiesel, Isaac Bashevis Singer, Emil Fackenheim, and Joseph Soloveitchik. The absence of many native-born counterparts to the great scholars and sages of Europe suggests the difficulty of developing on these shores the sort of Judaic culture that thrived before the Holocaust, and which has been transplanted and transformed in Israel. Religious vitality and creativity are not the most prepossessing features of Jewish life in the United States, where religious freedom is more passionately defended than used, where prayer is not widely assumed to be very effective, and a *tallis* is at best regarded as a fringe benefit.

The protagonist Nathan Zuckerman remarks in Philip Roth's most recent novel, *The Counterlife*, that "in our family the collective memory doesn't go back to the golden calf and the burning bush, but to *Duffey's Tavern* and *Can You Top This?*" Radio days thus mattered at least as much as holidays. Or consider the reminiscence of Larry Gelbart, a stellar television writer (*M*A*S*H*) and screenwriter (*Tootsie*), who acknowledged that the greatest literary influence upon his boyhood began—and virtually ended—with "Superman, Action Comics, first issue, June 1, 1938. Ten cents then, thousands now, but the memories are priceless. . . . Not a very lofty choice of reading material, but growing up on Chicago's West Side, I was more familiar with bookies than with books. Besides comics, the only literature in the house was the *Haggadah*, used for Passover *seders*—and I spoiled my enjoyment of that by peeking at the ending and finding out the Egyptians did it. To me, the ideal book would have depicted Superman helping the Hebrews during the Exodus."[38]

The familiarity of such experiences invites the inescapable suspicion that, as an addition to the cultural history of the Jewish people, the American community will not match the brilliance of the "golden ages" that have punctuated the history of the Diaspora. Of all the pivotal texts of the People of the Book, only the Bible itself was written in ancient Israel. Everything else is a product of exile. But the question of whether the most powerful and privileged of all Diaspora communities will enlarge the sense of holiness is merely a rhetorical one. Unable to retain a separate Jewish language, the American Jewish community has discovered no idiom with which to address itself alone in the reconstruction and rejuvenation of tradition.

Such was the view of several young intellectuals in the 1940s. Alfred Kazin, for example, had come "to accept the fact that I was Jewish without being a part of any meaningful Jewish life or culture. . . . The writing I have been most deeply influenced by—Blake, Melville, Emerson, the seventeenth-century English religious poets, and the Russian novelists—has no direct associations in my mind with Jewish culture; it has every association, of course, with the fact that, like many another American, I have had to make my own culture." Kazin added: "I have never seen much of what I admire in American Jewish culture." Lionel Trilling was, if anything, harsher, since modern Judaism had failed to produce "a single voice with the note of authority—of philosophical, or poetic, or even of rhetorical, let alone of religious, authority." The sterility of the American Jewish community was so devastating that "it can give no sustenance to the American artist or intellectual who is born a Jew."[39]

That was fair enough criticism a couple of generations ago. But if exceptions are made for the immigrant voices, those of the Holocaust survivors that still speak in foreign accents, the accusations of the secular intellectuals are almost as difficult to refute today. An echo of their criticisms can be found in Harold Bloom's recent assertion that "we do not yet have an American-Jewish culture. Our writers and speculators just have not been original enough until now, and probably will not be for some time to come." Because American Jewry has produced no Freud or Kafka, because its novelists do not equal fellow Americans like Faulkner or Melville or Hawthorne, because its poets cannot compare to the genius of their neighbors Whitman or Dickinson, Professor Bloom avers that a culture worthy of the name is missing. It is permissible to object that his standards are too exalted for even the very talented to match, that American Jewish writers have generally not sought to satisfy any such programmatic requirements or expectations to voice collective aspirations. It is also possible to argue that Judaic Studies in the academy may be applying the advantages of an American sensibility and methodology in reactivating the continuity of Jewish history. But what of Bloom's observation that American Jews have been losing the capacity to read and interpret the texts—the broken tablets—that are pivotal to culture itself, and certainly to Judaic culture?

Since so many Jewish readers have lost that capacity, the novelist Amos Oz has been among the Israelis to have indulged in *shlilat ha-galut*—the negation of Jewish communal life outside of Israel. "In terms of collective Jewish creativity, the post-Holocaust Diaspora has been barren," he has argued. "Individual Jewish creators in the Diaspora—to the extent that they remain Jewish, that is—are still living on the collective creativity of the non-existent Jewish centers of Eastern and Central Europe. They are living on an overdraft." The *kibbutznik* author has therefore considered it "only a matter of time before individual Jewish creativity there also fades away."[41] Amoz Oz does have a point, for a shrivelled community is not only unlikely to renew the sources of its own Judaism, it is also less able to nurture the sort of talent that a mass culture has so handsomely rewarded.

But the negation of the Diaspora can be countered. One way is to note, as Thomas L. Friedman did in a cover story in the *New York Times Magazine*, the extraordinary impact of American popular culture in the broadest sense among Israelis themselves; and to generalize that American culture itself, insofar as it is widely admired abroad at all, is deemed fascinating or worthy of imitation for having invented movies and for its popular music. Both Hollywood and Broadway (though not the recording studios of jazz and rock 'n' roll) have been primarily the locales of Jews, which suggests that the Diaspora has not been utterly uncreative, has not been running on empty. The erosions of assimilation have weakened the capacity of Americans to sustain and to enrich the legacy of Judaic culture. But the allure of an open society has also stimulated the distinctive contributions of Jews to an American culture. Perhaps the poignancy of the dilemma can best be illuminated by briefly noting the paths of two of the most gifted of American Jews. Both operated within the realm of high culture rather than the popular arts. But their careers have in retrospect suggested the differing directions that talent can take in serving the formation of an American Jewish culture.

One direction was taken by Harry A. Wolfson (1887–1974), who was born in Lithuania and was trained in the great centers of Judaic learning like Bialystock, Kovno, Vilna. He arrived in the United States at the age of eighteen and jumped, apparently without breaking stride, from a culture formed in the late Middle Ages to the campus of Harvard, from which he received his doctorate and where he taught for the remainder of his life. Wolfson held the chair in Hebrew Literature and Philosophy, in an institution where John Hancock had first endowed a professorship in Hebrew and theology prior to the American Revolution; and Wolfson became such a stunningly erudite scholar of Jewish, Christian, and Muslim philosophy that a chair was eventually named for him at the only Jewish-sponsored, non-sectarian American academic institution, Brandeis University.[42] He mastered medieval thought from Philo to Spinoza, which he categorized as a struggle to reconcile reason and revelation and which he conceived as a unity, with manifestations in three religious traditions and written in three languages (Latin, Hebrew, and Arabic). This was a singular achievement.

Wolfson was hardly an isolated figure and was as honored as any scholar of such recondite work could conceivably be. But this self-defined "unobservant Orthodox" Jew was also haunted by loneliness, just as Abraham Cahan's protagonist David Levinsky realizes how sadly different and estranged the successful cloak manufacturer had become from the boy who once poured over the pages of the Talmud. In the 1920s Wolfson had rejected an offer from the new Hebrew University of Jerusalem to create and lead its philosophy department. He later regretted his decision, and his explanation helps suggest the limitation of American Jewish culture: "My life would not have been happier, but I would have been what I started to be."[43]

A different life has been lived by Saul Bellow (1915–), who was born to Russian immigrants in Canada and raised in Chicago, where he too went to a *cheder* and argued with his parents in Yiddish. But then he checked out of the library the novels of Melville, Dreiser, and Anderson, and ended up producing an oeuvre that has garnered three National Book Awards and that, according to the verdict in Stockholm, has exhibited "exuberant ideas, flashing irony, hilarious comedy and burning compassion." When Bellow visited Israel, he too was invited to stay, and was told that a Diaspora existence was "inauthentic." Only as an Israeli, he was informed, could he re-enter history and be restored. The Nobel laureate, who is now the single most translated American novelist in the People's Republic of China, felt obliged to defend his choice, and in doing so affirmed the promise and the meaning of American Jewish culture. For all his concern for the security and well-being of Israel, Bellow professed to be "attached to my country and the civilization of which it was a part. . . . My life had [not] been illusion and dust. . . . Nor could I accept the suggestion that I repudiate some six decades of life, to dismiss my feelings for some of the sources of my being *because I am a Jew or nothing.* That would wipe me out totally. It would be not only impiety . . . but also self-destruction." For the novelist simply could not "despise the life that . . . [I was] born into. . . . If we dismiss the life that is waiting for us at birth, we will find ourselves in a void." To abandon the United States would, he feared, "destroy our reverence for the sources of our being." And so Bellow concluded that "the only life I can love, or hate, is the life that I—that we—have found here, this American life of the Twentieth Century."[44]

4

HUMOR

What is distinctive about Jewish humor, especially in its American setting? Students of the subject—and Jewish audiences —generally take its special qualities for granted, preferring to define it as Justice Potter Stewart once classified pornography: "I know it when I see it."[1] Others have tried harder, stressing the proximity of Jewish humor to the suffering that is an ineluctable feature of this ancient people's history. Literary critics have discerned a special verbal resourcefulness in Jewish wit. Freud stressed the aggressive quality of Jewish jokes, and once contemplated publishing an anthology of them. Yet one of his disciples, Theodor Reik, claimed that cruelty is absent from Jewish humor, adding that such "restraint prevents Jews from ridiculing the members of their family, especially the parents."[2] That definition would patently exclude such fictional revenges upon childhood and adolescence as Philip Roth's *Portnoy's Complaint*. A secondary character in that novel, the *kibbutznik* Naomi, contributes her own definition to the debate, scorning Diaspora humor because self-deprecation is so central to it.[3] Much of it has indeed invoked the derogatory stereotypes about Jews, who could blunt the impact of anti-Semitism by making their own variations on the themes of the greed and deviousness, the less-than-elegant profiles, the unclean habits that bigots ascribed to them. Modern American Jewish humor, the critic Albert Goldman has written, was therefore "the plaint of people who were highly successful in countless ways, yet who still felt inferior, tainted, outcast."[4]

No generalization can possibly cover all the cases; for one researcher has located eighty-six volumes of Jewish humor, published in the United States, Germany, and France in the past six decades.[5] No effort to encompass this multitude of material is likely to finesse all the problems of definition and conception, or resolve scholarly disputes arising from them—short of going into binding arbitration. The exceptions cannot be kept from bounding up to do their spiels as well. Many American Jewish comedians and comic writers don't seem to drip with suffering, for example. Show biz humor, at which so many Jews have succeeded, is usually too shallow for the likes of Alan King or Joey Bishop or Don Rickles to pass for sages. At best they are wise guys, not wisdom figures. Even though Dorothy Parker was only half-Jewish, our slightly dotty lady of the sorrows was twice as funny as the typical Borscht Belt headliner. Comedians like Ed Wynn, Danny Kaye, and Milton Berle performed creditably in serious dramatic roles, when called upon to do so; but the sadness that afflicts human life is not always an obvious source of most popular comedy. Neither Soupy Sales nor Buddy Hackett appears to have been born under the sign of Saturn.

Freud's stress upon disguised hostility would certainly seem to fit the agenda of the Friars' Club, the comedians' fraternity which has never had any trouble forming a *minyan*; and the nervous disclaimers of the insult comics, as they assure audiences just hit with friendly fire, "No offense, folks!," would suggest the aptness of his psychoanalytic observation. But no one familiar with, say, the frontier humor of the nineteenth-century American Southwest would dare to claim that Jewish aggressiveness is in any way unusual. Reik's discovery of the quality of mercy is also dubious. Indeed, to a philosopher like Henri Bergson, "a momentary anesthesia of the heart" is a precondition of laughter itself. It always signifies, the French Jewish thinker wrote, "an unavowed intention to humiliate."[6] Although Jewish comedians were almost entirely absent from the golden age of Hollywood silent comedy, and though they were largely instrumental in the development of the comedy record album beginning in the 1950s, verbal resourcefulness cannot be held accountable for the success of many others, from the Ritz Brothers and Three Stooges to their French cousin, Marcel Marceau, from the brilliant caricaturist David Levine to the cartoonist Rube Goldberg, from the goofy slapstick comedians like Sid Caesar and Jerry Lewis to the eerily enchanting Harpo Marx.

Nor is it safe to generalize that self-deprecation is a Jewish monopoly. Take the joke, which may be nearly a century old, about the talents and possessions that various races craved when they were created. The joke diverges from the Book of Genesis, but here is how it goes: The Anglo-Saxon asked for political domination, the Chinese wanted peace and isolation, the American Indian wished for a happy hunting ground, the black American for a million dollars, and the Jew for a few pieces of costume jewelry and the black man's address. Were the joke derived from a Jewish source, its facile assumption of Jewish cleverness would qualify any generalization about self-deprecation. But this insight into ethnic difference is actually taken from Afro-American folklore. Even Malcolm X, who issued the most searing jeremiads against self-hatred within the black community, repeated it in his *Autobiography*.[7]

Other claims are equally shaky. Jews are disproportionately represented among insult comics. But could any humor be more gentle than Sam Levenson's or endearingly cute than Danny Kaye's? A few comedians are political; most are not. Some exaggerated their politesse, like the comic persona of S. J. Perelman. Others have been ribald and "dirty"—including a high percentage of Jewish "funny girls" from Belle Barth and Totie Fields down to Bette Midler and Joan Rivers, whose faces launched a thousand quips. Some have specialized in mocking and trashing and denigrating themselves—most notably Rodney Dangerfield, whose baby picture was blown up into a poster by an organization advocating birth control; and even when Dangerfield became an adult, a prostitute once repelled his advances, protesting that she had a headache. Other performers have also depended for laughs upon their homeliness, like Britain's Marty Feldman, who became part of Mel Brooks's zany troupe. Feldman's "eyes, encased in protruding turrets, seemed to be independent of one another," Chaim Bermant has observed. "With his large head, and slight, tapering figure, he looked like a hydrocephalic lizard." Others also stressed their own puniness and vulnerability. But Sid Caesar, for example, was a *shtarker*, "the strongest comic in history," according to Brooks. "He could punch a Buick in the grille and kill it."[8] (Such power is ascribed to "King Kaiser," in *My Favorite Year*, the 1982 film based upon *Your Show of Shows*.) For every attempt to locate the essence of Jewish humor, all sorts of other counter-examples could also be cited.

So numerous are the complications that anyone foolish enough to generalize on the topic of American Jewish humor must *shlepp* past the bleached bones of earlier analysts who perished in the attempt. But some theories of the distinctiveness of the phenomenon are more persuasive than others. The *locus classicus* of the subject, in which its complexities are most engagingly encased, is *The Big Book of Jewish Humor*. Its editors, William Novak and Moshe Waldoks, nowhere formulate a single definition of a Jewish joke, though they do pass along the twin criteria that it is "one that no *goy* can understand and every Jew says he has already heard."⁹ More importantly, Novak and Waldoks have shown how indebted Jewish humor is to religious sources as well as to the minority condition from which such a sensibility could so naturally emerge. After elaborating upon these two elements, I would like to propose a third form of humor as distinctive to the culture or subculture that modern Jews have created.

The first category is almost tautological, since it bears the most intimate connection to the Jewish world itself, whose most important propulsive force has been religion. That is humor that is internal to Judaic belief and practice.

But first a brief comparison. In the carnivals that were celebrated in medieval and early modern Europe, Catholic authority could be mocked with impunity during the season preceding Lent. Inversion took the form of ridiculing the priests, putting Bibles on sticks, and committing other acts that reflected, according to the historian Emmanuel Le Roy Ladourie, "the Catholic scenario: Carnival embodied unbridled pleasure, the joys of life and the dance, [and] the pagan sins of the flesh." But while Purim could be considered a Jewish counterpart to carnival, the targets of impiety have differed. To be sure, Jews are enjoined to become too drunk to distinguish between the villain Haman and the hero Mordecai. But more significant is the Purim spiel, with its send-ups of Talmudic learning, its parodies of the flights of *pilpul*. Such drollery depended upon some intimacy with the intricate arabesques of rabbinic reasoning and thus gave a special cast to religious inversion.¹⁰

The rise of skepticism could draw upon Biblical knowledge for its own comic aims, as in the joke of Moses coming down from Mount Sinai and telling the Israelites that he had good news and bad news: "The good news is that I got Him down to ten. The bad news is that one of them is adultery." Or consider Novak and Waldoks's elaborate version of a tale from the late nineteenth century: Two very young Talmudic scholars from Lublin are invited from afar to marry the daughters of two wealthy families. The head of the yeshiva tells Menashe and Mendel that their prospective in-laws will be able to support Torah study all day or will even eventually enable them to go into the family business. The boys are put onto the train at the outskirts of the Pale. On the way Menashe asks Mendel exactly where they are going and why and is told: "You heard the Rosh Yeshiva. We're going to a place we've never heard of, to marry two girls we've never seen, to become part of two families we don't even know." The response causes Menashe to open the window of the compartment and jump from the train.

At the station the two excited entourages are astonished that only one *yeshiva bocher* gets off the train, so both prospective mothers-in-law grab Mendel to bring him home to their daughters. Each woman grabs one of the boy's arms, pulling in opposite directions as though he were a wishbone. They seem ready to pull him apart until the local rabbi begs the women to desist, promising a resolution of the dispute in his office the following morning.

That night the rabbi pores over the ancient texts in an effort to discover a solution, and is thrilled to realize that he—a provincial cleric—will be able to adjudicate a case so strangely similar to the case of the disputed baby that clinched King Solomon's reputation for sagacity. So the next morning the rabbi announces to the litigants: "My friends, only once before in the history of our people has a case of this sort passed before the eyes of a judge. The solution is therefore painfully clear: The boy must be cut in half."

Upon hearing the rabbi's pronouncement, one of the prospective mothers-in-law falls to her knees and urges a reversal of the decision. "Don't commit this terrible deed," she pleaded. "I will gladly give up my claim to this boy if you will only spare his life."

The second woman reacts quite differently, however, accepting with alacrity the rabbinic decision. "Go ahead," she says with a shrug. "Cut him in half. It's only fair."

At this point the rabbi jumps up, points to the second woman and proclaims: "Aha! *You* must be the *real* mother-in-law!"[11]

There could also be a post-Biblical, specifically Judaic form of humor that kids belief or custom. Though humor was not exactly integral to the sensibility of Paul Goodman, a litterateur who also published works in virtually every one of the social sciences and humanities, a 1945 play was entitled *Jonah: A Biblical Comedy with Jewish Jokes Culled Far and Wide*, in which the prophet sports a Brooklyn accent. It also happens that Goodman's favorite joke was about Mendele, "a loafer and a disgrace. The town council decided to give him a sinecure to get him off the streets. But every job requires a little effort, and Mendele wouldn't make any. Then they said, 'We'll make him the Messiah-blower, to blow the horn when the Messiah comes.' 'I should be the Messiah-blower?' cries Mendele. 'With *my* lungs? I couldn't lift the horn.' But the town councilors assured him that 'it's the year 5364, and the Messiah hasn't come yet.' 'With my luck,' says Mendele, 'with my luck the Messiah will come tomorrow.' "[12] A variation of this wry tale, with an equally ambiguous if less intense punch line, serves as the epigraph of Irving Howe's book on democratic socialism, *Steady Work*. This joke could only have sprung from those who had transferred at least the husk of religious faith to the secular politics that once inspired so many of them in Eastern Europe, in the United States, and in Palestine. In Chelm, the villager who is appointed to sit at the gate to await the coming of the Messiah complains about his low pay. The town councilors acknowledge that "the pay is low. But consider: the work is steady."[13]

Other writers have drawn upon the Bible for comic purposes, as in Isaac Rosenfeld's burlesque updating of the royal pains of "King Solomon" (1956); or Joseph Heller's recent novel about Solomon's father, *God Knows* (1984), which one critic dismissed as "the longest lounge act never performed in the history of the Catskills"; or Neil Simon's recasting of the Book of Job in Long Island, called *God's Favorite* (1974); or Arthur Miller's *The Creation of the World and Other Business* (1972), which treats human experience before the Fall and remains the only comedy in the playwright's oeuvre.[14]

But even if it could be demonstrated that contemporary Jewish writers may be a bit more likely than others to quarry comic motifs from the Bible, its stories and messages have hardly been a significant stimulus of modern humor. The Bible has of course so permeated the Western heritage, especially its literary traditions, that it could scarcely be confined to specifically Jewish expression. Even if space permitted allusion to other instances of Biblical satires, parodies, and burlesques, they would probably not add up to a corpus that was in any way synonymous with American Jewish humor.

For a second category does not affirm, however ambiguously, a particular religious tradition; instead, the powerful and universalistic faith that sprang from it almost two millennia ago becomes the target. Moritz Saphir (1795–1858) may well have been the first writer to perceive Jewish wit as "the defense and weapon of the oppressed,"[15] a way of getting revenge and a form of stress management. One

American illustration has a very pious Jew announce while on his deathbed his desire to convert to Christianity. His wife and children are shocked and puzzled, and wonder why so observant a Jew would wish to reverse so dramatically the course of his entire life. He explains: "Better one of them should go than one of us."[16]

In Christendom itself a lively tradition of anti-clerical jokes has shown no sign of expiring. But those that include rabbis as well as ministers and priests ought not to be interpreted merely as riffs on this theme. Since the rabbis usually prove to be the most clever of the clergymen, such jokes are almost certainly of Jewish origin. What is at work here is a way of getting even that deflects into comic directions the resentful memories of medieval disputations. These contests pitted Jewish apologists against Roman Catholic theologians, with salvation of the soul as the ultimate stake and the danger of forced conversion the price of dialectical failure. When a cardinal asks a rabbi, "When will you get rid of your silly and ridiculous dietary laws?," the rabbi's response ("At your wedding") means that salvation has become a laughing matter; and pluralism has replaced persecution. A hatchet has been buried—but not the differences.

A more direct assault on the majority faith reflects the persistent Jewish skepticism toward claims made about the Savior. Carl Reiner interviews the 2,000–Year-Old-Man, once a candy store operator in Nazareth, about the crucifixion; and Mel Brooks replies that, yes, he knew Jesus: "Thin, thin, nervous—wore sandals. Came in the store, didn't buy much, mainly water, wanted water—so I gave him water. Look! You have a business. You can't always make a sale. So when people want water, you give them water. But one thing I have to admit. He was a bit of a troublemaker. He beat up a couple of *rovs* on the steps of the *shul*—and *you know you can't do that!* But they didn't have to nail him up. They could have given him a severe lecture. I didn't agree with such a severe punishment."[17] Such routines also represent one of the sublime achievements of comedy, which is to reconcile us to a fate which is untouched by the transcendent and the heroic, to reduce the magnitude of the metaphysical to the proportions of the familiar, to exorcise the terrors of the unknown.

For all of Alex Portnoy's hostility to normative Judaism and its adherents, the beliefs of the majority hardly impress him as any more rational. He remembers a childhood during the holiday season, crossing over the line into Irvington, New Jersey, and was astonished that "not just children but grownups, too, stand around on the snowy lawns smiling down at pieces of wood six inches high that are called

Mary and Joseph and little Jesus . . ." Portnoy concludes: "The idiocy of the Jews all year long, and then the idiocy of the *goyim* on these holidays! What a country! Is it any wonder we're all of us half nuts?"[18] In Dr. Bruno Bettelheim's ingenious reconstruction of the notes of the equally fictional psychoanalyst, Portnoy may well have been a unforgivable patient, a disagreeable person and a deeply troubled Jew; he would also have made bad material for proselytization as well.[19]

Though Lenny Bruce (1926–1966) was also quite ecumenical in firing his satiric volleys at various sects and faiths, he could also poke blasphemous fun of the Savior. Internal evidence suggests the genesis of one of his most famous routines, "Religions, Inc.", in a Chicago nightclub: "You and I know what a Jew is—*One Who Killed Our Lord*. I don't know if we got much press on that in Illinois—we did this about two thousand years ago. . . . And although there should be a statute of limitations for that crime, it seems that those who neither have the actions nor the gait of Christians, pagans or not will bust us out, unrelenting dues, for another deuce."

Then Bruce flew through the other side of the envelope by announcing: "Alright, I'll clear the air once and for all, and confess. . . . Yes, we did it . . . I did it, my family . . . I found a note in my basement. It said: 'We killed him . . . signed, Morty.' And a lot of people say to me, 'Why did you kill Christ?' 'I dunno . . . it was one of those parties, got out of hand, you know' . . . We killed him because he didn't want to become a doctor, that's why we killed him.' "[20]

Please permit here the insertion of an odd historical footnote to Bruce's wisecrack that the Crucifixion may not have gotten much press in Illinois. Three years after Bruce's death, the chief attorney for the Chicago 7, William Moses Kunstler, tried to refute the judge's claim that this federal conspiracy trial was an ordinary criminal case. "Your Honor, Jesus was accused criminally," Kunstler argued, "and we understand really that was not truly a criminal case in the sense that it is just an ordinary—" But Judge Julius J. Hoffman demurred: "I didn't live at that time. I don't know. Some people think I go back that far, but I really don't." Then Kunstler retorted with some Jewish humor of his own: "Well, I was assuming [that] your Honor had read of the incident."[21]

Although the framers of the Bill of Rights probably meant to exclude blasphemy when they insisted that expression in the republic should be free, Bruce's routine—and perhaps Kunstler's rejoinder— are also signs of how tolerant popular culture had become. It was different in 1952, when George S. Kaufman, appearing a week before Christmas on the television program, *This Is Show Business*, was asked what he most wanted to get for the holiday. His dry, detached reply— "Let's make this one program on which no one sings 'Silent Night' "— provoked a firestorm of indignant phone calls to CBS and led to his removal from the show, though he was later rehired.[22] Such distance from the sancta of Christendom probably should not be compared to the in-jokes with which alumni of, say, Catholic parochial schools regale themselves.

But one joke in particular can be pressed into service to demonstrate the meaning of Jewish identity in America. Three converts to Episcopalianism are drinking together in their ritzy country club, when they begin explaining the reasons for their switch from Judaism.

" 'I converted out of love,' the first one said. Seeing the dubious looks on his friends' faces, he added, 'Not for Christianity but for a Christian girl. As you know, my wealthy wife insisted that I convert.'

" 'And I converted in order to succeed in the law,' the second one said. 'I would never have been appointed a federal judge if I hadn't become an Episcopalian.'

" 'I converted because I think that the teachings of Christianity are superior to those of Judaism,' the third one added.

" 'Whom are you trying to kid?' the first man answered with considerable heat. 'What do you take us for—a couple of *goyim?* ' "

Interestingly enough, Charles Silberman, from whom this joke is lifted, interprets its point as a reflection of the belief in the enduring qualities, the tenacious resilience of Jewish peoplehood, regardless of assimilation or even conversion.[23] If chuckles result, that means that something distinctive about being a Jew—even in America—remains an article of faith. *Am yisroel chai*—the Jewish people shall live.

But the joke is especially pertinent for other reasons. Its punch line reveals more than a hint of contempt toward a sister monotheism. It slyly stabs at the mental inferiority ascribed to non-Jews, whose religious creed is too preposterous to be credible. (The joke therefore constitutes a modern reversal of Tertullian's second-century profession that he believed in Christianity *because* it is absurd.) The joke serves as a slight manifestation of the Judaic culture that has continued to insist upon its divergence from the rest of Western civilization. And finally the presumption in the joke of intellectual superiority invites consideration of a third category that marks Jewish humor, which is its uneasy but discernible relation to the idea of culture itself, especially high culture.

This category is the most dubious and controvertible. It requires the fullest defense, and hence is also the most interesting. For the estimated 80% of professional comedians in the United States of Jewish origin[24] are among the legatees of a culture that has prized the exercise of mind. Even Biblical Jerusalem, as Max Weber writes in *Ancient Judaism*, was filled with an urban "stratum of intellectuals,"[25] with talkers in the city whom Deuteronomy 6:6–7 enjoined to teach the divine commandments "diligently unto thy children, and . . . [to] speak of them when thou sittest in thy house, and when thou walkest by the way, and when thou liest down and when thou risest up."

Or consider the utopia envisioned by Maimonides (1135–1204). As personal physician to Saladin, the sultan of Egypt, and as the great codifier of Jewish practice, Maimonides enabled his mother to boast of "my son the doctor" *and* "my son the lawyer." Book XIV of his *Mishneh Torah* made happiness the predicate of the contemplative life: "Sages and prophets longed for the messianic age not in order that they should dominate the world and rule over the gentiles . . . but solely in order to be free to devote themselves to the Torah and divine wisdom without oppression and hindrance . . . ." He added in the "Laws of Kingship": "Therefore [the children of] Israel shall all be great scholars; they shall know hidden things and attain to the knowledge of God as far as it is within human reach."[26] No wonder then that the feats of the eighteenth-century sage, the Vilna Gaon, who reportedly slept no more than two hours a night so that he could pore over and interpret the texts, were legendary. Such scholars reflected the image of a certain kind of deity. The rabbis once asked themselves what God does with His day. How, after the world has been created, does the Almighty spend at least part of the time? One answer was: studying the Torah.[27] The Eastern European Jews who studied the Torah themselves were often introduced to Hebrew by *melamedim*, who were usually impoverished. Two of them were once heard in conversation: "Ah, if I were Rothschild, I would be richer than Rothschild." "How could that be?" "I would do a little teaching on the side."[28] The evidence for the priority of mental cultivation in traditional Judaism need not be indefinitely extended.

The Purim spiel may be the distant ancestor of one emphatic form of American Jewish humor, whose line to high culture itself is a sinuous one—but it can be drawn. Among the Jewish comedians whose crossover dreams inspired them to achieve popularity in the wider society, the first two categories that have distinguished Jewish humor could not prevail. The mass audience simply would not "get" the allusions to texts which can take a lifetime to master, or to rituals that must seem as exotic as a Papuan cargo cult, or to Talmudic brain-teasers (like what happens if a mouse carries leavened bread into a home during Passover?) which seem ready-made for modern risibility. And of course modernity meant that most Jews themselves would become too secularized to grasp the references, to identify, say, the levity in Leviticus. The second category was also problematic. Just as Jews would hardly welcome the prospect of national exposure to self-deprecating jokes about disagreeable Jewish traits, so too the gentile majority could not be expected to relish the aggressive and insulting humor that was directed at non-Jews.

The popular entertainers emerged from a people that has long enjoyed a high opinion of itself, especially how smart its members were supposed to be. "Why did God create gentiles?" goes one riddle. The answer: "*Somebody* has to buy retail." Occasionally that curiosity could be aggressive. "You show a gentile carrots and peas, he eats carrots and peas," Jackie Mason has observed. "You show a Jew carrots and peas: 'Wait a minute. Why are there so many carrots compared to the peas?' "[29] Jews have harbored so immodest a sense of their own intellectual abilities that it was joked that the title page of a Yiddish rendition of Shakespeare, done by the editor of the *Jewish Daily Forward*, announced: "Translated and improved by A. Cahan." At the *bar mitzvah* of Alex Portnoy, the rabbi announces from the pulpit that the lad's IQ is 158. The congregants are "awed and beaming," Portnoy recalls for the benefit of his psychiatrist. Their "adoration I feel palpitating upwards and enveloping me there on the altar—why I wouldn't be at all surprised if when he's finished they didn't pick me up and carry me around the synagogue like the Torah itself."[30]

Jewish comedians sought to reach too wide an audience to bother to play off against their own religion, and the taboo against traducing it in front of the gentiles was usually powerful. But such comedians could mock (or pay inadvertent tribute) to high culture itself. Untutored in the intricacies of piety as they were often insensitive to the achievements of artistic genius, they could at least draw comic relief from their distance from such ambitions and pretensions. As involuntary heirs to a formidable tradition and prestige of learning, they were naturally alert to the comic possibilities inherent in their own diminished stature. Expected to play in the tackiest rooms in the house of intellect, the comedians made such incongruities pivotal to their craft and even on occasion to their sensibility and vision.

Perhaps that is why musical instruments, which are probably the most available symbols of artistic aspiration, have been so frequently associated with Jewish comedians.[31] Victor Borge made a specialty of parodying classical music, not only with his own tempos and substitutions (impossible to reproduce here), but also with verbal humor as well. When requested to play Bach, he asked: "Johann Sebastian or Offen-?" Nor was the violin very far from Benny Kubelsky, better known as Jack Benny; and he played charity concerts with serious orchestras. Danny Kaye conducted such orchestras as well. Though a clarinetist himself, Woody Allen made jokes about his own losing bouts in his childhood with the cello; and in his first full-scale film, *Take the Money and Run* (1969), he clumsily plays the cello in a high school *marching* band. Zero Mostel once cut an album of risqué songs that he claimed his mother, a *rebbetzin*, never taught him. The harp was an extension of one of the Marx Brothers, whose antic destructiveness one night may have inflicted permanent damage upon the dignified aura of opera. Aided by a script by George S. Kaufman and Morrie Ryskind, Chico all by himself came close to bringing the house down on *Il Trovatore*, while Groucho marched up and down the aisles hawking fresh roasted peanuts.

Billy Wilder's *Some Like It Hot* (1959), co-written by the Viennese-born director and the Roumanian-born I. A. L. (Iz) Diamond, takes a more angular shot at serious music, recognizing how vertiginously it had fallen when it lands at the all-female band which a saxophonist and a bass fiddler have joined. Tony Curtis and Jack Lemmon pretend to have studied at the Sheboygan Conservatory of Music, but soon a discrepancy in their announced resumés is exposed: less time is spent at the conservatory than they had once claimed. But they explain: "We got off for good behavior." The band's blonde singer claims to come from a musical family: her mother was a piano teacher, and her father was a conductor. "Where?" Tony Curtis asks her, to which Marilyn Monroe replies: "On the Baltimore and Ohio." Instead of direct assaults on the formidable demands of high culture, Wilder and his collaborators manage to convey the fun to be had among those who could only flunk those tests.

As a child Henny Youngman wanted to be a violinist, and has continued to make the fiddle a key prop in a stand-up comedy act in which the one-liners spew out like bullets from an Uzi submachine gun. Morey Amsterdam had been a cello-playing prodigy in Chicago who gained admission to college at the age of fifteen before making clear a preference for show business. As host of "The Texaco Star Theater" and then "The Morey Amsterdam Show," he was known for his theme song, "Yuk-a-Puk," which he played on the cello to punctuate the one-liners of his stand-up routine. Others had aspirations from which comic impulses deflected them: Sam Levenson was a schoolteacher; and Jackie Mason is an ordained rabbi, like his father and three brothers. While serving congregations in Pennsylvania and North Carolina, Mason "started telling jokes at *bar mitzvahs* and weddings. The jokes started getting better. I decided to charge a cover and a minimum."[32] Though narcotics convictions spurred Lenny Bruce to considerable adroitness in First Amendment law, he was far more of an uncultivated lout than a *poète maudit* (or a picaresque saint); and too often his profanity was mistaken for profundity. Yet, as Brandeis University's Milton Hindus may well be the only scholar to have noticed, Bruce's routine acknowledging the Jewish guilt for deicide quoted *Hamlet* (Act III, Scene 2) for an otherwise baffling shtick about "the gait of Christians, pagans."[33]

Indeed very few of the significant contributors to American Jewish humor enjoyed the benefit of much formal education. Perhaps the only one who did was Sidney Joseph Perelman (1904–1979), who graduated from Brown in 1925. Though he became most famous as a Marx Brothers scriptwriter, he came to resent his association with them; and when an editor tried to anthologize excerpts from his scenarios, Perelman's response was sulfurous: "If illiterates and rock fans (synonymous) can only be led to purchase my work by dangling before them the fact that I once worked for the Marx brothers, then let us find some other publisher." As a *New Yorker* luminary, "El Sid" was endowed with so freakish a command of English that, more than anyone else, he invested American humor with a linguistic turn. No wonder then that the comic work in which he most "re-Joyced" was *Ulysses*. When his daughter was despondent after reading *Crime and Punishment*, he assured her—and vindicated his own calling—by observing that "you can be as deeply moved by laughter as you can by misery." In pieces like "A Farewell to Omsk," for instance, Perelman proved to be a wicked parodist of the Constance Garnett translations of Dostoevsky's fiction.[34]

Russian literature itself has exerted much fascination for other Jewish comedians. In France, Marceau stretched himself past the bittersweet character of "Bip" to do an extended drama based on Gogol's *The Overcoat*. In America three former gag-writers for "Your

Show of Shows"—subalterns from Sid Caesar's palace—have paid their own forms of tribute. Woody Allen's *Love and Death* (1975) is itself a send-up of the genre, down to dialogue that includes the titles of Dostoevsky's novels. Mel Brooks's *The Twelve Chairs* (1970) is a rendition of Ilf and Petrov's 1920s Soviet satire, and he himself is on record as admiring not only Gogol but also the supreme diagnostician of crime and punishment. "My God, I'd love to smash into the casket of Dostoevsky," Brooks has announced with characteristic nuance and scruple and self-restraint, "grab that bony hand and scream at the remains, 'Well done, you goddam genius.' "[35] And Neil ("Doc") Simon once forsook his customary and immensely popular material to adapt some Chekhov short stories for *The Good Doctor*, a play which suffered an agonizing but quick death on Broadway in 1973.

But of all the Jewish comedians who have utilized high culture for their own purposes, by far the most important has been Woody Allen (1935–   ). No one else, for example, could have written the scene in *Play It Again, Sam* (1972), in which, newly separated from his wife, his alter ego of "Allan Felix" goes to an art museum in search of the opposite sex. His own favorite painter is Van Gogh, though Felix admits that he wouldn't cut off his ear for a woman unless he "really . . . like[d] her a lot." He boldly tries to meet another art lover standing in front of a Jackson Pollock, by asking her what the canvas means to her. She replies in an utterly flat monotone: "It re-states the negativeness of the universe. The hideous lonely emptiness of existence. Nothingness. The predicament of Man forced to live in a barren, Godless eternity like a tiny flame flickering in an immense void with nothing but waste, horror and degradation, forming a useless bleak straitjacket in a black absurd cosmos." Allan Felix immediately gets to the point: "What are you doing Saturday night?" She responds: "Committing suicide." Barely missing a beat, he then asks: "What about Friday night?," thus allowing a candid insight into the less-than-aesthetic motives of at least one museum-goer.[36] In its own way the scene echoes a short film for which Mel Brooks won an Academy Award, *The Critic* (1963), in which a Yiddish-accented *eiron*, a pickle-barrel sage, is baffled by abstract expressionism, and finally concludes: "I tink dis is a doity pitcher."

Other evidence from Allen's films would be overwhelmingly easy to cite. In *Take the Money and Run*, he tries to pick up Janet Margolin in a park, pretending to be a member of the New York Philharmonic. After she asks him what he thinks of Mozart, she becomes suspicious when he admits that he can't quite place the name. In *Bananas* (1971) he tries to impress Louise Lasser with his knowledge of Kierkegaard, whom he finds quite pithy; she agrees that the Danish theologian is indeed "full of pith." In *Hannah and Her Sisters* (1986), the character he plays hopes that Nietzsche's notion of eternal return will be proven false, because he cannot bear having to see the Ice Capades again. In *Annie Hall* (1977), which Allen first conceived as a novel, he cruelly teases Janet Margolin (again) by reporting that two magazines, *Dissent* and *Commentary*, have merged, forming a new journal called *Dysentery*. Proving that the magazine nursed no hard feelings, the promotion department of *Commentary* has used a still from *Bananas* in its advertisements, showing Fielding Melish (Woody Allen) reading the neoconservative monthly on the subway. Equally good-natured was the editor of *Dissent*, Irving Howe, who later joins other Jewish intellectuals, like Bellow, Bettelheim and Susan Sontag, in *Zelig* (1983); they constitute a chorus of parodists (self-parodists?) who ruminate on the severe identity crisis of the film's eponymous anti-hero. But none of Allen's films is burnished with a more touching scene than the existential moment in *Manhattan* (1979), when "Isaac Davis" tabulates what makes life worthwhile—from the face of his beloved to Louis Armstrong's rendition of "Potatohead Blues," from Groucho Marx to Cézanne's pears and apples, from Chinese food to a certain novel by Flaubert—and in praising it, Allen is savvy enough to skip the obvious title and pick as his favorite *Sentimental Education* instead.[37]

His essays betray a fascination with the idiom and posturing of intellectuals, such as "The Whore of Mensa" as well as his send-up of *Madame Bovary*, "The Kugelmass Episode" (which made Allen the only former backstage gag-writer ever to win a national prize for fiction, the O. Henry Award). Though he is the thinking person's comedian, having written a "Critique of Pure Dread," he has given differing accounts of why his formal college education came to an abrupt end. Either it was for cheating (which "was a delicate situation, because it was with the dean's wife"), or it was because of academic misconduct during a metaphysics final ("I looked into the soul of the boy sitting next to me"). But in one interview in the *New York Times*, Allen soberly acknowledged the cultural vacuum in his own immediate background: "I didn't go to a play until I was about eighteen years old, almost never went to a museum, listened only to popular music, and never read at all."[38] Nevertheless, the reach of Allen's films and feuilletons has often given even his most sophisticated fans the sense of being blessed (in Yiddish: *zelig*).

Another of the utterly unpredictable flash points of American cultural history is that the vaudeville clown Bert Lahr starred in the American premiere of Samuel Beckett's *Waiting for Godot*, one of the most daunting of avant-garde plays. It opened in 1956 in Miami, where the absurdist classic of the future Nobel laureate was billed as "the laugh hit of two continents." Lahr himself triumphantly repeated the role of Estragon on Broadway. *Notes on a Cowardly Lion*, the poignant biography that John Lahr wrote about his father, does not claim that the clown understood —except intuitively—the metaphysical bleakness that animates Beckett's dramatic vision; but Martin Esslin's standard account, *The Theatre of the Absurd*, traces Beckett's own indebtedness to the same comic tradition that Lahr himself adorned. Indeed the other great French absurdist, Eugène Ionesco, once remarked that the three greatest influences upon his work were Harpo, Groucho and Chico Marx—another sign of the proximity of Jewish humor to the most vital artistic impulses.[39] Perhaps that explains why the Minister of Culture in the government of François Mitterand, Jack Lang, bestowed his country's highest award for cultural achievement upon Jerry Lewis, three centuries after Molière's plays gave the French their first full taste of comedy. However obscure the link between *Le Bourgeois Gentilhomme* and *The Bellboy* and *Geisha Boy*, Monsieur Lewis is now—you should pardon the expression—a "Commander of Arts and Letters."

The major versions of American humor itself only rarely derive their force or offer pleasures by turning the forms of high culture inside out. The braggart of frontier lore, the little man of contemporary urban life, the wily confidence man—these are among the comic archetypes of the United States (and some of them can be located within its Jewish variant as well). But aiming at the *vita contemplativa* has been rare among the makers of the mirth of a nation. On that short list, Mark Twain's evisceration of "Fenimore Cooper's Literary Offenses" and James Thurber's solution to "The Macbeth Murder Mystery" certainly deserve high place. To be sure, the homespun cracker-barrel sages spouting horse sense have often japed at linguistic pretensions. When Harvard awarded Andrew Jackson an honorary Doctor of Laws degree in 1833, the rumor spread that the president had responded to the ceremonies, which were in Latin, as follows: "*Caveat emptor: corpus delecti: ex post facto: dies irae: e pluribus unum: usque ad nauseum: Ursa Major: sic semper tyrannis: quid pro quo: requiescat in pace.*"[40] Or recall Will Rogers's Depression-based put-down of those whose grammar may have been sounder than their bank accounts: "A lot of people who ain't sayin' 'ain't' ain't eatin'." It seems to be the essence of American folk wisdom to inquire of the intellectually puffed-up: "If you're so smart, how come you ain't rich?" But generally these are insignificant spin-offs from the orbit of American popular humor, whose targets and standards have been quite different; and therefore some sly recognition—de facto if not de jure—of high culture should be noticed as a special contribution of Jewish comedians.

It is *not* the argument of this chapter that all or even most of them can be credited with such contributions—only that Jews are more likely than others to be drawn to such themes. But even among Jews, beginning with the vaudeville veterans who went into radio and television and nightclubs and created the canon of film comedies from *The Cocoanuts* to *Bananas*, it was more common to mock the other familiar forms of mass culture than to furrow highbrows. This was almost as true of the essayists for the *New Yorker*, like Perelman and Allen and Marshall Brickman, as it was for the laureates of adolescent alienation who concocted *Mad* magazine. (Eustace Tilley, meet Alfred E. Neuman.) Take, for example, a skit like Mike Nichols and Elaine May's idea of a celebrity talk show, in which a spacey starlet reports that she has never dated Bertrand Russell even though the host assures her that "Bertie" is unlike other philosophers ("I mean, he's not pushy"); and the starlet plugs her forthcoming film *Two Girls in Paris* (the Hollywood version of Gertrude Stein's *Autobiography of Alice B. Toklas*). For all their allusions, such routines are really burlesques of popular culture itself.

Nor do I claim that popular entertainers are closet intellectuals. It is unlikely that, after a hard night regaling nightclub audiences with his failures to earn any respect, Rodney Dangerfield enjoys curling up with Kafka's "Metamorphosis." Or that Henny Youngman, after whining that his wife has a black belt in shopping, peruses Jane Austen for illumination into the dialectics of marriage. That is not at all the claim of this chapter. Andrew Bergman, who has written movie comedies like *Blazing Saddles* and *The In-Laws* and the Broadway hit *Social Security*, is most unusual in his academic credentials: he earned a doctorate in American history from the University of Wisconsin. Even more striking was Tom Lehrer, a former mathematics professor at MIT who became a cult figure because of the comedy albums he cut in the late 1950s and 1960s, leaving blood on the tracks with his wit. Far more typical, however, were the Marx Brothers (in *Horsefeathers*), Jerry Lewis (in *The Nutty Professor*) and Dangerfield (in *Back to School*), who were supremely qualified to spoof academic life—but not to enter it. Ditto the Harvard-polished psychiatrist whom Mel Brooks so unconvincingly plays in *High Anxiety* (1977), as he delivers a scholarly monograph at a professional conference while standing beneath giant posters of Doctors Freud, Jung, and Joyce Brothers. Ditto one of Sid Caesar's most memorable characters, an oft-interviewed "Professor" who arrived on "Your Show of Shows" with a bewildering variety of Teutonic names, dressed like a tramp and burdened with monumental ignorance—especially in his own field.[41] (Caesar's Professor elicited no imitators, interestingly enough, among the other television comedians of the era, non-Jews like Jackie Gleason or George Gobel or Red Skelton.) The craft of popular comedians can be enjoyed readily enough as an extracurricular activity, without demanding that their material be incorporated into a humanities curriculum. For the sort of art that gives life meaning, renders it intelligible, and does it justice is well beyond the reach of most of the familiar effluvia of popular culture, which provide the mass audience with the shlock of recognition and tend to have the profundity, complexity and subtlety of a high school pep rally.

The craft of these entertainers should not therefore be confused with the use of wit and parody to illumine particular features of intellectual life. Here the incomparable standards have been set by the playwright Tom Stoppard, who has offered brilliant criticisms of contemporary ethical theory in *Jumpers* (1972), which the logical positivist A. J. Ayer reviewed with admiration in the London *Sunday Times*,[42] and of contemporary language philosophy in *Professional Foul* (1977). In a similar vein, Philip Roth was not seeking to cut the literary vocation down to size in casting a senile sportswriter named Word Smith as the narrator of *The Great American Novel*. Parodying the coarse and blustery "Papa" who sat for Lillian Ross's *Portrait of Hemingway*, Roth has him object to a facile symbolist reading of the canon, declaring instead that *Moby-Dick* is "a book about blubber, with a madman thrown in for excitement. Five hundred pages of blubber, one hundred pages of madman, and about twenty pages on how good niggers are with the harpoon."[43] But the compression of Melville's epic to a fisherman's tall tale (itself proposed by a reductionist critic satirized in Wallace Markfield's 1964 novel, *To an Early Grave*) is also comically mistaken. Such lampoons suggest that Roth's tone and stance constitute a form of literary criticism (as Stoppard's plays are philosophical criticism). They are not to be understood as efforts to bridge or acknowledge the gap between high culture and mass entertainment.

But as though a mere alphabetic accident separates the comic from the cosmic, humor should not only be taken very seriously; it should also be considered risky business. One clue is the casualty figures that so many practitioners of American humor have racked up. Some go sour or crazy, or cannot limit themselves to being funny—from Mark Twain's late bitterness and misanthropy to Ambrose Bierce's compulsive morbidity, from Ring Lardner's descent into alcoholic self-destruction to Thurber's pessimism and cruelty, from Bruce's addiction not only to drugs but to his legal problems in assuming the role of shaman, to Mort Sahl's solemn obsession with conspiracies (such as the Kennedy assassination), down to Dick Gregory's abandonment of stand-up comedy for the sake of assaulting a host of injustices (such as eating meat). Here the transformation of the most important of American humor magazines can be taken as symptomatic. Its editor, William Shawn, explained in 1981: "I could enjoy life more if we could do nothing but be funny, which I love . . . but the *New Yorker* has gradually changed as the world changed."[44] The often strange and irrational conditions of contemporary life have enlarged the availability of the targets of humor, without making the psychological sources of comic creativity any easier to tap or sustain.

Humor may seem notably dependent for its effects upon the moment (which is why we groan at the jokes whose ancient lineage can be spotted, things which already seemed funny on the way to the Forum). Humor is also quite culture-specific (which is why the current Parisian intellectual fashion of *humour juif* seems so bizarre). But however susceptible it may be to the vicissitudes of taste and the risks of obsolescence, comedy may well be more durable than, say, tragedy. Debate still swirls around the question of whether a Christian tragedy is possible, or a modern tragedy; yet the status of comedy is much more secure. Depending upon the incongruities of the common life, it is the more pervasive of the genres that the Greeks invented. It is likely to last as long as human life retains its basic features, disclosing the distance from the ideals that have been far easier to formulate than to fulfill. That is why George S. Kaufman was wrong to define— and dismiss—satire as "what closes Saturday night." Nor was the Viennese satirist Karl Kraus accurate in predicting the course of his legacy: "X said disparagingly that nothing would remain of me but a few good jokes. That, at least, would be something, but unfortunately not even that will remain, for the few good jokes were stolen long ago—by X."[45] The corrosive and savage examination of "the last days of humanity" that Kraus presented added up to more than "a few good jokes," but—once the topical café wit has been discarded—rather to a more enduring and accessible vision of human corruption than most of the dramatists and tragedians and pundits of Kraus's era could manage.

For the quality control problems that surfaced as early as the Garden of Eden are destined to remain the butt of jokes; the problems of evil that are highlighted in the Bible are still alive to comic perspectives even when that book itself no longer exerts the hold upon the Western imagination that it once commanded. What was once ascribed to fate is now easier to apprehend as human folly; and comedy helps us to measure—if not mediate—the chasm between dream and reality, between spiritual claims and actual conditions. Even our most apocalyptic nuclear nightmares, as the director Stanley Kubrick demonstrated in *Dr. Strangelove* (1964), are amazingly amenable to satire. Such themes suggest the gravity that the topic of comedy should sometimes demand. Like other important and enduring subjects (such as religion), its very nature is interdisciplinary; and many different perspectives can enrich its meaning.

Students of Jewish humor therefore need not strike an apologetic note, even though their terrain seems so unpromising. For it is pockmarked with sources that range from joke collections, some of which at least are biodegradable, to show business biographies and autobiographies, which are usually parables of upward mobility from gags to riches that are rarely told with introspection or insight. The perpetrators of these books are still usually seated below the salt. But their artifacts of mass culture still need to be incorporated into the analysis of the American Jewish community, whose preferences—in charities and cuisine as well as candidates and causes—still differentiate them from other citizens.

That distinctiveness was illustrated at a banquet in which a Jewish organization honored a top black athlete as its special guest. A comic named Sy Kleinman, who was hired for the occasion, discovered that his Yiddish punch lines did not stop the athlete from laughing just as hard and as loudly as everyone else. Afterwards the surprised comedian asked the guest of honor whether he indeed understood Yiddish, to which the reply was: "No, but I have a lot of confidence in you people."[46] The virtual franchise that Jews have exercised over popular comedy may nevertheless be waning (an eclipse that the blazing talent of such tormented masters as Allen and Roth may well have obscured). But humor remains an important entree into the imagination of a group that has not been content with running out the clock until the Messiah arrives to bring history to an end, a group whose longevity has not yet stymied its creativity.

5

LIBERALISM

One of the most puzzling features of modern American politics has been the eccentricity of American Jews. In the 1984 Presidential race, for example, Ronald Reagan galvanized the enthusiasm of every measurable constituency of whites and carried 49 states. Yet perhaps the most affluent of such ethnic groups—the epitome of the success story of upward mobility—joined blacks, Chicanos, and welfare recipients in preferring the Democrats' Walter Mondale. In repudiating Reagan at the apex of his popularity, the Jews were among the very few exceptions to Art Buchwald's reversal of the democratic wisdom of Abraham Lincoln: you *can* fool all of the people all of the time.

Even as the consultants for the next candidates for office zero in on the shopping malls and factory gates where the flesh can most effectively be pressed, even as the pollsters plumb the attitudes of the couch potatoes in preparation for the next set of races, the voting habits of most American Jews are worth pondering. For they constitute an irrational number in the equation of national elections. They have violated one of the few axioms of the discipline of political science, which is that the higher the income, the bigger the margin for the GOP. By and large, Jews do not seem to define their interests in the terms that others in their class manage to do. To elucidate the oddity of the Jewish suffrage requires the comparative method and—

perhaps more than anything else—an exploration of the past, if only because the historical imagination so affects such voters themselves.

A respect for idiosyncrasy allows us to begin in Dublin on June 16, 1904. In Barney Kiernan's tavern, in the century's most admired novel, Leopold Bloom becomes most explicit about his own membership—however nominal—in "a race . . . that is hated and persecuted. . . . Plundered. Insulted. Persecuted." When asked whether he is referring to "the new Jerusalem," Bloom responds: "I'm talking about injustice." James Joyce's protagonist is an Everyman, incarnated as a commonplace Jew, who is nevertheless endowed with the insight that "it's no use. . . . Force, hatred, history, all that. That's not life for men and women, insult and hatred. And everybody knows that it's the opposite of that that is really life." But not everybody—whether in Dublin or elsewhere—knows what Bloom knows. In this "Cyclops" episode (the most "political" in the novel), Leopold Bloom asserts that love is "the opposite of hatred."[1] For it confers upon human existence whatever shred of numinous purpose and redemptive hope that it can offer.

This thirst for justice, this desire to terminate a history of hatred, this idiom of moralism can be lifted out of Joyce's literary context and converted into the template of the Jewish approach to American politics. To make such a claim hardly implies that those qualities are unique to Jews, who certainly hold no hammerlock on either the theory or practice of ethics. But the historical record and the data of political science disclose that Jews are more susceptible than other voters to a vision of human brotherhood, to ideologies and programs that can be packaged in ethical terms, and to politicians who can present themselves as apostles of social justice. More so than other Americans, Jewish voters are inspired by appeals that can be contrived to echo the prophetic assault upon complacency and comfort. Theirs is a distinctive political subculture.

The policies that Jews support and the causes that they champion, the values that they cherish and the appeals that charm or alarm them do not correspond with the political profile of any other group. Arguments of immediate expediency and calls for ethnic loyalty find them less receptive than any other minority. To be sure, when party machines and local bosses were dominant, Jews mostly voted for the conventional candidates. But they have also differed from the Irish, the Poles, the Italians, and others in their participation in crusades designed to end the bribery and corruption that contaminated such machines. In this respect they have mostly resembled patrician Protestants of Anglo-Saxon stock in their Progressive hostility to the "old politics" of the bosses. So idealistic a stance has persisted, for Jews were manifestly more critical of the Watergate scandal than non-Jews, of whom 29% still "approved" of the Nixon administration in 1974 and regretted his resignation. The corresponding figure among Jews was 6%.[2] The comedian Jackie Mason at least partly reflected Jewish attitudes to Nixon: "I love a crook who knows his business. . . . Every week they caught him and every week somebody else went to jail." Though very much a layman, Mason offered his own diagnosis that Nixon suffered from syphilis after leaving the White House: "You can't screw 200 million people and end up with phlebitis."[3] Even though American politics bears some resemblance to professional wrestling—with its fake pains and screams, its relative harmlessness and absence of danger—Jews have been conspicuously involved in seeking alternatives, in reform movements and especially in socialism, which promised a cooperative commonwealth that would transcend the barriers of class and tribe and extinguish hunger and want and poverty.

The demand that the world conform to standards of social justice might be contrasted with Tolstoy's claim that the whole of the Gospels could be compressed into the injunction: Resist Not Evil. He was among the heirs of the prophetic imperative that warns us that, when we finally check out of here, we should not expect to be judged by how much wealth or power or glory we have attained, but rather by how righteously we have lived. That is a tradition of conscience, a conception of redemption, that Christians and Jews share. But the Jews have often drawn peculiar political implications from that warning. Their motto has often been: *resist* evil, which could be recognized and challenged through the incorporation of idealism in politics.

Unlike blacks, who have felt the weight of evil more than other Americans, whose situation has been so historically shaped by the stigma that whites have attached to skin color, Jews are (in the formulation of the Zionist historian Ben Halpern) an "ideological minority."[4] Commanded to be "a kingdom of priests, a holy people" (Exodus 19:6), they *choose* to be different according to a particular value system, a complex of symbols and ideas that impose meaning and coherence upon their lives. Daily existence may have been reduced to pressing pants, or delivering milk, or (like Leopold Bloom) canvassing for advertisements. But what could give life purpose amidst poverty, and give confidence amidst oppression, was a set of ideals that their own ancestors had developed and had hoped would elevate the human condition. Those beliefs were Biblical in origin. It must have been exhilarating as well as burdensome for Hebrew to be considered the native tongue of ethics, and for the statement issued from the world's first summit conference—on Mount Sinai—to become a foundation for Western civilization itself. The influence of Hebraic ethics has been pervasive and incalculable, defining in large measure the aspiration (if hardly the achievement) of most contemporary Americans—Christians and sinners alike. How much residual prestige those moral standards confer can be detected in the recent defense articulated by Congressman Daniel Crane, the pro-family conservative Republican censured for sexual relations with an adolescent Congressional page: "I still believe in the Ten Commandments. I broke one of them. And I think they're just as good today as they were then."[5]

The assumption that life is given dignity insofar as it can be infused with ethical idealism has, however, exerted a special attraction for Jews, and took a form indigenous to their religious tradition. That may be a small part of the continuing importance attached in the United States to the Passover *seder*, currently the most widely observed of Jewish holidays. To be sure, as the sociologist Marshall Sklare has shrewdly noted, its popularity is boosted by several relevant factors: it occurs only once a year rather than once a week (like the Sabbath); the calendar places it close to a Christian holiday (Easter) that can compensate for feelings of exclusion; it embraces children. But unlike, say, harvest festivals, Passover is also readily invested with modern meaning.[6] Recording the first experience of exile, the *Haggadah* could be read as a reminder that, even in America, Jews were still in a sense in Egypt, so long as others were in "Egypt," in bondage to poverty or subjected to tyranny. Passover is a celebration of freedom that is touched with the tears of injustice, an expression of national independence that is designed to reinforce a sense of solidarity with others who are oppressed, an annual invitation to comfort and pleasure that also recalls degradation as well as deliverance, an index of the meaning of exile that assures participants that there is a promised land.[7]

Whatever the actual impact of such holidays on the attitudes and behavior of Jews, there is no doubt of the singularity of the religious heritage that incorporated the Passover ethos and helped sustain them in the millennia of exile. One of their enemies, Charles Maurras, wrote in 1899 that Hebrew thought was permeated with "dreams of justice, beatitude, equality and inner revolt"—an accusation from the founder of Action Française that would have made many Jews proud. Coming from the opposite end of the political spectrum, the attorney Louis D. Brandeis noticed the distinctiveness of the Judaic legacy in 1914, upon assuming the leadership of the American Zionist movement. "I have been to a great extent separated from Jews. I am very ignorant in things Jewish," he admitted. "But experiences, public and professional, have taught me this: I find Jews possessed of those qualities which we of the twentieth century seek to develop in our struggle for justice and democracy—a deep moral feeling which makes them capable of noble acts; a deep sense of [the] brotherhood of man; and a high intelligence, the fruit of three thousand years of civilization."[8]

Some of this praise can of course be discounted as self-congratulation, by a figure whose fierce desire to be included in a movement of national restoration may have produced an excess of chauvinism. But the very fact that Brandeis approached Jewish life more or less from the outside licensed him to see more clearly than those who had absorbed its beliefs by osmosis the strangeness of its emphasis upon a moralistic patrimony, which American Jews have generally translated into liberalism, progressivism, a proclivity for reform. It was therefore not coincidental that in the film *Manhattan* (1979), a character with the thoroughly WASPish name of Yale (played by Michael Murphy) berates the neurotic Jewish seeker of integrity (played by Woody Allen) for allegedly trying to be God. Allen exculpates himself with a celebrated line: "I—I gotta model myself after *someone!*"[9] In that exchange is a clue to the character of Jewish politics in America.

A defect of such politics is its over-investment in ideas at the expense of the concrete, its seduction by the allure of humanitarian rhetoric. The makers of American foreign policy, for example, have sometimes grasped how deftly such sentiments could be manipulated, how readily pieties could serve as surrogates for decisive action. The ease with which the Roosevelt administration could pretend to help alleviate the suffering of refugees from the Holocaust has now become a staple of the diplomatic historiography of the Second World War, but it had a precedent in the administration of his cousin. In 1902, after the Roumanian government intensified economic discrimination against its Jewish population, co-religionists in the United States persuaded the Department of State to send a diplomatic note that would chastise such oppression as "repugnant to the moral sense of liberal modern peoples." Such notes made a hero of Secretary of State John Hay, who smirked privately about "the Hebrews . . . poor

dears! all over the country think we are bully boys." After the awful
Kishinev pogrom in czarist-ruled Bessarabia a year later, New York's
genteel "uptown" Jewish leadership—which was sensitive to what
motivated the immigrant masses "downtown"—sought to deflect the
outrage that was seeping from the Lower East Side. A petition
campaign was organized. Burnished with prestigious signatures, this
was a slow and tedious process that was never expected to reach the
proper address in Russia. John Hay's solution, when confronted with
a petition whose promoters never intended to deliver it anyway, was
to bury it in the archives of the Department of State. "In the future[,]
when students of history come to peruse this document," he proclaimed during the ceremony of interment, "they will wonder how
the petitioners, moved to profound indignation by intolerable wrongs
perpetrated on the innocent and helpless, could have expressed
themselves in a language so earnest and eloquent. . . . It is a valuable
addition to public literature, and it will be sacredly cherished among
the treasures of the Department."[10]

Words—the more inflated the better—are the most respected currency of Jewish politics, whose communal agenda has rarely been
devoted to the satisfaction of more immediate or parochial interests.
In the American version of the great game of politics, Jews may be
the most voluble players, the heirs of the people of whom Erasmus
was already complaining during the Renaissance that they "spread a
kind of fog over everything . . . words, words, words . . ."[11] The
former Speaker of the House of Representatives, Tip O'Neill (D-
Mass.), artfully combined old-fashioned organization politics with
New Deal liberalism, and happened to have had as a chief aide an
Orthodox Jew named Ari Weiss. But when the congressman wanted
to be redistricted to drop the posh suburb of Brookline, he is supposed to have cracked: "I love the Jewish people deeply. But they
write too many letters." The same impulses help account for their
disproportionate representation among the speech writers, the media
consultants, the publicity agents, the communications directors, the
lawyers, the analysts, the reporters, the activists associated with the
various causes—Common and uncommon and Barry Commoner's—
that the authors of the Federalist Papers could not have foreseen as
voices in the dialogue of popular sovereignty.

The wish that parochial narrowness be transcended also explains
why Jews may be less impressed than other groups when their own
brethren seek or secure public office. The reason may be found in
the response that Foreign Minister Golda Meir gave when she visited

Washington early in the 1960s. Attorney General Robert Kennedy is supposed to have told her that American pluralism had become so plastic that "we now have a Catholic President. Maybe in twenty years, we'll even have a Jewish President." "We already have one," she allegedly replied. "It doesn't help."[12] The ethnic identity of candidates is not a negligible consideration for Jewish voters, but it usually weighs less heavily than issues or personality and character. This might be contrasted with the close-as-handcuffs cohesiveness of Irish politics, as traditionally practiced in our major cities, or with the importance that blacks in recent years have attached to the election of black office-holders. Consider the indifference of Jews however to such often symbolic gestures. No Jews were included in President Reagan's inner circle of advisors, and more Jews were playing major league baseball (to be precise, one) than served in his cabinet. Nor was the ill-fated nomination of Douglas Ginsburg to succeed Lewis Powell on the Supreme Court tendered to reestablish a "Jewish seat," and Jews failed to rally quickly around Judge Ginsburg because of a common origin. When President Nixon nominated an undistinguished ex-segregationist judge in 1970 to succeed Abe Fortas, a Republican senator from Nebraska, the Honorable Roman Hruska, justified the mediocrity of G. Harrold Carswell as follows: "We can't have all Brandeises, Frankfurters, and Cardozos and stuff like that there."[13] But neither Nixon nor Reagan was penalized for such lapses in patronage.

It was not until 1973 that New York, a city whose population is more than a quarter Jewish, elected a Jew as its mayor; and in 1982 the liberal Mario Cuomo defeated Lewis Lehrman, a conservative Republican gubernatorial candidate who had not yet converted to Roman Catholicism, by two to one among New York's Jewish voters. Perhaps something still endures of Rabbi Stephen S. Wise's argument that "the only excuse for a Jewish [bloc] vote is to keep bad Jews out of office. We can leave it to the fairness of the American public to elect good Jews."[14] That faith has been vindicated, resulting in a legislature in which the proportion of Jews within it is well above their 2.5% of the general population. In the 99th Congress the eight senators of Jewish birth represented such states as New Hampshire and Nevada, and the twenty-nine members of the House of Representatives did not come exclusively from Jewish population centers. But not even those congressmen from districts that are models of what Jimmy Carter once called "ethnic purity" could take for granted a voting bloc signed, sealed, and delivered over to them because of a common ancestry.

Perhaps no group takes more seriously the ideal of popular sovereignty or is so inspired by the rhetoric of democratic responsibility. Jews are twice as likely to vote as other Americans, constituting about 6% of the electorate. They do not march to the polls under the ancient slogan of the corrupt bosses ("Vote early, and vote often"), but because they cherish the right to vote more deeply than their neighbors. Such devotion to the suffrage pays off because of the very unrepresentative system known as the electoral college, which quite inadvertently places a heavy thumb on the scales of Jewish residential patterns. Almost half of all American Jews live in the two most populous—and therefore politically critical—states: New York and California.[15] In other states whose size casts a shadow in presidential campaigns, such as Illinois, Pennsylvania, New Jersey, and Florida, Jews constitute at least 5% of the electorate (12% in California). Jews happen to be massed in states that provide 166 electoral votes. To demonstrate the electoral impact of the Jewish proclivity to concentrate in states of urban density, let's crunch some numbers. About a quarter of the voters in New York state, for example, are Jewish. In 1976 they went about 80% for Carter over Gerald Ford, enabling the Democrat to carry the state and with it the presidency. Had Carter and the incumbent evenly split the Jewish vote of New York, Carter would have *lost* the state and with it the White House.[16] Thus, the influence of a tiny minority is magnified in an incorrigibly anti-majoritarian, winner-take-all system; and that is why their attitudes and impulses have counted ever since the political alignment that began in 1932.

It might be contended that during the New Deal, the era that essentially inaugurated the Jews' modern political style, they voted their pocketbooks as unhesitatingly as other disadvantaged groups. The promise of recovery from the Great Depression, so it could be conjectured, is sufficient to explain the whopping electoral majorities conferred upon Franklin D. Roosevelt. The New Deal was indeed resourceful and pragmatic—and moderately successful—in its effort to repair a capitalist system that badly needed overhaul. But other factors must be summoned to account for his popularity. Roosevelt managed to symbolize the progressive spirit of communal claims against a rampant individualism, an ethos of solidarity toward which Jews were already sympathetic; and in drawing upon the talent of a few high-profile advisors, like Henry Morgenthau, Jr., Benjamin V.

Cohen, and Felix Frankfurter, the president demonstrated his own triumph over the snobbery of his class. During the 1936 campaign, his speech writer Sam Rosenman offered not to accompany the president on a swing through the Bible Belt of the Midwest. Roosevelt is supposed to have repudiated the suggestion as follows: "That's no way to handle anti-Semitism. The way to handle it is to meet it head-on."[17] A final factor in elevating FDR to Olympian stature among the Jews was the leadership that the commander-in-chief embodied in the Allied struggle against the Third Reich, the counterweight that the "Four Freedoms" represented amidst the horror of total war.

His four elections have set the standard against which subsequent Jewish devotion to Democratic liberalism has come to be measured. The depth of this fervor can be observed in microcosm with the Schechter brothers, who were in the kosher poultry business in Brooklyn. They had been convicted of selling diseased chickens, and of violating the wage and hour stipulations of the National Industrial Recovery Act. Instead, the Schechters claimed that the National Recovery Administration, a keystone of New Deal regulation, was hurting them unfairly, and therefore challenged the legality of the NRA. In a landmark 1935 decision, the Supreme Court agreed with them. Yet in the presidential election the following year, all sixteen votes in the Schechter family went to Roosevelt. So did the Chicago ward that was the most completely Jewish in the United States—by a margin of 96%,[18] the sort of unanimity bettered in the New World in recent years only by the likes of "Baby Doc" Duvalier in Haiti, who ran unopposed. In the 1940 and 1944 elections, Roosevelt racked up 90% of the Jewish vote. Other Americans were as impoverished, as devastated by the Great Depression, as the Jews were. But no other group has clung so tenaciously to the liberal wing of the Democratic Party.

American Jewish voters can hardly be expected to give a future Democrat the sorts of whopping landslides that Roosevelt received. Indeed, after all the historical evidence that has accumulated in the last two decades of research into the indifference of his administration during the Holocaust, not even the reincarnation of Roosevelt himself would do as well. The earthquakes he registered on the political Richter scale should not be permitted to serve as a fair test of the Jewish commitment to liberalism—in part because the New Deal helped give many Jewish families the cushion so that they would have more to conserve today, in part because liberalism itself has undergone so many fluctuations and permutations in the past half-century.

The Jewish vote has nevertheless puzzled political scientists because, ever since Roosevelt, it cannot be correlated with other groups of whites who have ascended to similar socioeconomic heights. Even after Jews became firmly implanted in the upper bourgeoisie, they have not behaved according to the same definition of their political interests as their peers and neighbors. They have exhibited as little class discipline as Spanish anarchists. As early as the 1920s, Jews have identified so strongly with the Democratic Party that, in presidential elections, they have voted for its nominees by an average of about 25% more than the general electorate.[19] The historical and statistical evidence for this pattern is so consistent, and so overwhelming, that it can be presented without even working up a sweat.

Eisenhower had been the military leader of the crusade in Europe. It was he who, upon having headed the army that liberated a subsidiary labor camp of Buchenwald, turned pale at the evidence of Nazi barbarism, and ordered nearby units to see Ohrdruf: "We are told that the American soldier does not know what he is fighting for. Now, at least, he will know what he is fighting *against*."[20] As a civilian, Eisenhower remained first in the hearts of his countrymen. But because he was also first in the heart of his country club, a pal of Republican millionaires, Adlai Stevenson got almost two out of every three Jewish votes, even in 1956, when prosperity was manifestly including the Jews, who were increasingly nestled in suburbia. By 1960 political scientists were desperate to explain why John F. Kennedy won a higher percentage of votes among Jews than among his fellow Catholics. Or why in 1964, campaigning against the grandson of an Arizona peddler named Morris Goldwasser, Lyndon Johnson received proportionately as many Jewish votes as any president since Roosevelt. Or why, when George Wallace tried to be a racist spoiler in primaries and general elections, Jewish voters rejected his candidacy as decisively as blacks did. Or why, in 1968, the margins of Hubert Humphrey's victories in Jewish neighborhoods so closely mirrored his successes in black slums and Chicano barrios that Milton Himmelfarb coined the aphorism that his brethren lived like Episcopalians but voted like Puerto Ricans.[21]

The year 1972 was supposed to be a turning point—but somehow it never turned. The famous news photo of Sammy Davis, Jr. embracing Richard Nixon did not prove to be prophetic of how the entertainer's fellow Jews would respond to the president, whose campaign incorporated an ethnic pitch that had all the subtlety of a recruitment poster. The campaign was also very effective among whites, especially high-income whites, who bestowed three-fourths of their ballots upon the Republican incumbent. Senator George McGovern was the most liberal Democratic candidate in memory, a prairie Plekhanov who tilted his party further to the left than any other nominee had ever done. He won less than a third of the white gentile vote, but he got two-thirds of the Jewish vote. Indeed, so far were the Jews from the category of lapsed liberals that, if the rest of the country had voted by similar margins in 1972, Senator McGovern would have won the greatest landslide in American history.[22]

Or how could political scientists explain 1976? Because of Watergate the nominee of the Democratic Party gained the White House for the only time in the five national elections after 1964. Though his first cousin is an Orthodox Jew, Jimmy Carter was a born-again Baptist, a career naval officer, a peanut farmer from a tiny Georgia town—not the sort of resumé that would have been expected to comfort typical Jewish voters. He was a regional candidate—urging Southern campaign audiences to put in the White House someone who did not have an accent. Yet a white Southerner was much *less* likely to have cast a ballot for Carter than was a Northern Jew. In fact, had it not been for the black vote, the Democratic candidate would have lost every Southern state except his native Georgia. But he did attract 71% of Jewish ballots, and it is permissible to speculate that had an even more liberal Democrat been nominated—say, Edward M. Kennedy or Walter Mondale—the Jewish margin would have been even more enthusiastic.[23]

Four years later Carter received more of the Jewish vote than Governor Reagan did. But for the first time since the Pleistocene era before the formation of the Roosevelt coalition, a Democratic candidate could not secure a majority of that vote. Two of the polls—a CBS exit poll and a later one by the American Jewish Committee—indicated that Carter won a plurality of about 44%, compared to Reagan's 39%. Congressman John Anderson received about 15% of the Jewish vote,[24] having firmly repudiated his earlier drive for a Constitutional amendment that would have declared the United States a Christian nation. This was a politically quixotic and theologically dubious effort to which the best riposte had been offered earlier in the century by Mark Twain, who drawled, upon hearing that twenty-two clergymen were delivering a resolution to the White House that declared that America was after all a Christian nation: "So is hell."[25]

Jews voting for Anderson as a third-party protest vote were apparently willing to forgive him. It is fair to assume that he attracted the votes of Jews who would nominally consider themselves Democrats and/or liberals, since the 10% of American Jews who think of themselves as Republicans would have had little warrant for preferring Anderson to the conservative, equally pro-Israel, far more electable Reagan. Almost 60% of the Jewish vote therefore remained in the Democratic and/or more liberal column in 1980. Reagan nevertheless bettered even Eisenhower's percentage of the Jewish vote, leading Marshall Breger, the Reagan administration's chief liaison to the Jewish community, to dream that Mondale's appeal to the Jewish community in 1984 could be capped at 60%.

After spending about $2 million in that effort, the GOP failed to reach that goal. Its failure is astonishing. After a recession early in his first term, Ronald Reagan presided over a more prosperous economy than the one he had inherited four years earlier. By 1984 the rate of inflation had dropped to its lowest point in twelve years; the rate of economic growth had climbed to its highest point in thirty-four years. Even the unemployment rate was skidding. Indeed, to his question, "Are you better off than you were four years ago?," not only would most citizens, including most Jews, have been obliged to answer in the affirmative, so, too, would Mondale himself, who had left the vice-presidency in 1981 with a net personal worth of only $15,000.[26] John Zaccaro, the husband of Congresswoman Geraldine Ferraro, would also have responded in the affirmative; and Jesse Jackson was also better off than four years earlier. Moreover, Reagan was firmly opposed to interpreting affirmative action as quotas, as were 64% of American Jews.[27]

On foreign policy the president could boast that, during his administration, not one square inch of territory had been yielded to the Communists. The administration, to be sure, had been unable to protect U. S. Marines from terrorism (which was, incidentally, the president's rationale for his high absenteeism from church). But he presided for four years over a country which—apart from the brief invasion of a tiny Caribbean island—had not been at war. (Jackie Mason again deserves quotation: "I'm proud of Reagan because, ever since then, Grenada has never attacked this country.")[28] The administration did take some positions that could certainly be interpreted as antagonistic to Israel. AWAC planes—brandishing military equipment too sophisticated even for our NATO allies—were sold to Saudi Arabia, after a bruising fight with many congressmen and with the

American Israel Public Affairs Committee. A few supporters of the sale aired accusations of dual loyalty, insinuating that opponents preferred Begin to Reagan. Members of the latter's executive branch were also unleashed to condemn the bombardment of the nuclear reactor in Baghdad as well as Israel's invasion of Lebanon. And a peace plan was offered that the Likud government believed was too risky to pursue; the proposal was rejected. But these actions occurred early enough in Reagan's term to be largely ignored even by many Democrats who voted for Mondale—and even by Prime Minister Yitzhak Shamir and Defense Minister Moshe Arens, whose timely praise of the president in the fall of 1984 could have been interpreted as amounting to a Likud endorsement. As in earlier electoral campaigns, support for Israel was not an issue that divided the two candidates.[29]

And even though the GOP spent four times as much as did the Democrats to snare the Jewish vote, the party still could not gain any traction. Even though the incumbent did 8% better among the general electorate than he had done in 1980, President Reagan did worse by the same percentage among Jewish voters. In getting 66% of Jewish ballots, Mondale touched a more enthusiastic constituency only among blacks and the unemployed. This response was so mystifying that a few neo-conservatives cried foul, grousing that pollsters did not properly weigh the conservative ballots of the more pious, less chic Jewish neighborhoods. But the argument that Mondale appeared to do better only "because poor Jews were not sufficiently sampled," Nathan Glazer has concluded, still makes the Jews bizarre: "They are a group where you have to sample the poor in order to find the Republicans."[30]

Of course, Jews willing to vote Republican could be found elsewhere: among neo-conservative intellectuals, among the Orthodox, and among some of the wealthy—especially in the Sun Belt.[31] But the proportion of Jews willing to label themselves conservatives has been barely a quarter (compared to 35% of the rest of America in 1984). The figures for liberalism are the reverse: 36% of Jews are willing to be identified with it, compared to 25% among Americans generally.[32] By every contemporary criterion (from environmental regulation to reproductive rights, from national health care to marijuana, from welfare programs to busing to achieve racial integration), Jews still occupy a more port-side stance than other whites, with whom attitudinal differences are often immense.[33] In the aftermath of the 1984 election, one historian, Edward S. Shapiro, was among several conservatives who were compelled to concede that "Jewish liberalism will . . . persist despite the fact that it has become irrelevant and counterproductive. . . . The Jewish infatuation with the Left should end," he argued; but neither Shapiro nor other Jews on the right seemed to expect such an affinity to evaporate. Liberalism this persistent—after a generation or two within the upper middle class—could not be changed with a lug wrench.[34]

The state races in 1986 only reinforced the gloom of those who wanted "the Hebrews! poor dears" to vote their class interests, to behave like everyone else. In the senatorial campaign in California, the liberal Democratic incumbent, Alan Cranston, beat Ed Zschau, a conservative Republican, by only two percentage points. Among Jewish voters however, Cranston whipped Zschau by 4:1. In the California gubernatorial race the conservative Republican, George Deukmejian, beat the liberal Democrat, Tom Bradley, by almost 2:1. Among Jewish voters the ratio was reversed. In Florida a moderate Democrat, Bob Graham, defeated the incumbent senator, Paula Hawkins, a conservative Republican, by ten percentage points. But she lost the Jewish vote by sixty percent. In Maryland a conservative Republican, Linda Chavez, ran for the Senate against a liberal Democrat, Barbara Mikulski, who beat her 3:2. Among Jewish voters Mikulski clobbered Chavez by over 8:1. In New York the incumbent senator, Alfonse D'Amato, a Republican, defeated a liberal Democrat, Mark Green, by 58% to 41%. Among Jewish voters the proportions were the reverse— 64% for Green, 34% for D'Amato, who did as well as he did only because of his conspicuous championing of Israel. Orthodox Jewish neighborhoods backed the incumbent very heavily. When D'Amato ran for the Senate six years earlier, he had gotten only 8% of the Jewish vote. Meanwhile Governor Mario Cuomo remained in Albany, thanks to receiving 65% of the suffrage of his state in 1986; the Jewish margin for the liberal Democrat was 15% higher.[35]

In such races the liberal Democratic candidates may well have been able to project the social concern that engendered the welfare state itself, but that explanation may no longer be sufficient. The recalcitrance of poverty, the deepening spiral of dependence, the wretched failures of the educational system, the ugliness of crime in the underclass have all undermined the once-unquestioned equation of liberalism with the effort to make the world more attractive. The struggle to promote social justice can no longer be assumed to require an ever-expanding governmental bureaucracy as its only—or chief— instrument. By the 1970s many Jews came to acknowledge the force of this argument, which cannot be spun out here; and the Reagan administration did much to check a liberalism that was already chastening itself. And yet if the Jews themselves did not completely jettison their allegiance to the progressive causes that the Republican Party has scorned as anachronistic, if not dangerous, the explanation can be found in the kind of America which the GOP has seemed willing to foster. Its association with the Moral Majority, and the militant Christianity conveyed at the prayer breakfast during the Dallas nominating convention in 1984, stirred some of the anxieties that neither social status nor economic success could completely stifle. The rise of the New Right has been more disturbing to Jews than the circulation within the Democratic Party of Third World sympathies and attitudes that collide with Israeli interests. If many Jews worried about what in God's name the Republican Party has been up to, that is because of the way that historical forces have shaped most Jews— supremely modern, urban, educated, secularized. For them the Moral Majority has represented bad karma.

Public opinion polls have revealed that, even though their families have been traditionally famous for their integrity, Jews have tended to be more tolerant than Roman Catholics or Protestants of extramarital, premarital, and homosexual relations. Traditional Judaism hardly holds a brief for such conduct, but what is more noteworthy is that the sexual tolerance of American Jewry clashes with what proportionately more Christians have deemed sinful in *all* circumstances. That is why Jews did not enlist in such crusades as the "Family Protection Bill," which was introduced by President Reagan's best friend in the Senate, Paul Laxalt (R-Nev.). Jews restrained their enthusiasm for a bill which would have allowed parents to review textbooks before their assignment in the public schools, which would have prohibited federal funding of abortions for poor women, and which would have blunted federal protection of the civil rights of homosexuals. A political party that opposed so fundamental an ideal of fairness as the Equal Rights Amendment could not elicit much Jewish support, especially when, according to one poll, a Jewish man was slightly more likely to favor the E. R. A. than was a gentile woman. Vice-President George Bush's proposal that an abortion performed on a woman impregnated by a rapist or a relative should not be considered a crime made him look to many Republicans like a dangerous moderate. That helps explain why the GOP has not been attractive to Jews, who supported the 1973 *Roe v. Wade* decision even more than the majority of other Americans and who were unpersuaded by Reagan's campaign logic that "every-body who's for abortion has already been born."[37]

Puritanism is not an outgrowth of Judaism, which in the Diaspora has not promoted hedonism either (though the founder of "Club Med," Gilbert Trigano, is Jewish). The precariousness of centuries of exile instead encouraged the ideals of temperance and moderation, scorning both instinctual repressiveness and excess. Jews in the United States have generally resisted the efforts of moralists and religious zealots to make personal habits a target of public policy, to invade the barroom and the bedroom. Most American Jews have feared the intrusions of the fanatic, whom Finley Peter Dunne's affable Mr. Dooley once defined as "a man that does what he thinks th' Lord wud do if He knew th' facts iv the case."[38] Having tasted enough fanaticism in their history, the Jews are generally inclined to confine religious questions to enclaves of privacy. It was Louis Brandeis who first asserted that privacy is "the most comprehensive of rights and the right most valued by civilized men."[39]

Prayer is of course a more complicated question, since the protection of all forms of worship, the wall of separation between church and state, the disestablishment of religion were never intended under the First Amendment to stifle expressions of faith from public life. Even as late as *United States v. Macintosh* (1931), the Supreme Court declared without hesitation or reflection that "we are a Christian people";[40] and even though later Justices invalidated prayers as well as moments of silence in public schools, the Court itself opens its sessions with invocations of divine guidance. The trickiness of the problem of church-state relations was suggested when Reagan winked at the Religious Roundtable in Dallas at the 1984 Republican convention: "You can't endorse me. But I can endorse you." (If *that* is the choice, the reverse relationship would be more compatible with the First Amendment.) At the prayer breakfast the morning after his renomination, the president attacked opponents of voluntary class-room prayer for their "intolerance." He added that "religion and politics are necessarily related," for "there are, these days, many questions on which religious leaders are obliged to offer their moral and theological guidance. And such guidance is a good and necessary thing." The Dallas convention manager later acknowledged that such remarks "probably cost us some Jewish votes, but the test of the pudding was in the eating, and it ate pretty well."[41]

Nevertheless, the New Right is not anti-Semitic and has not directly imperiled the faith of Jews. When the president of the Southern

Baptist Convention, Reverend Bailey Smith, asserted that "God Almighty does not hear the prayers of a Jew," he was enunciating something that a devout Christian might plausibly believe. It is a strong implication—though not the only possible conclusion—derived from a complete acceptance of Christian belief, which holds that no salvation is possible for those who spurn the opportunity to accept Jesus as their savior. Yet Reverend Smith's assertion generated an outcry greater than anything aroused by his coarser statements (such as "I think they [i.e., Jews] got funny-looking noses"), because his description of a hearing-impaired deity diminished the legitimacy of the Jewish community itself. That is why many Southern Baptists repudiated Reverend Smith's claim that Jewish prayer was in vain, why so many Southern Baptists insisted that Reverend Smith did not speak for them, and why he himself apologized to American citizens of Jewish faith and the following year showed up at a *seder*.[42] Because religious intolerance is widely perceived as un-American, because the civic equality of Jews with more numerous Protestants and Catholics has been established, evangelical ministers can be forced to realize the political and moral liabilities of seeming to criticize Jews. Indeed, the myrmidons of the New Right sometimes learn this lesson a little too well. When Reverend Dan T. Fore, the head of the Moral Majority in New York, was accused of anti-Semitism in 1981, he responded to the charge by insisting: "I love the Jewish people deeply. God has given them talents He has not given others. They are His chosen people. Jews have a God-given ability to make money, almost a supernatural ability to make money. They control the media, they control this city [of New York]."[43] It is one of the healthier paradoxes of American politics that such classic stereotypes can be uttered in the accents of benevolence.

Nevertheless, Jews have commonly perceived the champions of militant Christianity as threatening to their interests. According to one exit poll after the 1984 elections, only 20% of the Jews gave Jesse Jackson a favorable rating (more than any other group of whites); but only 5% approved of Jerry Falwell. Eighty percent disapproved of the president of the Moral Majority, which is as close to communal consensus as American Jewry is likely to attain.[44] For evangelicals in politics like Reverend Falwell have sought to destabilize the status quo in which the religious neutrality of the public sector—or the equitable treatment accorded to Catholics and Jews as well as Protestants within it—could almost be taken for granted. Most Jews consider it self-evident that a prayer recited in unison in a public school, even if no mention is made of the Savior, violates the prohibition against the establishment of religion. The ostentatious entwining of politics and religion under Reagan accentuated the difference between the majority faith and those who remain dubious about the resurrection of Christ. That is why many key figures in Christianity have challenged the New Right as well, warning of social friction and fragmentation, insisting (as did Reverend Falwell's fellow Virginians, Jefferson and Madison) that religion operates best when the plug of state support is pulled. When Jefferson praised the construction of the "wall of separation" in 1802, he did so for the sake of comity; but Roger Williams had advocated it as early as 1644—not so much for political reasons, but so that religion itself could thrive.[45] The desire to worship in an uncoercive atmosphere therefore need not be an issue that differentiates, in the charming dichotomy of former Secretary of the Interior James Watt, "liberals and Americans." But it is an issue that has kept Jews wary of signing up as Republicans, just because their tax brackets are comparable.

For GOP strategists, winning the allegiance of 2.5% of the citizenry may not be critical, since they have done quite nicely in the late twentieth century without the Jewish vote. As the *National Review* has relished pointing out, Jimmy Carter is the only Democratic presidential nominee in the four elections between 1972 and 1984 to carry more than one state (a feat he accomplished twice). But that 2.5% minority remains precisely that, and is therefore heavily dependent on allies and friends—not to secure its rights, which are safe—but rather to help it defend its interests. And whatever else it is, the True Believers who have injected so much juice into the New Right have proved themselves to be ardently pro-Zionist. This is the predicament that currently faces the American Jewish electorate.

Because the security and welfare of Israel are so pivotal to Jewish destiny and to the future of the Jewish people everywhere else, pro-Zionism has become the prerequisite for the practice of Jewish politics in America.[46] Not all liberals have appreciated the full value of a democratic Jewish homeland, and not all the champions of Israel have been liberals. The source of much of the unsolicited pro-Zionism of evangelical Christianity should, however, offer scant comfort to Jews, whose conversion is considered the necessary prelude for the Second Coming of Christ. Conversion will be made simpler if they have gathered in one place, and what better place for them than Israel? Such is the evangelical vision of the climax of Jewish history, though there is no reason to assume that contemporary American evangelicals will succeed when, after two millennia, Christendom has already failed to carry out this eschatological assignment. Among its relatively few successes was the ironist Heinrich Heine, who converted only out of convenience and who once pungently explained the futility of Christian efforts at proselytization: "No Jew can believe in the divinity of any other Jew."[47]

But the motivations of the evangelicals may matter less than the conclusions, which is why some Jewish leaders have been grateful that such a formidable segment of Christendom has helped to guarantee a strong Israel. Because the sympathies of the Moral Majority enhance the diplomatic support of Israel's only major arsenal, the former national director of the Anti-Defamation League, the late Nathan Perlmutter, became the most prominent advocate of prudent cooperation. He believed that Jews should be willing temporarily to endanger their souls and their chances of salvation, while nevertheless forging an alliance with such reliable friends of Israel: "If the Messiah comes, on that very day we'll consider our options. Meanwhile praise the Lord and pass the ammunition." Perlmutter's colleague Oscar Cohen also warned: "Today the fundamentalists are on our side; but if Jews work hard at it, they won't be."[48]

Entanglement with such strange bedfellows is what most Jews have apparently remained willing to avoid, for they are the legatees of the residual commitment to an open society that soft-pedals the imperatives of faith itself. A "community of fate" cannot easily extinguish its memories, which for Jews include the suffering that the ideological fervor of religious majorities can inflict. Though fewer Jews than in the past exhibit the symptoms of messianism, many are still cognizant of how their peculiar history has given them no warrant for complacency, no expectation of security. They are a people that is extrasensitive to warning signals, that seems to believe that if everything is coming your way, you are probably in the wrong lane. Poised between hope and memory, comfort and anxiety, their idealism is easy to tap, even as their politics is designed to sniff danger as well.

In accounting for the aberration of Jewish electoral behavior, history matters more than economics; sensibility matters more than status; and ethos matters more than expediency. So long as the Democratic Party continues to present itself as the party of compassion, so long as its version of the rainbow coalition can assure its respect for diversity, an "ideological minority" that is enjoined to remember having been slaves in Egypt is unlikely to welcome the advances of a Moral Majority and its affiliates. A penchant for liberalism, however enfeebled, has become one of the ways American Jews differentiate themselves from their neighbors, while still honoring the aspirations of their parents and grandparents. "Remove that thinning measure of social commitment," Irving Howe has conjectured, "and the problem of Jewish distinctiveness must become increasingly severe." This warning is not of course a case for the validity of liberalism, but it is an argument that the cohesiveness of Jewish identity will be affected by the abandonment of progressivism and social activism.[49] Perhaps that is why the straight line projections of a Jewish shift to the Republican Party have so far been falsified, and why future Tuesdays in November may continue to reveal the presence of at least one group of voters who define their interests as their ideals.[50]

6

RADICALISM

After the Yom Kippur War of 1973, the foreign-born Jewish intellectual then directing American foreign policy paid his first visit to Saudi Arabia, where Henry Kissinger was obliged to listen to what was widely known as King "Faisal's standard speech. Its basic proposition was that Jews and Communists were working in parallel, now together, to undermine the civilized world as we knew it." The secretary of state wondered whether Faisal was "oblivious to my ancestry—or [was] delicately putting me into a special category." But in any event, "Faisal insisted that an end had to be put once and for all to the dual conspiracy of Jews and Communists." A later meeting allowed the king to repeat his warning to Kissinger, who concluded that the king's absorption in "the epic conflict between good and evil" made issues like an armistice on Israel's northern front seem trivial by comparison.[1]

What mattered to Faisal should, in this case, also intrigue historians of modern Jewry as well. For the association between political radicalism and the Jewish people continues to smack of certainty, to ring with the conviction of dogma. That the Balfour Declaration and the Bolshevik Revolution both occurred within five days of one another did not strike some American foreign policy experts as coincidental, and during World War I they warned that a Jewish Commonwealth would nurture radicalism in the Near East.[2] It is also worth remem-

bering that the *Fuehrer* whose country Kissinger himself later fled
could not distinguish between Jews and Bolsheviks and believed that
the headquarters of world Jewry were located in Moscow. If such a
belief in the intertwined nature of Jewry and radicalism can also
penetrate all the way to the desert kingdom of the Saudis, it is a
subject worth investigating, even though limitations of space restrict
the observations in this chapter mostly to the United States. It is also
a ticklish topic, as William B. Saxbe, an attorney general under Nixon,
discovered in 1974 when he committed the logical fallacy of composition, expressing relief that Jewish intellectuals were no longer "very
enamored of the Communist Party."[3]

Even when the passions of American radicalism became exhausted
in the aftermath of the 1960s, after Jerry Rubin became a Wall Street
analyst and Eldridge Cleaver and Rennie Davis pursued even more
sacred endeavors, the social roots of Marxist as well as anarchist
beliefs deserve to solicit scholarly attention. Only a fraction of American Jews have been radicals, but a conspicuous number of radicals
have been Jews who have shaped the singularity of the Jewish style in
politics. They have contributed, however unwittingly, to the differen-
tiation of Jews from others who have shared American citizenship,
without agreeing on how its obligations ought to be met. It is the aim
of this chapter to offer a brief historical overview of the relationship
between American Jews and radicalism, to suggest its cultural and
psychological texture, and to account for this relationship.

The impression of such a copula can be traced virtually to the
birth of the modern era itself. In seventeenth-century England, as
the Puritan revolution of the saints was liquidating the legitimacy of
monarchy, Oliver Cromwell denounced his left flank, the millenarian
Fifth Monarchy men, as "Judaisers."[4] This term of reproach was
hardly noticed in the midst of the simultaneous cataclysms of Jewish
history, such as the Chmielnicki massacres in Poland and the Ukraine
and the messianic movement of Sabbatai Sevi that swept from Yemen
to Hamburg. But John Calvin had also dismissed the image of utopia
as the "foolish" concoction of the Jews,[5] so that well over a century
before emancipation in France and the Germanies—the prototypes of
the Jewish encounter with the modern world—the descendants of the
Biblical prophets were perceived as harbingers of social change and
messianic hope. More often Jews were merely liberals, however, who
believed in progress through greater representation under the rule
of law. For example, this was the stance of the *Allgemeine Zeitung des
Judentums*, which conjectured that Jewish radicalism had sparked the

1881 pogroms in Czarist Russia. This main organ of liberal German Jewry therefore advised its Russian brethren to abstain from "secret conspiracies and subversive activities," which would discredit Jewry in general.[6]

But in the first two waves of Jewish immigrants to the United States, through the middle of the nineteenth century, dissidents like Ernestine Rose and the abolitionist David Einhorn were rare; and the fragmentary Jewish communities established in North America in the colonial and early national periods harbored few radicals. Only the arrival of two million Jews fleeing persecution and poverty in Eastern Europe fostered the rise of radicalism—a polysemous term which in this chapter is intended to encompass the varieties of Marxian socialism, anarchism and the more estranged forms of youth activism in the 1960s. The ideologies that the fin-de-siècle immigrants professed, the causes that they espoused, and the institutions that they created established the standards against which subsequent versions of Jewish radicalism have been judged.

Even after allowances have been made for the conventional, moderate politics and even indifference of perhaps the bulk of the Jews, what was special about the first generation or so of Eastern European immigrants to the Northeast and Midwest was how authentically they consolidated political radicalism with other manifestations of Jewish life. On its masthead the *Jewish Daily Forward* proclaimed slogans like "Workers of the world, unite" and "The freeing of the working class must be the task of the working class itself." At its peak the circulation of this newspaper was a quarter of a million, making it the most widely read Yiddish paper on earth. Daniel Bell concluded that "the *Forward* bound together the Jewish community and made it socialist." The newspaper usually put ethnic claims above ideological loyalties, and honored such claims when socialism was mute, as when—early in its history—the *Forward* supported the bourgeois Dreyfusards in France and did not oppose the imperialist Spanish-American War.[7]

Socialism may have helped satisfy some of the idealistic yearnings of the Jewish community, but that community did even more for the radicalization of the American labor movement and for the promotion of a more humane economic system. The garment trade unions and their associated Workmen's Circle provided the Socialist Party of America with much of its organizational and financial strength. They maintained their allegiance to socialism long after other militant unions had fully reconciled themselves to the capitalist order. The International Ladies Garment Workers Union, one labor historian has noted, "used its considerable vote at AFL conventions on behalf of radical resolutions . . . more consistently than almost any other trade union." In opposing immigration restriction (more for ethnic rather than class reasons), in supporting women's suffrage and Negro rights, and in encouraging the growth of socialism in Europe, unions like the ILGWU exhibited "a humanitarian, idealistic, and deeply held desire for equality and social justice. . . . But perhaps the most distinctive contribution of the ILGWU," Professor John Laslett added, "was its various provisions for the health, education, and general welfare of its members, which went far beyond the sick, death, and other benefits provided by most other American trade-unions. It was on the educational program of the union, however, that the greatest emphasis was laid." Even in the 1920s, despite the pressures of the open-shop movement and the bitter factional struggle with the Communists, the ILGWU fostered the revival of post-war radicalism and continued to contribute to the coffers and the morale of the socialist movement.

Only when it endorsed Roosevelt for president in 1936 (as did the *Forward*'s editor Abraham Cahan himself) did this relatively long chapter in American radical history come to a close. For other imperatives and values within the Jewish community sapped a sustained working-class militancy. The promises of the wider society and the impulses of upward mobility among its own membership weakened the ILGWU's commitment to class consciousness. Italian-Americans transmitted the skills of the needle trade to their children, and therefore became increasingly important in such unions. But Jewish workers generally recommended educational advantages and property acquisition instead.[8] Despite the stirring words of the *Forward*'s masthead, the Jewish working class did not free itself. Instead it taught its own children to free themselves *from* the working class.

The allegiances of other Jews shifted to Bolshevism, which exerted a disproportionate appeal before that particular god failed. Jewish involvement was extensive despite the policies of the Party. In the late 1920s the Comintern supported Arab rioters against Jewish settlers in Palestine. In the 1930s the Stalinist purges claimed uncounted thousands of innocent Jewish victims, and Foreign Minister Molotov proclaimed in 1939 that Fascism was merely "a question of taste." Early in the Second World War, the NKVD handed Jewish prisoners over to the Gestapo, and after the war Yiddish culture and its custodians were systematically extinguished under Stalin. The anti-Semitism of Stalinism eventually caused the membership and support of the Party to be depleted of thousands of Jews who had been attracted to the promise of a militantly effective universalism and "progressivism."

Of the intellectuals who publicly proclaimed their support for the Communist ticket of William Z. Foster and James Ford in 1932, almost a third were Jewish. Only later did most of them realize that they had been trying to thumb rides on "the road to serfdom." Even Sidney Hook, the first Marxist professor in the United States, explained to readers of *Modern Monthly* "Why I am a Communist" (1934). The Stalinist group that Whittaker Chambers later charged Alger Hiss with having joined, and which was burrowed in the Department of Agriculture, included John Abt, Lee Pressman, and Nathan Witt. At the end of "the red decade," leading fellow travelers, including many Jews, signed an ad criticizing those who believed that totalitarianism linked the Soviet Union and Nazi Germany. The timing of the ad was unlucky: it appeared shortly before the Nazi-Soviet pact was signed in Moscow. (It must be added that most of their opponents in such organizations as Americans for Intellectual Freedom—including by this point Hook himself—were also Jews.)[9] The historian Daniel Boorstin, by 1953 a conservative who told HUAC that his support of the Hillel Foundation at the University of Chicago demonstrated his hostility to Communism, had been a Party member for a year or so before the Molotov-Ribbentrop Pact undermined his reasons for joining—his opposition to Nazism and anti-Semitism.[10] Such reasons were commonplace.

Even more than Stalinism, the movement led by Leon Trotsky won the loyalty of many Jewish radicals. The heresiarch himself was of course born Lev Davidovich Bronstein. The interest of this multilingual intellectual in literature and his fluency of expression were overshadowed by the flair for action—political and even military—that his remarkable career exhibited. It is true that James Cannon shared with Max Shachtman the leadership of the Trotskyist movement in the United States, until their split in 1940. But the rank-and-file were, apart from the truckers of Minneapolis, probably almost exclusively Jewish. Several of the younger members later rose to prominence as intellectuals, critics, and scholars, among them the late Martin Diamond, Leslie Fiedler, Gertrude Himmelfarb, Irving Howe, Irving Kristol, Seymour Martin Lipset, Marvin Meyers, and the late Isaac Rosenfeld. Even Bernard Cornfeld, the erstwhile "Midas of mutual funds," was a Trotskyist in his youth. It therefore made sense for Saul Bellow to send Augie March to Mexico intending to serve as

Trotsky's bodyguard, and to make Hyman Lustgarten, the black marketeer in post-war Europe in "Mosby's Memoirs" (1968), a former Trotskyist. American Trotskyism taught Kwame Nkrumah the operations of an underground organization, before he returned to Ghana and became its *Osayegfo* ("redeemer"). Near the end of his life, Malcolm X was tentatively interested as well.[11] Nevertheless, for all the efforts primarily of Jews to keep this version of revolutionary Marxism alive, the verdict upon it must be the same as that which Trotsky himself pronounced upon Martov and the Mensheviks. "You are miserable isolated individuals" was Trotsky's curse in 1917. "You are bankrupt. You have played out your role. Go where you belong, to the dust-heap of history."[12]

It was a place to which more than the Trotskyists were consigned. Even though a disproportionate number of American radicals were Jews, it is also worth asking why so few Americans were deeply dissatisfied with their society and eager to seek alternatives. The Jewish contribution to radicalism is all the more striking because of its unattractiveness to so many other Americans. There are many reasons—perhaps as many as twenty-seven, according to one scholarly survey of why there is no socialism in the United States.[13] But one aspect that ought to be highlighted here shows the character of American society as well as any other. That is its relative openness to political reform and social change, its capacity to roll with the punch. Consider the editorial published on November 15, 1909 in the Socialist daily, the *New York Call*, which listed immediate demands to end the exploitation and misery of the working class. This agenda was "so revolutionary," the editorial insisted, that mere amelioration could not fulfill such demands as labor laws, employer liability, the right of unions to control their own treasuries, legalization of the boycott, the elimination of the labor injunction, government inspection of work places, reduced working hours for women and children especially, and serious efforts to bring to an end the terrible loss of life in mines and factories. But the joke on the *New York Call* and other socialists was that not only were these demands conceivable; they were, after much struggle, attained—in most instances within one generation.[14]

The role of reform as the nemesis of radicalism can be measured through Jewish biography. In his youth the Dutch-British immigrant Samuel Gompers had flirted with socialism which, in the United States, he considered unnecessary and even dysfunctional; and his stewardship of the American Federation of Labor had much to do with making the immediate demands of the *New York Call* conceivable after all. Gompers claimed to share the ideals of socialism, differing—at least initially—only over tactics. As a trade unionist here, he asserted that he would have been a nihilist in Russia, a socialist in Germany.[15] Or consider Sidney Hillman and David Dubinsky, who were radicals in czarist Russia. In America they were militant trade union leaders whose leadership of strikes did not land them in jail—or in the equivalent of Siberia. Abraham Cahan escaped from Russia because czarist police discovered his involvement in a revolutionary organization. By 1936 he too was supporting the squire from Hyde Park.[16] Another immigrant, Frank Tannenbaum, came to the United States in 1905, quickly became involved with the Wobblies, and in 1914 was convicted of disturbing the peace when he tried to lead New York's unemployed and hungry in seeking refuge in churches. He was imprisoned on Blackwell's Island. The warden of Sing Sing encouraged Tannenbaum to go to college, so he went to Columbia, graduated Phi Beta Kappa, and became one of its most distinguished professors. And when Tannenbaum published a book about the warden of Sing Sing, Roosevelt himself wrote the introduction.[17]

With the prosperity and comity that pervaded so much of post-World War II America, with the embourgeoisement of much of the labor movement, and the virtually complete integration of Jews into the polity and economy, dissidence could not have been expected to sustain itself; and "the end of ideology" was one way of writing its death warrant. No scholar or political analyst of the 1950s could have anticipated how dramatically the corpse of radicalism would be jump-started in the following decade. Perhaps many young Jews still felt a little like strangers in the land of Egypt, expressing their marginality through civil rights activism, anti-poverty campaigns, the movement against the Vietnam War, feminism, and through support of Third World causes. During the Great War and the Red Scare that followed, Jewish radicals like Emma Goldman, Jacob Abrams, Victor Berger, Benjamin Gitlow, Rosika Schwimmer, and Yetta Stromberg had been unable to stay out of the line of fire; and their names became attached to important civil liberties cases. Jewish radicals in the 1960s and 1970s were no more successful in avoiding trouble. Captain Howard Levy was prosecuted for refusing to train Green Berets. The Chicago 7 included Abbie Hoffman, Jerry Rubin, and Lee Wiener. The indicted co-conspirators of Dr. Benjamin Spock and the Reverend William Sloane Coffin were Mitchell Goodman, Marcus Raskin, and a Unitarian, Michael Ferber. Though Daniel Ellsberg was never a radical, strictly speaking, his exposure of the Pentagon Papers, the unsavory methods used to prosecute him, the plumbers' rifling through his psychiatrist's files, and his vindication helped bring to an end both the Vietnam War and the Nixon administration itself.

Even in unexpected places, Jews cropped up. Martin Luther King, for all his militancy and activism, was not a radical. Nevertheless, one of the key advisors of this Baptist preacher was Stanley Levison, a pivotal money manager for the Communist Party and a close associate of its top leadership prior to his intimacy with King. Their friendship became the justification for the FBI's squalid bugging campaign against the civil rights tribune.[18] The organizing struggle of Cesar Chavez in the fields of California drew upon the resources of Catholic commitment and Mexican-American ethnic solidarity (*La Causa*). But Saul Alinsky, the son of immigrant Orthodox Jews, helped tutor Chavez in the tactics of peaceful but forceful confrontation. The pacifist and nonviolent mood of the folk music movement was much influenced by Joan Baez, who was in turn influenced by Ira Sandperl. And the letters from Folsom Prison which gave shape to Eldridge Cleaver's nascent militancy were addressed to his attorney, Beverly Axelrod, to whom *Soul on Ice* is dedicated. According to one journalistic account, the first wave of civil rights workers to go South in the early 1960s was more likely to quote Harry Golden than Gandhi or Thoreau.[19]

It is also worth recording the tactics of SNCC's Stokely Carmichael, who bravely went into Lowndes County, Alabama to encourage voter registration. None of the county's 12,000 blacks was listed on the voter registration rolls, whereas the whites were so enthusiastic about their version of "participatory democracy" that 117% of them were eligible to vote. To break down the climate of fear that enveloped the black community, Carmichael taunted the sheriff, mocked his stride, and insulted him with a Yiddish term—an anatomical invitation unsuitable for quotation in a scholarly work. The graduate of Bronx High School of Science guessed correctly that Southern whites did not understand Yiddish, which he used in Lowndes County as a disruptive force of delegitimization. In any case, Carmichael had felt little respect for his Southern white adversaries after the jailers had confiscated his Camus and DuBois paperbacks but left him in his cell with C. Wright Mills's apologia for Castroism, *Listen Yankee!*, which they mistook as a warning to Northern agitators. Not that the influence of Jewish radicals couldn't be found in the Caribbean as well. In the early 1960s in then British Guiana, whose population was about evenly divided between East Indians and blacks, the leader of the

People's Progressive Party was a Marxist dentist named Cheddi Jagan. His wife was a former member of the Young Communist League from Chicago, Janet Rosenberg; and Jagan once told President Kennedy how much he admired the *Monthly Review*, particularly the writings of Leo Huberman and Paul Baran.[20]

The last bloody clash of the civil rights movement took place in Greensboro, North Carolina, where the peaceful sit-ins had begun almost two decades earlier. On November 3, 1979 five members of the Communist Workers Party were murdered by the Ku Klux Klan and its associates. The dead included two Jews, and another Jew was seriously wounded. They were the last white victims in the struggle of solidarity with Southern blacks, a chain of martyrdom that had begun with Andrew Goodman and Michael Schwerner, killed along with a local black, James Chaney, in Philadelphia, Mississippi, in 1964. Goodman had been in the state for only a few hours when he was abducted and killed by a group of whites who knew Schwerner as "the Jew-boy with the beard." The murderers even argued with one another for the honor of killing "the two Jews and the coon."[21] Their deaths suggested the continuity of a certain dedication to social justice, even amid prosperity, reform, and the decline of anti-Semitism.

In some ways the most baffling aspect of that commitment involved the student power movement. Here the Jewish propensity for radicalism was most intriguing, because its militancy could not be explained as easily as the immigrant working class socialism of the New Leftists' grandfathers, or in terms of the desperation that the Great Depression engendered. The student radicals who rebelled at Berkeley, Columbia, and Harvard, and who were also inclined to protest on other Ivy League and Big Ten campuses, were privileged. They were not motivated by material self-interest and unhampered by prejudice and discrimination. Jews constituted about a tenth of all college students in the 1960s, yet they were often half or more of the radicals on leading American campuses. Under the auspices of the American Council of Education, a survey of 1966–67 asserted that the most accurate single predictor of protest was the matriculation of a substantial minority of Jewish students. Even during the Berkeley sit-in of 1964, according to one report, *Hatikvah* was sung; and Students for a Democratic Society was packed with Jews, whose Jewish identity was often disguised or downplayed.[22]

Few made their origins a source of self-consciousness or reflection about their motives or their ideals; and when it came to camouflaging,

Hollywood did the rest. The best-known memoir to emerge from the campus rebellions was probably James Simon Kunen's *The Strawberry Statement* (1969). Yet in the film version, the Columbia campus of the book was shifted to a mythical Middle America; and the swarthy urban rebels who seized buildings at Columbia became the sorts of blondes whom Jesus is generally depicted as resembling. The Judaization that Oliver Cromwell had linked to radicalism was therefore bleached out. Hollywood's grip on the social reality of the 1960s can also be gleaned from the casting of Stanley Kramer's *RPM* (hyperbolically an abbreviation for "revolutions per minute"), in which the university president is played by Anthony Quinn and a graduate student is played by none other than Ann-Margret.[23] Such casting has thwarted sociological understanding.

Something of the texture of the Jewish involvement in the radicalism of the 1960s can be seen in Roger Simon's novel, *The Big Fix* (1973), also a film, a detective story whose protagonist is himself a former political activist from Berkeley. A secondary character is based on ᐟAbbie Hoffman, thus already transfigured into legend, imagined as having a disguised identity in which "Howard Eppis," chairman of the Free Amerika Party and the author of *Rip It Off*, makes it big in the advertising business. In the film, the protagonist was played by Richard Dreyfuss, whose thespian career had begun in a Chanukah play and who was later granted conscientious objector status because of his opposition to the Vietnam War. The protagonist has an aunt who is still a Stalinist while living in a Jewish old-age home. In the movie itself, one of the books shown on his shelf is a novel by Alan Lelchuk, *American Mischief* (1973), itself a depiction of a radical rebellion among Jewish students, led by Brooklyn-born Lenny Pincus, at a university strikingly like Brandeis University (called Cardozo College in the novel). In the Lelchuk novel, Pincus attempts to fulfill the logic of literary radicalism by shooting Norman Mailer, who was to write a glowing introduction to Abbie Hoffman's autobiography seven years later, *Soon To Be a Major Motion Picture*.[24] The lines could scarcely be more taut.

But it is much easier to tabulate the impact of the Jews upon radical movements and ideas in the United States than to account for such influence. Four theories have been devised to explain this historical propensity for the left, but none has the compass or ingenuity—the formulaic authority—to compel assent.

One theory stresses Judaic culture itself, with its yearning for *tikkun olam* ("repair of the world"), its commitment to social justice, and its insistence on speaking prophetic truth to power. The appeal for social justice is one strain in Jewish tradition, but it is certainly not the only one; and the long history of the Diaspora prior to Emancipation fails to disclose many antecedents for modern radicalism or even modern liberalism.[25] The rabbis and sages who wrote the commentaries on the Bible and the commentaries on the commentaries, who codified the laws and explicated the customs, would not have received 100% ratings from the Americans for Democratic Action, and they certainly would not have been vulnerable to red-baiting. The terrors of much of premodern Jewish life, with its incessant threats of extortion, pariahdom, pogroms, and expulsion, promoted a wary conservatism that cannot convincingly be invoked by Jews in quest of sanctions for their radicalism.

Albert Einstein, himself a socialist, nevertheless believed in a connection between socialism and Judaism, for both are based upon the sense of "solidarity of all human beings." But he could not claim a logically necessary connection between a radical ideology and a religious source.[26] Even those who professed to find in holidays like Pesach and Chanukah the inspiration for subsequent struggles against tyranny, as Julius Rosenberg did in his letters to his wife in Sing Sing, failed to acknowledge the nature of the despotism that they themselves freely chose to serve. They identified with the executioners, not the victims of Stalinism, which means that what needs to be explained is how, say, leftist Jews have selectively applied their religious heritage. Radicals in the post-Emancipation era have distanced themselves from both pious and impious homes. But it has become a commonplace that the most observant are rarely radical, and the most radical are rarely observant. The more radical the Jew, the less he or she is likely to know (or care) about normative Jewish life.[27]

But the skepticism that this thesis engenders does not require its complete abandonment. For it allows us to take ideas and values seriously; and if what has distinguished the Biblical Hebrews and their descendants from those around them has been their religion, then perhaps something in the value system of the Jews has made them susceptible to modern radicalism. Misery alone is an insufficient explanation. It propelled neither American blacks nor Russian *muzhiks* to the varieties of Marxism. Among the Jews, as indicated by the privileged partisans of the New Left, suffering is not even a necessary—much less a sufficient—cause of attraction to radicalism. That cause should be sought elsewhere. Denial of the importance of ideas in the formation of the Jewish people would defy common sense. To be sure, in a universe which is reputed to be curved as well as pockmarked with black holes, an appeal to common sense is risky. Nevertheless some tropes and values must have been transmitted in such a way that Jews even in the United States nourished more radicals than comparable groups. One does not have to be an intellectual historian to consider an analogy with Yogi Berra's description of baseball: "90% of this game is half-mental."

The observation that Orthodoxy co-exists with radicalism far more rarely than religious ignorance and indifference is also problematic. Much depends upon the implication that *Halacha* (Talmudic law) has frozen Judaism into a rather unchanging mold, that Reform Judaism, for example, places undue weight upon the evolutionary aspects of Judaism and excessive stress upon prophetic ideals of social justice. It may well be the case, as Alexander Orbach has pointed out, that only this feature of Judaism—the stress on *tikkun olam*—got transmitted to emancipated Jewry. This emphasis is not to be confused with the whole of Judaism, but it may be the husk of what has remained for much of modern Jewry. In any event, scholarship does not require the acceptance of only an Orthodox definition of Judaism. Perhaps Gershom Scholem can be quoted out of context: "I do not . . . view the events of Jewish history from a fixed dogmatic standpoint . . . [nor do I] know exactly whether some phenomenon is 'Jewish' or not." Scholem rejected the "assumption that there is a well-defined and unvarying 'essence' of Judaism, especially . . . where the evaluation of historical events is concerned," and found it impossible to know a priori which sorts of beliefs were tolerable within Judaism.[28] The argument that ancient messianic hopes have been injected into modern politics therefore cannot be summarily rejected.

The hospitality of Judaism to diverse beliefs can be underscored by a comparison with Roman Catholicism. Papal encyclicals against socialism by Pius IX and Leo XIII may well have retarded the growth of socialism in the late nineteenth century. The Church—what Lenny Bruce later called "the only *the* Church"—was ideologically opposed to systematic political efforts to redistribute or abolish private property. So hostile was it (even in some cases to trade unionism itself), so frequent were the warnings uttered by parish priests all the way up the hierarchy, that ecclesiastical opposition helps account for the failure of socialism to sink deep roots in American soil. The movement was condemned as "a heresy, a rampant heresy," and to be both a Catholic and a socialist was considered a contradiction. But even though some socialists were anti-clerical and anti-religious, even though Jewish radicals sometimes deliberately flouted traditional rituals and piety, American rabbis did not consistently oppose radicalism.[29] Unlike rabbis, Catholic priests and Protestant preachers were occasionally radicals. But rabbis did not categorically stigmatize socialism either, or make adherence to its creeds in any way incompatible with Judaism or with membership in *k'lal yisroel* (the people of Israel). Indeed a major strain of Zionism was based upon a socialist ideology, and emphasized a natural affinity between the destiny of the Jewish people and an egalitarianism and collectivism pivotal to socialist doctrine.

A second possible explanation is anti-Semitism, which provoked Jews to struggle to alter societies that denied their rights and disparaged their merits and dignity. And since the Jews were the pariahs of Europe, radicalism and revolutions were intelligible responses to the frustration of full equality. In the United States, anti-Semitism has been far milder, especially by the time the New Left emerged in the 1960s. But the experience of discrimination and the fear of bigotry, abroad as well as in the United States, nevertheless motivated Jews to subscribe to and support radical causes, especially Communism in the 1930s and 1940s. The advantage of this theory is that some Jews themselves explained their attraction to communism in the light of its militant opposition to Nazism. The HUAC testimony of Daniel Boorstin, already cited, may be taken as representative.

One problem with this theory is its fudging of the distinction between liberalism and radicalism—quite apart from other reactions to anti-Semitism, such as Zionism. Nor is there any way of matching the extent of such deprivation to the popularity of radicalism among the Jews. The severity or scope of persecution does not correlate with the extent of adherence to radicalism, and those who have been turned down or turned away do not necessarily turn left as a consequence. The Lower East Side, which was the burnt-over district of American socialism, was probably far less aware of "status deprivation" and the incongruities of social and civic position than were the liberal and even conservative "uptown" Jews of the same era.

Moreover, if status deprivation were so decisive a motivating factor, one might have expected American Jewish radicals to hope that the Jews themselves, so stung by prejudice and discrimination, would become an important constituency for political change. This was rarely, if ever, the case. The "Jewish" garment workers unions were not consolidated along ethnic but rather economic and class lines, and made a point of their alignment with others in the garment trades, like the Italians. No American equivalent of the Bund emerged, although Jewish labor leaders appreciated its work and accomplishments in Eastern Europe and were touched by its fate. But a Jewish separatist labor socialist movement did not emerge in the United States; battles were conducted instead from the left flank of the American Federation of Labor. Though there were Jewish sections of the Communist Party in the 1920s, it is not too hyperbolic to state that Jews became experts on the revolutionary potential of every oppressed group in the United States except their own. The Party simply could not speak (even in Yiddish) in a special way to Jewish group interests. Israel Amter's famous salutation, "Workers and peasants of Brooklyn!," was unlikely to rouse the masses. If such radicals thought that status deprivation made their fellow Jews embittered and indignant, such knowledge was successfully repressed.

A third explanation, again originally propounded to account for liberalism (by Werner Cohn), has been extended by W. D. Rubinstein to incorporate radicalism as well. These scholars argue that the leftist orientation of modern Jewry is due to the historical circumstances of post-Emancipation Europe and beyond. The right was inhospitable and uncongenial because of its allegiance to tradition, hierarchy, and privilege, and (in Maurice Barrès's terms) to *la terre et les morts*. The right was nostalgic for an era in which Christianity was preeminent, which means that it was no accident that the first Western thinker to uncouple religion from politics was a Jew, Spinoza. Rubinstein has observed that, at least until recently, a certain set of historical circumstances kept the Jews away from the right: its anti-Semitism, its association with elites that excluded them, its defense of privilege at a time when most Jews were impoverished and disadvantaged. The left was, by contrast, impelled to reduce the particularities of religion, tradition, and even class.[30]

Here the connection with Jews was evocatively drawn in the mid-nineteenth century by a German socialist, J. L. Bernays, a Jew who asserted that his people had "rescued men from the narrow idea of an exclusive fatherland, from patriotism. . . . The Jew is not only an atheist, but a cosmopolitan, and he has turned men into atheists and cosmopolitans; he has made man only a free citizen of the world. . . . The Jews took their revenge upon the hostile world in an entirely new manner . . . by liberating men from all religion, from all patriotic sentiment . . . from everything that reminded them of race, place of origin, dogma and faith." This connection between universalist hope and revolutionary Jews was, for Bernays, a source of pride, reflecting the distance from rightist politics, which was defined in opposition to such atheism and cosmopolitanism.[31]

This set of historical circumstances no longer prevails, at least not as sharply as it did in the nineteenth century. Until 1945 the lethal enemies of the Jewish people were primarily on the right. Since then the political constellation has shifted considerably. The Holocaust taught many of its surviving remnant of the failure of European emancipation, the violation of the hopes once invested in the promise of civil equality. Israel was the most notable result of the disillusion with atheism and cosmopolitanism, for it reminded Jews of precisely what Bernays boasted that his people had liberated Europe from: race, place of origin, dogma, and faith. Now Jewish interests and welfare, without which Jewish moral values cannot be perpetuated, are dependent upon a secure and thriving Israel, whose enemies in the world arena have usually emanated from the left, from the putatively revolutionary regimes of the Third World. Anti-Zionism in Europe is almost entirely a phenomenon of the left and especially of Communism. The European center of anti-Semitism has been relocated to where it was, under czarist auspices, in the nineteenth century: in Moscow. Jews have increasingly realized that a tyranny so vast that it encompasses eleven of the world's twenty-four time zones, where a city like Vladivostok is closer to Honolulu than it is to Leningrad, has been brazen enough to support the Arab claim that Jewish sovereignty encompasses too large a corner of the Middle East. Moreover, the conservative forces in the United States have been detoxified of most of their anti-Semitism, and barriers have been lowered to others besides Henry Kissinger. The Jewish proletariat has largely disappeared, thus eliminating the class basis of socialist ideology.

And yet, while the historical circumstances that might have produced the Jewish slant toward radicalism have largely evaporated, the Jewish stance remains more tipped to the left than to the right. Wherever radicalism in the United States can still be found (apart from black separatism), Jews are within its ranks. Leftist traditions—and perhaps even the Judaic value system—still block the reorientation of Jewish politics. What caused immigrants to be socialists may not resemble what drew some of their grandchildren toward the New Left, but social and economic conditions have neither changed so drastically nor overcome inertia in leading most Jews away from either their allegiance to liberalism or their tolerance for radicalism. If historical circumstances alone produced the Jewish propensity for the left, the disproportionate number of Jews coagulating in the New Left could scarcely be explained.

There is no reason to assume that historical change since the eighteenth and nineteenth centuries somehow skipped the Jewish family, whose dynamics have given rise to the fourth theory for the origins and perpetuation of Jewish radicalism. As religious authority yielded to the lure of secular Western civilization, as some forms of traditional piety became more rigid and opportunities in business and the liberal professions widened, as ghetto walls tumbled down and the winds of modernity rustled through the *shtetl*, the family was obliged to bear an increasing burden in reconciling the tensions and antinomies of Jewish life. The roles of fathers and mothers and children altered, sometimes subtly, sometimes searingly; and even when the tensions ran silent, they ran deep.

As the Jewish family struggled to gain and restore its cohesiveness, it sanctioned political heterodoxy. "To other people, I'm a professional radical," Saul Alinsky once observed. But to his mother, "the important thing is, I'm a professional."[32] Literary evidence can also be cited. Sholom Aleichem's Tevye realizes the destruction of tradition, and faces—both figuratively and literally—a new world. Nevertheless, he cannot abide the romantic involvement of one daughter, Chava, with a gentile, and mourns her inclination to accept the consequences of putting private happiness ahead of peoplehood. But another daughter's marriage to a revolutionary is not a disgrace to Tevye, however baffled he may be; for Hodel and Pertschik remain part of the Jewish people. Similar indulgence is granted in America as well. In Jules Feiffer's play, *Grownups*, a New York couple bubbles with pride that their son is a journalist for the *New York Times*. That is their emblem of making it, the certification of success. A jarring note is injected when the son informs them that he is writing a book blasting the political system as corrupt and immoral, but the parents don't skip a beat in exuding *naches* (joy). It does not seem to matter whether the system is rotten, so long as their son wins recognition for exposing it.

Nathan Glazer has argued that Jews were disproportionately attracted to the New Left simply because they grew up in families which already nurtured earlier dissidents: "Jewish political traditions, traditions of liberalism and socialism, open young Jews to the *possibility* of influence by liberal and socialist views. Young Jews are more likely to be aware of a variety of left-wing political creeds." Glazer has suggested that the presence in so many Jewish families of older radicals has given the young a sense of political alternatives. In such families upward mobility was authorized and encouraged in various ways, but Marxists were still hanging around—undoubtedly more adhesively than in gentile families. No character is more greedy and ambitious than Mordecai Richler's Duddy Kravitz, but the Uncle Benjy who runs a dress factory is shown—in both the novel and the film—as wealthy but still a Stalinist.[33]

Compare, on this point, two novels of upward mobility according to the American Dream, in which young men who start impoverished become wealthy, only to taste the ashes of emptiness and disenchantment. *The Rise of David Levinsky* (1917) allows its protagonist to realize that he was not necessarily destined to become a successful clothing manufacturer. Had he chanced to hear a speech by Karl Marx, Levinsky speculates, he might well have become a socialist (as was his creator, Abraham Cahan). Yet the eponymous protagonist of *The Great Gatsby* (1925) never imagines a similar alternative. Or take the two most famous Beatnik writers of the 1950s. Jack Kerouac's heritage was French Canadian, which may have helped make him surprisingly old-fashioned, from his vices (alcohol) to his politics (Republican). Kerouac liked Ike in the 1950s, preferred Nixon to Kennedy in 1960, and had reacted to the televised McCarthy hearings by announcing that the junior senator from Wisconsin had "the real dope on the Jews and fairies." By contrast, Allen Ginsberg's father was a poet who had published in the bohemian socialist magazine, *The Masses*. His mother was a Communist whom Ginsberg memorialized in perhaps his greatest poem, "Kaddish" (1959), attributing to her the haunting advice: "The key is in the window, the key is in the sunlight at the window. I have the key. Get married Allen don't take drugs." (The advice was ignored, but Ginsberg nevertheless became so rich from poems denouncing Moloch that he has incorporated himself for tax purposes.)[34]

The phenomenon of the "red diaper baby" appears to be almost exclusively Jewish; and, while the case is undoubtedly exceptional, the sons of Julius and Ethel Rosenberg, Michael and Robert Meeropol, were themselves involved in SDS. For every Mark Rudd and Abbie Hoffman, whose fathers were fairly conservative if not apolitical, there was a Bettina Aptheker, a Berkeley activist whose father has been a Communist historian and publicist; or a Kathy Boudin, whose father has been prominently engaged in the legal defense of Communists and fellow travelers. And even Rudd's parents made a point of supporting him during the Columbia insurrection, bringing him food and referring to him as their son, the revolutionary.[35] Karl Marx's mother is supposed to have wistfully remarked how much better it would have been if her son had only *made* some capital instead of just writing about it. But Henrietta Marx did not disown him.[36] Nor did the father of David Dubinsky, who grew up in Lodz, where the Jewish working class toiled from twelve to fifteen hours a day. At thirteen young Dubinsky quit school; at fourteen he was a master baker in his father's shop. At fifteen, as secretary of the bakers' union, he struck, helping to shut down his own father's shop. But when the police came to take him to jail, Dubinsky's father gave him money and a *tallis* (prayer shawl).[37]

"Marx said it: Abolish such families!" cries the grandfather in exasperation in Clifford Odets's *Awake and Sing* (1935), as Jacob's relatives wound one another trying to survive the Depression.[38] But exactly how such families spawned radicals is a matter of dispute, and the theories are incompatible. For Glazer and Seymour Martin Lipset, radical offspring wished to extend and make operational what liberal parents did not fully practice. These analysts of the New Left of the 1960s have stressed the continuity in the values of the two generations, with the younger generation attempting to live up to the pieties of social justice with which they had been inculcated. The positive support of such parents gave the young confidence in the rightness of their values and in the propriety of their engagement in the civil rights movement, in anti-poverty campaigns, in battles for student power, and in their resistance to American military intervention in Vietnam. Impressionistic evidence is given along this line in Midge Decter's *Liberal Parents, Radical Children* (1975). Social science supports this view in the monographs of Kenneth Keniston and Richard Flacks, admittedly based on small samples but clearly dependent upon psychological investigation of Jewish as well as non-Jewish New Leftists, plus the more recent and far more comprehensive *Roots of Radicalism* (1982) by Stanley Rothman and S. Robert Lichter.[39] The children thus discovered a fresh way to obey the Fifth Commandment.

An alternative—and indeed contradictory—reading of the relation of parents to radical children is most forcefully advanced in Lewis Feuer's *The Conflict of Generations*. His relevant evidence is drawn not only from Jewish student radicals in the United States but from Russian Jewish students in the late nineteenth century as well. Feuer emphasizes not only the self-destructiveness and nihilism of student movements but—in the special case of the Jews—a disgust with the fathers' "passive recipience of persecution," leading them to identify with the sufferings and struggles of other groups, notably blacks. He explains the Jewish predilection for student radicalism in the 1920s and 1930s by referring to the nature of American culture itself and by the eagerness of the second generation to distance itself from the ways of the immigrant parents. The cycle of irrational rejection was to be perpetuated in the 1960s.[40]

The evidence for the "de-authorization of the fathers" is partly autobiographical; accounts by Morris Raphael Cohen and John Gates, for example, are cited. But *The Conflict of Generations* leaves unclear why it is aberrant to repudiate the culture of, say, immigrant parents (even when, as in the case of Cohen, such rejection was neither violent or suicidal). Nor does Feuer elucidate his own assumption that the only proof of rationality would have been duplication of the values and life-styles of the elders. He also fails to acknowledge the possibility that many young Jews identified with and supported the civil rights movement because racial segregation and discrimination constituted a far more shameful violation of the promise of American democracy than any other social problem, including anti-Semitism. Certainly some signs of Oedipal strains should be mentioned which buttress Feuer's case, as in the wilder rantings of Jerry Rubin, as in Bob Dylan's advice to parents in changing times not to criticize what they could not understand, as in the admission of a former 1960s student in Lawrence Kasdan's retrospective film, *The Big Chill* (1983): "Half the stuff I did, I did to piss off my parents. And it worked." In Feiffer's satiric *Grownups*, the Jewish parents are so obtrusive and inescapable that when the adult daughter whimsically proposes killing them, her brother demurs: "That would be only a short-range solution." Here, too, Abbie Hoffman's rambunctious autobiography is revealing about its filial conflicts.[41]

Nevertheless, the Feuer thesis is in general unconvincing. Even if he is right about the self-destructive irrationality of student movements in the 1960s, no links are firmly forged to Oedipal relations to parents. Social scientists and others who have investigated young radicals' attitudes toward their parents disclose neither such hostility, nor disgust with the passivity of their parents. Far from subsuming their own ethnicity in a romantic identification with the uprisings of oppressed peoples and minorities, many Jewish members and sympathizers quit the New Left after 1967, when it became hostile to Israel. Nor does Feuer's theory explain the phenomenon of young radicals who insisted upon the compatibility of their politics with

Jewishness and Judaism, a synthesis which flourished largely after publication of *The Conflict of Generations*.[42] The traditional strength and cohesiveness of the Jewish family have undoubtedly been decisive in shaping the identities of the rebels who emerged from homes that—unlike their grandparents' English—were rarely broken. But bonds of continuity and affirmation appear to have been more powerful than the friction and disaffection which could also be detected. Why some families produced radicals, and most others liberals, nevertheless remains an enigma.

There is another theory that has been given almost no attention. It is advanced here only tentatively, because there are reportedly many places in purgatory reserved for those scholars who allow generalizations to outstrip their evidence. The explanation is given a fleeting glance in Lawrence H. Fuchs's early and influential study of liberalism, *The Political Behavior of American Jews*, in Glazer's reflections on student radicals (which is confined to America in the 1960s). In accounting for a penchant for radical ideologies and movements, scholars have given little, if any, weight to what the sociologist Talcott Parsons considered the most distinctive characteristic of the Jewish people: its intellectuality.[43]

Even the word "intellectual" itself arose thanks to Jews; for it was coined during *l'affaire* in France to categorize the Dreyfusards, some of whom were the captain's co-religionists. If Jews have been disproportionately radicals, it may be because they have been disproportionately intellectuals. Randolph Bourne and Thorstein Veblen were among the first Americans to recognize the spectacular impact that Jewish intellectuals were making upon Western culture, but the remarks of Nikos Kazantzakis are even more to the point. "Ours is an age of revolution," the Greek writer said of the inter-war period: "That is, a Jewish age." Modern life had become fragmented and decomposed, and "the Jews have this supreme quality: to be restless, not to fit into the realities of the time; to struggle to escape; to consider every status quo and every idea a stifling prison. This spirit of the Jews shatters the equilibrium . . ."[44]

They were often indifferent to or highly critical of the pieties of national honor, of blood and soil. Morris Hillquit, for example, wrote the Socialists' St. Louis Declaration of 1917 that branded the Great War a crime. He was consistent in his opposition to militarism and "the false doctrine of national patriotism" even after czarism had been overthrown and the world more plausibly made safe for democracy. Thus an editorialist for the *New York Times* could take a swipe at

Hillquit, whose "singular genius" was to try "at once to betray the land of his birth and the land of his adoption." No wonder then that T. S. Eliot, at the same time as Kazantzakis, imagined a Christian society that would, for "reasons of race and religion," exclude large numbers of "free thinking Jews." From Eliot's perspective, such a minority would endanger the social stability and ideological coherence of his ideal order; and he warned against "a spirit of excessive tolerance."[45]

Revolutionary politics was a natural outlet, for Béla Kun and Georg Lukács in Hungary, for Gustav Landauer and Ernst Toller in Bavaria, for Rosa Luxemburg in Berlin, for Trotsky and Karl Radek and Julius Martov and Lev Kamenev and Grigori Zinoviev in Russia, for Mikhail Borodin in China, and innumerable others. In the United States, intellectuals were less driven to such extremism; but their presence gave the Jewish labor movement much of its distinctiveness. The early leaders of the ILGWU, for example, were almost invariably former students who, according to a labor historian, "found themselves in the garment industry as a matter of necessity, not of choice." But their experience in Russian revolutionary movements gave Benjamin Schlesinger, Julius Woolf, Saul Metz, Abraham Boroff, and others a certain stature as well as militancy; and therefore "the Jewish workers turned instinctively to the intellectuals for help and were grateful for the leadership which they were able to provide." More than any other immigrant group, the Jews harbored intellectuals among their tired, huddled masses; and they fostered a radical spirit and outlook. Noam Chomsky, for instance, has recorded his own indebtedness to the "radical Jewish working class milieu" to which his family belonged: "It was a very unusual culture which I don't think exists anymore, a mixture of a very high level of intense intellectual life, but at the same time it was really working class."[46]

That is why the Jews differed from other members of the proletariat, and remained sympathetic to radicalism even when nestled in the middle class. For in America in particular, radical movements have failed to appeal to their ostensible constituencies, have flunked the assignment of dialectical materialism. Nearly all the oppressed and impoverished have ignored the agitation of radicals, have listened only in moments of crisis, and have lapsed back into moderation or political indifference when special pressures were released. Because radicalism is an *ism*—that is, a modern ideology, those groups pervaded by the presence of intellectuals have been most likely to sustain it. Consider a *New York Post* headline in 1950: "Einstein Red Faker,

Should Be Deported, Rankin Screams." In insinuating that independence of mind and political dissidence were the signature of Jews in particular, even a venomous crank like the Mississippi congressman was groping for a partial truth. And in a way Attorney General William Saxbe was right after all, when he attributed the earlier strength of American Communism to the power of Jewish intellectuals yearning after strange gods that eventually failed.

Not only defense agencies should reiterate, however, that most Jews have not been radicals. Even most Jewish intellectuals have not been radical. Such persons—and not serfs, or slaves, or peasants, or black sharecroppers—have nevertheless been overrepresented in revolutionary movements, almost as predictably as queens beat jacks in poker. In describing the homes of Jewish New Leftists, Glazer has singled out the importance of books, lectures, and "cultural style" in promoting a greater responsiveness to the social environment. He isolates certain measurable indices, such as college attendance and choices of fields of concentration; but he did not speculate upon intellectuality itself as a susceptibility to radical impulses. It is curious that Glazer himself should dwell on "cultural style," because his own youthful radicalism was barely shaped by reading as such. His own family—which had to go on welfare in Harlem during the Great Depression—was so unfamiliar with his own vocation as a writer and an editor that his mother, once asked to describe his occupation, vaguely asserted that he was "in the pen business."[48] A hypothesis that emphasizes such vocations and such inclinations does not require the ascription of intellectuality to the Judaic faith itself, as the source of a certain tendency toward radicalism. That is another advantage of the theory.

One final note should be sounded, whatever the vitality of the Jewish future, whatever the momentary quiescence on the left. Radical movements have attracted the best as well as the worst of humanity; but however equivocal the record of socialism in the annals of human freedom, the pain of the dispossessed ought to continue to disturb even those whose well-being is partly derived from the travail and the martyrdom of earlier radicals. Among those who gave themselves to such struggles, many paid the price of passion, embroiling themselves more than other mortals in folly and tragedy. Like all the other members of our species, however, they were subjugated to the ordinances of time and place, even as they dared to press against the limits that only social arrangements seemed to impose. They also dramatized the process of disenchantment, of putting into secular form longings for redemption that were once expressed in a religious idiom. It may still be appropriate to relate their ambiguous pursuit of brotherhood to the hope of Natalia Victorovna Haldin, the character in Joseph Conrad's *Under Western Eyes* who "believe[d] that the future will be merciful to us all. Revolutionist and reactionary, victim and executioner, betrayer and betrayed, they shall all be pitied together when the light breaks."[49]

The radical heritage is, at its most sublime, difficult to perpetuate; and the Jewish intellectuals who once embraced such movements sometimes found their way toward a more enduring set of values within their own religious tradition. Under American conditions, which are so hospitable for Jewish comfort and so risky for Judaic culture, the question remains whether this tiny people can still distinguish itself by the disproportionate numbers of sons and daughters that it can produce who are famished for justice.

7

JOURNALISM

The subject of the relationships of Jews to journalism is entangled in paradox. Their role in the press has long been an obsession of their enemies, and the vastly disproportionate power that Jews are alleged to wield through the media has been a staple of the anti-Semitic imagination. This manifestation of bigotry has been so intense that it has dwarfed the interest that scholars or Jews themselves have shown in the problem. Such disparity merits the slight correction and compensation that this chapter is intended to offer.

This feature of Judeophobia was perhaps inaugurated in a significant way in the squalid and murky origins of *The Protocols of the Elders of Zion*, the most ubiquitous of anti-Semitic documents. Itself a forgery, the *Protocols* were based upon a chapter of Hermann Goedsche's novel *Biarritz* (1868). Entitled "In the Jewish Cemetery in Prague," that chapter formed the contours of the "Rabbi's Speech" that exposed the methods of the conspiratorial ambition to dominate Christendom and indeed the planet. "If gold is the first power in this world," the rabbi informs his co-conspirators, "the second is undeniably the press. . . . Our people must become the editors of all daily newspapers in all countries. Our possession of gold, our skill in devising means of exploiting mercenary instincts, will make us the arbiters of public opinion and enable us to dominate the masses." With this influence, the rabbi fiendishly predicts: "We shall dictate to the world what it is to have faith in, what it is to honor, and what it is to curse. . . . Once we are absolute masters of the press, we will be able to transform ideas about honor, about virtue, about uprightness of character, we will be able to deal a blow against . . . the family, and we will be able to achieve its disintegration. . . . We shall declare open war on everything that people respect and venerate."[1]

This passage from the precursor to the *Protocols* has been quoted at some length because it foreshadowed the conception of Jewish power in and through journalism which was to be repeated for over a century. That anti-Semitic fears were stirred by the Jewish involvement in finance is commonly known; it is insufficiently realized how often this phobia was coupled with animus against the Jewish participation in journalism. As a locus of sinister or repellent Jewish influence, the newsroom was second only to the bourse. A little over a century ago, the historian Heinrich von Treitschke warned that "across our Eastern borders there pushes . . . a troop of ambitious, trousers-selling youth, whose children and children's children will someday dominate Germany's exchanges and Germany's press." Nor did the Swiss historian Jacob Burckhardt fail to notice that Jews exerted special impact upon the "venal" press.[2]

The final German example is extracted from *Mein Kampf*, whose preface explains the book's purpose as an account of the Nazi movement and of the political development of its *Fuehrer*. The author does so "insofar as it may serve to destroy the foul legends about my person dished up in the Jewish press." Before even getting to the text itself, he reveals his paranoia and his rage—not by alluding to race, or to the dangers of pollution and infection, or to the stock market, or to religion. In the sole reference to Jews in the preface of *Mein Kampf*, only "the Jewish press" is mentioned. The chapter retracing the author's steps in becoming an anti-Semite bristles with memories of the degenerate Jewish journalists who operated as liberals or as Marxists in fin-de-siècle Vienna. "For one Goethe," the inmate of Landsberg Prison concludes, "nature easily can foist on the world 10,000 of these scribblers who poison men's souls."[3]

In more muted form and with shifting emphases, this theme crosses the Atlantic as well. On the subject of one immigrant group, Secretary of State John Hay remarked, Henry Adams was "clean daft. The Jews are all the press, all the cabinets, all the gods and all weather. I was amazed to see so sensible a man so wild."[4] The patrician historian was not unique. The most mischievous and important of American Judeophobes was Henry Ford, who was probably the wealthiest citizen of the world's wealthiest country as well. More than anyone else, Ford made the *Protocols* internationally famous. This forgery permeated the editorial policy of the weekly that he owned, the *Dearborn Independent*, which from 1920 until 1927 ran anti-Semitic columns. The series entitled "The International Jew" was later published in book form; the first column (May 22, 1920) set the tone. After observing the tentacles of Jewish financiers within the American economy, the editorial announced that "Jewish journalists are a large and powerful group here. . . . They absolutely control the circulation of publications throughout the country." Later in 1920 Ford's newspaper warned that from the northeastern section of the United States, "poisonous infections of revolutionary doctrine" were being "spread throughout the country upon the wings of 'liberal' publications subsidized by Jewish money."[5]

One ambition ascribed to Jews in journalism was to implicate the United States in war. This is a theme not readily found in German anti-Semitism, probably because the United States has been far less hospitable to militarism, and also because the American tradition of isolationism was—until fairly recently—so tenacious. A little-known example of this charge of warmongering can be located in the writing of H. L. Mencken, an ornament of American letters who was the most inescapable journalist of the 1920s. But during the First World War, Mencken's opposition to the conflict and to American intervention made him a beleaguered and rather subdued figure. He was no anti-Semite, and yet he was impelled to comment in 1922: "Fully four-fifths of all the foreign news that comes to the American newspapers comes through London, and most of the rest is supplied either by Englishmen or by Jews (often American-born) who maintain close relations with the English. . . . I was in Copenhagen and Basel in 1917," Mencken added, "and found both towns—each an important source of war news—full of Jews representing American journals as a sideline to more delicate and confidential work for the English department of press propaganda."[6] What is peculiar about this appraisal is its direct collision with the assessment of the British ambassador in Washington, Sir Cecil Spring-Rice, who wrote on November 13, 1914 that the American Jewish bankers of German ancestry were "toiling in a solid phalanx to compass our destruction. One by one they are getting hold of the principal New York papers . . . and are bringing them over as much as they dare to the German side." Spring-Rice stressed the power of this lobby so adamantly that he may well have curtailed his own career. For his government believed him enough to replace him in Washington with a prominent Jew, Lord Reading (Rufus Isaacs), possibly in the hope of placating the American press.[7]

An even more vigorous opponent of American intervention in the Great War than either Ford or Mencken was a Midwestern congressman, Charles A. Lindbergh, Sr.; and in the 1930s his son entered the political cockpit to urge the United States to keep out of another European conflict. In a radio speech in Des Moines, Iowa, on September 11, 1941, the aviator identified "the three most important groups which have been pressing this country toward war . . . the British, the Jewish and the Roosevelt administration." Speaking of the Jews, he warned: "Their greatest danger to this country lies in their large ownership and influence in our motion pictures, our press, our radio and our government." Although distrust of Eastern bankers and financiers had fueled his own father's isolationism, Colonel Lindbergh himself underscored Jewish control of what later came to be called the media. He also provided the helpful advice that, by pushing their case for military intervention against Germany, Jews would only encourage anti-Semitism.[8]

When Vice-President Spiro Agnew blasted the liberal slant of the eastern "establishment press"—primarily television—in 1969 (in the same city as Lindbergh's speech of almost three decades earlier), it was the most vigorous, deliberate assault by a leading official on the press in American political history. Unlike Lindbergh, Agnew made no mention whatsoever of Jews. That did not prevent some of his more excitable supporters from drawing one conclusion from the vice-president's condemnation of news organizations in which Jews happened to be prominent, and media figures as well as the American Jewish Committee noticed an increase in anti-Semitic hate mail. Even as Agnew protested that he was being unfairly smeared for having instigated this vitriolic attack, he told Barbara Walters on NBC's "Today Show" that a "Jewish cabal" exercised mastery of the American media, permitting "Zionist influences" to tilt American policy unduly toward Israel. Agnew repeated this charge in published interviews and even in his novel, *The Canfield Decision* (1976). Two ex-speechwriters for the vice-president, William Safire and Victor Gold, denounced Agnew's remarks, which President Ford called "wrong, both substantially and morally."[9] One recent aspirant for Gerald Ford's former job, the Reverend Jesse Jackson, has also discerned Jewish influence on American banks and the media.[10]

And yet the paradox mentioned at the outset of this chapter bears emphasis: the subject has captivated the adversaries of the Jews far more than it has fascinated either Jews themselves or independent scholars. In a biography of Mordecai M. Noah, the first significant journalist of Jewish origin in the New World, Professor Jonathan D. Sarna states categorically: "There is no history of Jews in American journalism."[11] The researcher is therefore required to begin with specialized monographs, such as biographical portraits of individuals appearing in encyclopedias and reference works. One journalist's book, Stephen D. Isaacs's *Jews and American Politics* (1974), does include a chapter speculating on the apparent overrepresentation of such journalists on the contemporary political landscape. But the topic is not treated in a historical—much less in a general scholarly—way; nor is the overview on the subject of journalism in the *Encyclopedia Judaica* interpretive. It too is primarily biographical in orientation, tracking the careers and achievements of reporters, editors, and publishers in various countries—one of whom, Theodor Herzl, even became the prophet and father of the Zionist state. The only previous scholarly article on the role of Jews in American journalism highlights the critiques that have been rendered of the problematic nature of the press itself.[12] The rest is "no comment."

In breaking this silence, a scholar must weigh without apology the validity of the claim of Jewish overrepresentation in the media. An argument is not ipso facto false because it is repeated by a disgraced vice-president of the United States. The law of averages works in a fashion that allows for the possibility of even a crook or a demagogue—or an anti-Semite—hitting upon the correct answer some of the time. But however exaggerated or unwarranted the beliefs of bigots may prove to be, the conspicuous attractiveness of journalism for many Jews merits analysis and explanation, within the context of modern Jewish experience.

The raw statistics utterly belie the expectations envisioned in the Prague rabbi's speech of dominating the daily press. Over 1700 daily newspapers are currently published in the United States. Jews own about fifty, or less than 3%, which is the proportion of Jews in the general American population. Even when these particular newspapers' circulation is taken into account (8%), it is evident that newspaper publishing is hardly an awesome sign of Jewish entrepreneurship.[13] There are nearly 9,000 radio stations and 1,000 television network affiliates, but no data on the ethnic and religious identification of their owners appear to be extant. According to the only published figures on the percentage of Jews among American editors and reporters, the 3.3% so identified is only slightly above their proportion in the general population.[14]

The two most newsworthy American cities do, however, seem to be covered by a large fraction of journalists of Jewish birth. According to a 1976 study, a quarter of the Washington press corps was of Jewish background. A volume of Jewish economic history published a year earlier claims that "it has been estimated that . . . 40% of . . . [New York's] journalists are Jews." Marcus Arkin fails to disclose the basis of this estimate or even its source. But since New York is the media capital of the country, and not only the most populous concentration of Jews on the planet, the proportion of Jews in the general population is more relevant than their percentage in the city itself. Arkin's estimate is therefore almost certainly too high, perhaps much too high.[15]

Numbers do not of course correlate with influence, nor participation with impact; and the prestige of certain papers cannot be quantified. Here, too, analogs in European history can be found. In the Weimar Republic as earlier in the Second Reich, special distinction was conceded to the Jewish-owned *Frankfurter Zeitung* and the publishing houses of Ullstein and Mosse. And the Jewish editorial control of the *Berliner Tageblatt* and the *Vossische Zeitung* typified the Jewish presence across the spectrum of the liberal and leftist press, even though the conservative and right-wing press (dominated by the Hugenberg trust) enjoyed greater circulation. The most prestigious newspaper in Central Europe was undoubtedly Vienna's *Neue Freie Presse*, which Jews published and to which they contributed *feuilletons*. In the more remote provinces of Franz Josef's empire, some visiting cards contained the following boast below the engraved name of the bearer: "Subscribes to the *Neue Freie Presse*."[16]

In the United States as well, as Agnew's own partisan speech implied, some news organizations are more respected and important than others. According to one survey, the reporters whose beat is Washington, D. C., acknowledge the supremacy of the following influences: 1) television networks, 2) weekly news magazines, 3) the wire services, and 4) four daily newspapers—the *Washington Post*, the *New York Times*, the *Washington Star* (now defunct), and the *Wall Street Journal*.[17]

With the exception of the wire services (the Associated Press and United Press International), these branches of the Fourth Estate are institutions in which Jews have tended to congregate. A 1979 survey revealed that 27% of the employees of the *Times*, the *Post*, the *Wall*

Street Journal, Time, Newsweek, U.S. News and World Report, the three networks, and the Public Broadcasting System were of Jewish origin. Fifty-eight percent of the producers and editors at ABC were Jews.[18] They were conspicuous at the top. The Sulzberger family retains its ownership of the *New York Times,* of which the executive editor is Max Frankel, the managing editor is Arthur Gelb, the associate editor is A. M. Rosenthal, and the editorial page editor is Jack Rosenthal. Eugene Meyer had bought the *Washington Post* at an auction in 1933; and it was under the leadership of his daughter, Katharine Graham, raised as a Lutheran, and executive editor Benjamin C. Bradlee, a Brahmin, that the newspaper became the chief rival to the *Times.* For the *Post's* Pulitzer Prize-winning exposure of the Watergate scandal, the two most famous local reporters in history benefited from the support of editors Howard Simons, Harry Rosenfeld, and Barry Sussman. "More than any other editor at the *Post,*" Carl Bernstein and Bob Woodward claimed, "Sussman became a walking compendium of Watergate knowledge, a reference source to be summoned when even the library failed." The city editor was essentially "a theoretician. In another age, he might have been a Talmudic scholar."[19]

Other Jews who have occupied pivotal positions in the media should also be mentioned. Warren Phillips was editor of the *Wall Street Journal,* whose current managing editor is Norman Pearlstine. Marvin Stone was editor of *U. S. News and World Report,* long the extended shadow of David Lawrence; it is now owned by Morton Zuckerman. Edward Kosner was editor of *Newsweek.* The managing editor of *Time* was Henry Anatole Grunwald, who began his career at the magazine as its part-time copy boy. William Paley was chairman of the board of CBS, while Fred Friendly and Richard Salant were presidents of its news division. The Sarnoff family was long dominant at NBC, whose news division was headed by Richard Wald. Leonard Goldenson was president of ABC, while the executive producer of its evening news was Av Westin. The president of the Public Broadcasting System was Lawrence Grossman. The president of National Public Radio has been Frank Mankiewicz, the son of the co-scenarist of Hollywood's most brilliant film, a portrait of a press lord, *Citizen Kane* (1941).

Statistical measurement cannot convey the impact which Jews have exerted upon American journalism. How can the prestige of the *New York Times* be tabulated? In its authoritativeness as the newspaper of record, in its reputation for accuracy and comprehensiveness, the *Times* is in a class by itself. It has a news staff of 550 in New York alone, where its Times Square newsroom covers 1.3 acres. For the

Times to communicate "all the news that's fit to print," six million trees are chopped down annually. The Sunday edition typically runs over four hundred pages, printed in enough copies for the sheets to paper over the island of Manhattan twice.[20] But what does it mean for its editors and reporters to realize that their words will be read and pondered in the White House and in the Kremlin, in City Hall and in the libraries and archives of posterity?

Or how does the scholar measure the impact of Walter Lippmann (1889–1974)? He was probably the most admired American journalist of the twentieth century; and one reputable historian considered him "perhaps the most important [American] political thinker of the twentieth century" as well. Because Lippmann's approach to journalism was oriented to interpretation, he made little impression on the process of news gathering. But it was said in Washington during his prime that foreign governments formally accredited their ambassadors to the president and by private letter to Lippmann, who seemed to stride above the norms of diplomacy when it suited him. His regular pilgrimages to Europe were so rigorously arranged that, in 1961, Nikita Khrushchev's request to delay Lippmann's Soviet visit by a few days, due to an unanticipated political crisis, was rejected. The Russian dictator then rearranged his *own* plans so that he could meet the American journalist. (The resulting interviews earned Lippmann a second Pulitzer Prize.) Quantification of his stature can sometimes be attempted. When Lippmann spoke at the National Press Club to celebrate his seventieth birthday, more correspondents were in attendance than had come to hear Khrushchev speak in the same room a little earlier.[21]

Or how is the impact of Herbert Bayard Swope (1882–1958) to be assessed? He won the first Pulitzer Prize for reporting (in 1917) and gained fame as the executive editor of the *New York World* in its heyday, the 1920s (when Lippmann ran the editorial page). He coined the term "op ed" page, a feature for which he was primarily responsible. From a Roosevelt campaign speech of 1932, Swope singled out the phrase "new deal," thus labeling an administration and also an era. When both were over, he coined the phrase "the cold war" (which Lippmann gave currency).[22] Swope instituted the newspaper practice of capitalizing the word "negro"; and under his direction the *World* won a Pulitzer Prize for a series exposing the Ku Klux Klan. Lord Northcliffe of the London *Daily Mail* considered Swope the finest reporter of his time. Late in the 1920s, when the promising humorist James Thurber sat down in a speakeasy and was told only later that

he had been in the company of Swope, Thurber feigned astonish-
ment. He'd been under the impression that Herbert Bayard Swope
was a legend. The editor's mansion on Long Island had so impressed
F. Scott Fitzgerald that it was the inspiration for the East Egg home of
Tom and Daisy Buchanan in *The Great Gatsby*. Swope brandished so
much *chutzpah*, RCA's David Sarnoff once remarked, "that if you
wanted to meet God, he'd arrange it somehow." Maybe that was an
exaggeration, but Swope *did* seem to know everyone else of importance, and never underestimated the value of wire-pulling—sometimes quite literally, as when Swope complained directly to Sarnoff
when a friend's television set went on the blink. Swope was so famous
that he became one of the first *Time* magazine cover subjects, so
arrogant that he listed among his favorite books not only the Bible
and the *World Almanac* but also any volume containing a reference to
himself, so imperious that he could scoop other reporters by dressing
exactly like a diplomat and getting a front row seat at the Versailles
Peace Conference. The impression he made was so distinctive, effu-
sive, and flamboyant that, after deluging a convalescent Ring Lardner
with get-well messages, the humorist wired back: "CAN YOU SUG-
GEST ANY WAY TO END THIS CORRESPONDENCE AMICABLY
STOP MY PERSONAL PHYSICIAN SAYS EXCITEMENT OF
HEARING FROM YOU DAILY IS BAD FOR ME . . ." Swope's written
legacy is surprisingly sparse and brittle, but his hellzapoppin' personality made him into the most formidable newsman of his age.[23]

Let one other biographical illustration suggest the elusiveness of
measuring the Jewish role in American journalism. If Swope lived the
myth of American journalism, Ben Hecht (1894–1964) not only
enjoyed it as fully but also, more than anyone else, created it. It is
from Hecht that Americans learned that newspapermen could be
corrupt, cynical, wenching, dissolute, coarse, drunken rogues, insensitive to anyone's privacy, oblivious to puritanical codes—and therefore having more fun than anyone else. Born on the Lower East Side
of New York, Hecht began his professional career in Chicago at the
age of sixteen. His first assignment, which the publisher of the *Chicago
Journal* gave him, was to write obscene verses for a stag party. Over a
decade of such intimacy with the vulgarities of his profession and the
raunchiest features of city life gave Hecht material for *1001 Afternoons
in Chicago* (1922), for later autobiographical novels like *Gaily, Gaily*
(1963), and for his spirited memoir, *A Child of the Century* (1954). But
Hecht's greatest achievement as a myth-maker was *The Front Page*
(1928), in collaboration with Charles MacArthur.[24] This piece of

gallows humor, which incidentally is Tom Stoppard's favorite American play, has bobbed up in three Hollywood versions, the last directed by the Viennese *bon vivant*, Billy Wilder, who had learned in the pages of Karl Kraus's *Die Fackel*, among other forums, of the pertinence of journalism as a peephole into modern malaise.[25] Newspaper experiences were the capital that Hecht drew upon for writing fiction and films, and his recounting became the standard against which the vicissitudes of the profession came to be measured.

Since such examples could be multiplied, the limitations of space make it impossible (as newsboys used to scream) to "read all about it." It is preferable to elucidate such impact rather than illustrate it.

History must be appealed to, in accounting for the special responsiveness of many Jews to opportunities in professions such as journalism. There has to be some sort of "fit" between skill and milieu, between potentiality and circumstance. That is why the *Encyclopedia Judaica* dates the Jewish contribution to European journalism at the beginning of Emancipation itself, conjecturing that a people already relatively urban and literate found itself "in the right place at the right time." Moreover, the encyclopedia asserts, the "gift of adaptability permitted the Jew to act as an intermediary, the link between the event and the reader, as the journalist has often been called." The press offered "brightness and novelty," an outlet for a people that felt little if any devotion to pre-modern tradition. Also pertinent here are the speculations of sociologist Arthur Ruppin that "city life forces people into intensive interaction, into an exchange of goods and ideas. It demands constant mental alertness. . . . The great mental agility of the Jews . . . enabled them to have a quick grasp and orientation in all things . . ."[26]

Such comments get us closer to the truth, though they would appear to be more applicable to the nineteenth century than to the twentieth. They are more useful in explaining the initial attraction that journalism might have exerted on the newly emancipated, not why—if anything—the Jewish involvement has persisted without noticeable loss of intensity. By the twentieth century, especially long past its midpoint, the relative historical advantages which literacy and urbanity might have conferred should have become quite marginal. The conjectures of the encyclopedia and of Ruppin undoubtedly apply more directly to Europe than to the United States, which was post-Emancipation from its inception as an independent nation and has imposed no official restrictions upon Jews.

This theory, like others, suffers from the disadvantage of blurring or ignoring the distinction between journalists themselves and their employers. With some important exceptions, Jews often achieved prominence on the business side before the expressive side. This distinction was put most cogently by A. J. Liebling, who realized early on that he "did not belong to a joyous, improvident professional group including me and [publisher] Roy Howard, but to a section of society including me and any floorwalker at Macy's. Mr. Howard, even though he asked to be called Roy, belonged in a section that included him and the gent who owned Macy's. This clarified my thinking about publishers, their common interests and motivations."[27] Liebling himself wrote primarily for the *New Yorker*, where there was publisher Raoul Fleischmann before there was editor William Shawn.

But the persuasiveness of the generalization depends in part on what one makes of Joseph Pulitzer (1847–1911), certainly among the most inventive and spectacular figures in journalism at the turn of the century. The format and style of the two newspapers he owned, the *St. Louis Post-Dispatch* and the *New York World*, established the rules for layouts, features, and photography that still govern the modern newspaper. In the late nineteenth century, as American anti-Semitism was peaking, Pulitzer bore the handicap of being considered a Jew, without enjoying the spiritual advantages that adherents of Judaism can cultivate. His father was part-Jewish, his mother was a Catholic, he himself was at least nominally an Episcopalian, and his children were not raised as Jews. In the haunted, afflicted years of his greatest wealth and fame, Pulitzer employed a series of secretaries to read to him the news that his failing eyesight prohibited him from following. There is some grandeur in his insistence that his secretaries be capable of literate and sparkling conversation. There is nothing admirable in the advice that the young men were given not to speak to the publisher on the topic of Jews.[28]

Adolph S. Ochs (1855–1935), who bought the *New York Times* in 1896, harbored his own sensitivities on the topic of *am-echad* ("a certain people"). But his identity as a Jew was not in doubt. He married the daughter of the most innovative of nineteenth-century rabbis, Isaac Mayer Wise; and he and his descendants, the Sulzbergers, remained members of the flagship Reform synagogue, Temple Emanuel. "Religion is all that I stand for as a Jew," Ochs announced in 1925. "I know nothing else, no other definition for a Jew except religion." So constrained a classification exhibited a logic of its own. Faith was so private and minor a feature of family life that his descendants and relatives generally were informed that they were

Jewish on the eve of their departure for boarding school. Having severed the bonds of peoplehood, the Sulzberger family through its foundation gave a pittance to Jewish philanthropies: $1,800 to the United Jewish Appeal in 1973, $900 the year after the Yom Kippur War.[29]

But limiting Jewishness to religious belief did not keep the family that has owned the *Times* from realizing that others might be troubled by Jewish "clannishness" and cohesiveness, and therefore much effort was expended to limit the perception of the *Times* as a "Jewish" newspaper. If the business side preceded the expressive and editorial side, that was because it was undoubtedly a matter of *Times* policy. Under Ochs, his son-in-law Arthur Hays Sulzberger, and *his* son-in-law Orville Dryfoos, no Jew rose to the position of managing editor. That barrier was finally scaled by A. M. Rosenthal, but only after the chief foreign correspondent, Cyrus L. Sulzberger, had kept him from covering a UN conference in 1948 by announcing the following quota: "One Jew in Paris is enough." In 1952, when Daniel Schorr, then a *Times* stringer in the Low Countries, asked for a staff position, C. L. Sulzberger rebuffed him with the observation that "we have too many Jews in Europe."[30] It is commonly believed that Theodore Bernstein, the newspaper's authority on usage, the "technical genius" of the bullpen, could have risen to the post of managing editor had he been a gentile. It is also widely assumed that *Times* policy once disguised the given names of Jews, so that bylines were given to A. (for Abraham) M. Rosenthal, A. (for Abraham) H. Raskin, et al. The current editor of the editorial page, Jacob Rosenthal, forced the *Times* to break its rule against informality; the masthead lists him, rather incongruously, as Jack Rosenthal.[31]

The history of American journalism cannot exclude Jews whose interest was not in deadlines or headlines but merely in the bottom line. Terms like "brightness and novelty," or bridging the gap "between the event and the reader" make little sense in evaluating the career of Samuel I. Newhouse (1895–1979). He took charge of his first newspaper, the *Bayonne* (New Jersey) *Times*, at the age of seventeen. By the time of his death, Newhouse owned thirty-one newspapers, seven magazines, six television stations, five radio stations, twenty cable-TV stations, and even a wire service. Only two other newspaper chains were larger; none was more profitable. But profit was all that mattered to Newhouse; no publisher was less interested in the editorial policies—which varied—of the newspapers he owned. He didn't bother to read his own products, preferring to peruse the *New York*

Times instead. Newhouse's credo was simple: "Only a newspaper which is a sound business operation can be a truly free, independent editorial enterprise." His sons now direct his empire.[32]

Entrepreneurship having nothing to do with expressiveness also characterized the career of Moses Annenberg (1878–1942), the immigrant who founded Triangle Publications (the *Daily Racing Form*, the *Philadelphia Inquirer*, and the *New York Morning Telegraph*). His son Walter founded *Seventeen* as well as the magazine with the second greatest circulation in the United States, *TV Guide*, which has over 17 million readers.[33] Dorothy Schiff, the former publisher of the *New York Post*, whose grandfather was the venerable communal leader and banker Jacob Schiff, undoubtedly spoke for her peers when she confirmed an axiom that, "once you reach a certain financial level, people don't think of you as anything but very rich." Unpredictable and frivolous, she ran the *Post* from 1939 till 1976 in a style akin to the very last line in *Citizen Kane*: "I think it would be fun to run a newspaper!"[34] They belong to the history of American business, not in the *Oxford Companion to American Literature*.

Other explanations for the Jewish predilection for journalism also merit scrutiny and criticism. In *Jews and American Politics*, Stephen Isaacs argues that the intellectual and verbal resourcefulness that Jews have historically cherished is rewarded in the mass media.[35] By now Isaacs's explanation smacks of a commonplace—which does not mean that it is false, only that it is familiar. Truisms are often hard to separate from truths, and this one at least has the virtue of identifying the core of values that may be the matrix of a Jewish occupational proclivity as well as a contrast with other values stressed among gentiles. If the Jewish encounter with modern society does differ from the experience of others, the explanation may well be connected to alternative beliefs.

But Isaacs's theory is also quite restricted. Almost no publishers or network executives have been intellectuals. The celebrated journalists who grew up ignorant of the Judaic religion and its stress upon the Word would make a long list. Nor does the explanation incorporate those journalists whose success has been visual rather than verbal. The most prestigious award of the National Cartoonists Society, for example, is called the "Reuben," in honor of the first president of the society, Rube Goldberg. The most honored of political cartoonists is the *Washington Post*'s Herbert Block ("Herblock"). Al Capp (né Caplin) created the Dogpatch of *Li'l Abner*, which was syndicated in 500 newspapers and has entered the mainstream of popular culture.

Verbal resourcefulness had nothing to do with the photojournalism of Erich Salomon in Germany, Alfred Eisenstaedt in Germany and then with *Life* magazine, or Robert and Cornell Capa, Budapest-born brothers whose original name was Friedmann. Probably the most famous shot ever taken by an American photojournalist was Joe Rosenthal's depiction of the four U. S. Marines raising the flag on Iwo Jima—an icon of heroism and patriotism. And since President Reagan himself was a former sports announcer, it would be patronizing to ignore such figures as Mel Allen and Howard Cosell, or Nat Fleischer of *Ring* magazine, whose approach to subjects like the New York Yankees and Muhammad Ali has shown little trace of Talmudic learning.

Stephen Isaacs also notes the Jewish representation in a field which, "like all forms of mass education, prizes the non-ethnicity of universalism" and especially the ideal of objectivity. Those opting for journalism as a career might therefore hope to be judged by their merit, not their religious or national origin.[36]

This generalization is partially valid, for the Jews attracted to it have usually been quite assimilated and deracinated, eager or anxious to blend into civil society. One of the most brilliant editors of the *Neue Freie Presse*, Theodor Herzl, was far down that road himself; and after he had been irrevocably stung by the spectacle of anti-Semitism, he dreamed of a mass conversion of Jews at St. Stephen's Cathedral in Vienna.[37] Perhaps this is not too farfetched a context to discuss the star foreign correspondent of the *New York Daily Tribune* from 1852 till 1862, Karl Marx. His parents having converted, Marx was formally baptized as a Lutheran; and he grew up into an atheist. It is less well known that the only occupation for which he was ever paid was journalism. When Marx edited the *Rheinische Zeitung*, he depended on Jewish businessmen in Cologne for support; but his greatest success was writing for the American newspaper that Horace Greeley edited. Marx submitted 350 articles that he himself wrote, plus another dozen in collaboration with F. Engels. The *Tribune*'s managing editor, Charles A. Dana, once announced that Marx was "not only one of the most highly valued, but one of the best-paid contributors attached to the journal." The contributions ceased in 1862, however, when Greeley fired Dana, who had permitted anti-Semitic material to be published in the *Tribune*. Several articles infected with such material had been submitted by Marx.[38]

Perhaps the epitome of the "non-ethnicity of universalism" was Lippmann. In the more than ten million printed words of wisdom and counsel that he imparted in his lifetime, Jews were seldom mentioned. But he did write an analysis of anti-Semitism for the *American Hebrew* in 1922, blaming the excrescence of bigotry primarily on the vulgarity and ostentatiousness of nouveaux-riches Jews themselves. No one was more anxious to sever whatever bound him to the community of Israel. He agreed that his alma mater, Harvard College, was correct in imposing a limit on Jewish admissions. More than 15% of the student body, Lippmann suspected, would generate a *Kulturkampf*; and his own "sympathies are with the non-Jew [, whose] . . . personal manners and physical habits are, I believe, distinctly superior to the prevailing manners of the Jew."[39] From 1933, no column by the most influential pundit of his time mentioned the persecution of Jews in the Third Reich, though two columns in 1938 did suggest that the "surplus" population of Europe should be sent to Africa—the very continent which the Zionists had tumultuously rejected four decades before. During the Holocaust Lippmann wrote nothing about the camps; afterwards he wrote nothing either. Though he never converted to any version of Christianity, Lippmann's efforts to obscure his own origins reached ludicrous proportions. Ronald Steel's excellent biography records the nervousness that one friend experienced in playing Scrabble with Lippmann. She worried that the letters forming the word "Jew" might come up, perhaps upsetting the champion of disinterested reason, the Apollonian savant who wrote in 1915: "Man must be at peace with the sources of his life. If he is ashamed of them, if he is at war with them, they will haunt him forever. They will rob him of the basis of assurance, will leave him an interloper in the world."[40]

A. J. Liebling (1904–1963) constitutes a final case of how fiercely such journalists tried to bleach out their origins. A crack reporter for the *New York World* under the direction of Swope, he became the inventor of modern criticism of the press and was among the most savvy monitors of its performance. Liebling bragged that he could "write better than anyone who could write faster, and faster than anyone who could write better." Both of Lippmann's wives were gentiles; so were all three of Liebling's. Identifying with the Irish toughs among whom he was raised, attending Dartmouth when it was perhaps the most religiously restrictive of Ivy League colleges, Liebling became a *New Yorker* war correspondent who was more pained by the devastation that Nazi Germany was wreaking on France than by the Holocaust itself. His third wife commented: "Even Hitler didn't make him an intensely self-conscious Jew." Liebling once declined to attend a literary salon on Manhattan's Upper West Side because "sheenies who are meanies will be there." He was an eccentric as well as a witty and facile craftsman who suffered the strangest of deaths, because he was a gourmand who became a glutton. Devouring the forbidden foods like lobsters, clams, and oysters, Liebling simply ate himself to death.[41]

There are of course exceptions to Isaacs's generalization; a few American journalists did not propel themselves furiously from their Jewish origins for the sake of a neutral or abstract universalism. Although Mordecai Noah (1785–1851) was a "restorationist" rather than a genuine forerunner of Zionism (before the term had been coined), he was an advocate of Jewish rights as well as an adept polemical journalist who helped usher in the form of mass communications associated with the liveliness and sensationalism of the penny press.[42] Ben Hecht, for whom a boat transporting refugees illegally to Palestine was named, was certainly the most fervent Jewish nationalist to emerge from American journalism. He became a leading champion of the Irgun, and an indignant critic of the first prime minister of Israel, David Ben-Gurion. But Hecht's blazing opposition to Nazism and commitment to Jewish rights came after his newspaper career had essentially been abandoned. Swope's support of the Jewish Telegraphic Agency, his presence at the creation of the Overseas News Agency, and his fund-raising for the United Jewish Appeal also transpired after he had ceased working for the *World* or for any other newspaper. He had nothing to do with the astonishing decision of his brother, Gerard, once the president of General Electric, to bequeath the bulk of his estate (nearly $8 million) to Israel's leading engineering institute, Haifa's Technion, in 1957.[43] A younger example of comfort with Jewish identity is Martin Peretz, who edited the campus newspaper as an undergraduate at Brandeis University and in 1974 became the editor-in-chief of the *New Republic* (which Lippmann had helped to found six decades earlier). Peretz has presumably been responsible for the considerable interest that the magazine has shown in the Middle East, primarily from a Labor Zionist perspective.[44]

If the rarity of such figures tends to corroborate Isaacs' point, an even more striking phenomenon invalidates it. For if objectivity and universalism are supposed to endow the profession with so much appeal, the influx of Jews to journals of opinion and to partisan organs would not be so large. Neutrality would hardly characterize the *New Republic* from Lippmann and Walter Weyl through Gilbert Harrison to Peretz, nor the *Nation* under Victor Navasky, nor *Dissent* under Irving Howe, Lewis Coser, and Michael Walzer, nor the *Progressive* under Morris Rubin, nor *Partisan Review* under Philip Rahv and William Phillips, nor the *New York Review of Books* under Robert Silvers and Barbara Epstein, nor the *Public Interest* under Daniel Bell, Irving Kristol, and Nathan Glazer. Norman Cousins, for three decades editor-in-chief of the *Saturday Review*, played an influential role in the genesis of the nuclear test ban treaty of 1963. Cousins had already helped found SANE (Committee for a Sane Nuclear Policy) when President Kennedy asked him to organize a citizens' committee for a nuclear test ban treaty to press for senatorial ratification. Cousins contributed $400,000 of his own money in that effort, even selling the *Saturday Review* to do so—a triumph of political belief over journalistic professionalism. The Nixon administration's "enemies list," which was provided to the Senate's Watergate investigating committee in 1973, included CBS's Daniel Schorr ("a real media enemy") and Marvin Kalb; NBC's Sander Vanocur; and columnists Sydney Harris, Joseph Kraft, Max Lerner, and Frank Mankiewicz.[45] The underground press that surfaced in the 1960s also made no pretense of reaching for the asymptote of objectivity. A short list of its luminaries would include Paul Krassner (the *Realist*), Marvin Garson (the *Berkeley Barb*), Jeff Shero (*Rat*), Allan Katzman (the *East Village Other*), and Jesse Kornbluth and Marshall Bloom of the Liberation News Service. Like other radical journalists beginning at the dawn of the twentieth century, their writing was a direct extension of their politics and was indistinguishable from it—and indeed was often a substitute for political action.

Even the slightest nod in the direction of comparative history would sabotage Isaacs's stress on the attractiveness of objectivity. American newspapers have generally developed in the direction of defining themselves in terms of the gathering and dissemination of information, as quickly as possible, under the aegis of impartiality. But European newspapers, say, from the Congress of Vienna until the rise of Nazism, operated according to other principles—pronouncing (and therefore forming) opinions, promoting a set of political and cultural attitudes. Such journalism was a forum for the *Weltanschauungen* of publishers, editors, and writers. And yet Jews flourished as fully in that environment as have journalists of Jewish birth in the United States. It was not because of the allure of objectivity that Herzl won success as a *feuilletoniste* for the *Neue Freie Presse*, nor Léon Blum as a critic in the French socialist press, nor Arthur Koestler as a correspondent for the Ullstein house in Berlin.

Even within the context of American media, objectivity is not universally prized, quite apart from the growing suspicion that it may be impossible to attain. Lippmann and David Lawrence largely invented the syndicated column of opinion and interpretation.[46] Its eminent practitioners in recent years have included David Broder, Anthony Lewis, and the late Joseph Kraft. Moreover the career of William Safire suggests how misleading it would be to remove the study of journalism from cognate fields. Safire began as a public relations counselor (once called "press agent"), became a speechwriter for Richard Nixon in particular, then a lexicographer, a novelist, and primarily a columnist—honored with a Pulitzer Prize—for the *New York Times*, all without breaking stride. Swope saw no conflict between his role as an editor and his services as a publicity flack for Bernard Baruch.[47]

There is another possible explanation for the disproportionate impact that Jews have exerted in the American media. It is advanced tentatively, because it is at best only partly satisfactory; it cannot cover all the cases or withstand all objections. No theory on this subject can. But it enjoys the advantage of taking into account the experience of other countries in the Diaspora, and applies especially well to the particularities of the American framework. The speculation allows one to acknowledge the historical singularity of the Jewish people without requiring for its theoretical validity the journalists' knowledge of or fidelity to Judaic tradition and values.

This thesis holds that the press has been a key instrument in the recognition that we inhabit one world—not one village or valley or province or nation. Journalism is not only a bridge between reader and event, as the *Encyclopedia Judaica* avers, but between people and people. And a certain dispersed and vulnerable minority might be especially sensitive to the recalcitrant problems that human diversity and plurality can pose. Exile made the Jews aware that the world is larger than parochial and even national boundaries, and some Jews became hopeful that those borders might be transcended. Positioned as outsiders, they were vouchsafed the knowledge of relatives and other co-religionists abroad, were given at least a glimmering sense that there *was* an abroad, a life elsewhere. Jews were therefore responsive to cosmopolitanism, or trans-nationalism; they tended to want to see the world as one.

Such a marginal situation and such an international spirit have commonly been appreciated by scholars explaining the Jewish penchant for trade, even though the Biblical Hebrews were not famous for their business acumen. In describing the comparatively large number of Jews working for American newspapers prior to the Civil War, Professor Sarna has observed that "journalism . . . permitted the kind of independence and mobility that Jews have often looked for in their occupations. . . . Commerce on a large or small scale," he added, "depends on information. Jewish merchants, travellers, peddlers and, of course, relatives served as 'reporters' long before the public press had any interest in printing the news." But other scholars have not extended or tested Sarna's claim that "Jews had the kind of cosmopolitan outlook which journalism demands."[48] Too little curiosity has been piqued by this explanation for the Jewish attraction to journalism.

The cosmopolitan character of mass communications can be verified biographically. The effort to reduce the gaps of time and distance was especially pronounced in the career of Israel Ben Josephat (1816–1899), a rabbi's son who was baptized in Berlin in 1844 and moved to London in 1851. He became best known for founding the news agency Reuters, for he eventually became Baron Paul Julius von Reuter. He began with pigeons, then cable, and then telegraph—just as he followed political reports with commercial news and then general news. Reuters thus became perhaps the leading international news agency.[49] The inventor of the press interview, the prime "pseudo-event," was Henri Blowitz-Opper (1825–1903). He was born in Bohemia, wrote for Parisian newspapers, and became a French citizen, but achieved widest recognition as a correspondent for the *Times* of London.[50]

It was not necessary, however, to be an immigrant to seize the possibilities of communicating to newly literate, increasingly enfranchised and empowered masses. Joseph Moses Levy (1812–1888) owned and edited the *Sunday Times* for a year; but he is more important for having published, beginning in 1855, London's first penny morning newspaper, the *Daily Telegraph*. Levy simply cut the previous price in half. The *Daily Telegraph* was Liberal until 1879, after which it switched to the Conservatives. Levy's eldest son, Edward Levy-Lawson, succeeded him, making the paper livelier in its presentation of news and famous for its crusades.[51] Thus, father and son played roughly the same roles in British journalism that were performed by two quite different figures in the United States. The most important American innovator of the penny press was not a Jew, but he was an immigrant: James Gordon Bennett, a Scotsman. An even more pivotal practitioner of mass journalism was Pulitzer, the immigrant from Hungary. The tableau of his final years—with teams of secretaries reading to Pulitzer his favorite German and French literary works in their original languages—is a sign of how cosmopolitan a figure he cut in American journalism.

Of course the case is complicated by the obvious fact that the United States has been a nation of immigrants; and a thesis that is scientifically elegant would have to demonstrate that immigrant Jews, or immigrants generally, were represented in journalism more fully than in the American populace. Such validation is probably impossible, and impressionistic evidence will have to be substituted.

It is striking that Adolph Ochs of the *Times* and William Paley of CBS were the sons of immigrants; David Sarnoff of RCA/NBC was born in Russia. Lippmann had made many trips to Europe as a child and was attuned to advanced European thinkers like Bergson, Wallas, and Freud. Swope, Hecht, and Liebling were also the sons of immigrants; and Liebling's dying words could not be understood because they were uttered in French.[52] The closest American equivalent of the *feuilleton* was undoubtedly "Topics of the Times," whose anonymous but much-admired author was Simeon Strunsky, born in Russia. Even today, long after the era of mass migration of Jews is over, the executive editor of the *Times* is Max Frankel, born in Germany. His predecessor, Abe Rosenthal, was born in Canada to immigrants from Russia. Henry Anatole Grunwald, who became the chief of all Time, Inc. editorial enterprises, was born in Vienna. It might be added that Luce himself, the co-inventor of the news magazine, was born in China to Presbyterian missionary parents (who could hardly have been thrilled when he briefly worked as a legman for the bawdy Ben Hecht); and the Calvinist sobriety and rectitude of the *Times*'s James Reston may well have stemmed from his Scottish birthplace. Such biographical data do not snap the case shut, but they are suggestive.[53]

There is, however, no philosopher's stone that can transmute the unstable mixture of competing theories into the purity of a single explanation. Even though monocausality lacks credence, a stress upon the cosmopolitan sympathies of Jews would rectify scholarly neglect.

Complications will continue to bedevil the study of Jews in American journalism. Even though the subject cannot be studied in isolation, confined to the twelve-mile limit of the shores of the United States, it must also be fixed within the compass of a society in which an independent press has flourished and in which the talented, the ambitious, and the lucky could often be handsomely rewarded. Freedom of the press has occupied a central place in the democratic

design; and even wayward pressmen could point out that their occupation is one of the few businesses (along with religion, firearms, and
liquor) that is granted Constitutional protection. Jefferson idealized
liberty of the press so fervently that he once committed the logical
flaw of the excluded middle term when he expressed a preference
for "newspapers without a government" over "a government without
newspapers."[54] But his extravagant tribute to journalism was to echo
for nearly two centuries of the Republic, even though individual
journalists have been hated and vilified (some by Jefferson himself),
lost duels, been beaten up, and tarred and feathered and murdered.
Their power has been respected even when it has not always been
exalted. It failed to strike Americans as odd that one of the legendary
lawmen of the Old West, "Bat" Masterson (1853–1921), ended up as
an editor of the *New York Morning Telegraph*.[55] It was also natural for
the comic-book creators of Superman, Joe Shuster and Jerome Siegel,
to provide the man of steel and righteousness with the earth-bound
identity of a newspaper reporter, Clark Kent of the *Daily Planet*.
Among the most beloved of recent presidents, John F. Kennedy was
first employed as a journalist (the only time he was off the public
payroll). Had he lived long enough to retire from the White House,
Kennedy had contemplated becoming a publisher. Like Citizen Kane,
he too thought that it would be fun to run a newspaper. (The Orson
Welles film had as its working title *American*.)[56] Jews could succeed as
journalists in part because journalists could succeed in America.

Finally, what will continue to render this topic enigmatic is the
larger question of Jewish identity in modern times. This book is not
the place to explore the definition of who a Jew is; I have enough
problems. But it is certainly fair to assert that *at most* only a segment
of ethnic identity or religious heritage has ever been implicated in
what journalists have done, and therefore the task of determining a
distinctive Jewish contribution is complicated when so many Jews have
blended so successfully into the structure of social organization. What
they have achieved as individual journalists betrays only the most
tenuous link to their sensibility as Jews, but that is why any study of
their influence and motivations promises to shed further light on the
elusive meaning of Jewish modernity in mass society. During a historical period when it is hardly a disability, and indeed something of an
asset, to be a Jew in America, journalism is among the indices of full
participation in the host society. The press badge is a certificate of
"making it." Far from signifying a cabal or a conspiracy, dispropor-

tionate representation in the mass media demonstrates the hospitality of the American environment, the congruence of American values— and the benign challenge that is thereby posed to Jewish singularity and survival.

8

MOVIES

In the 1950s a Hollywood producer named Ross Hunter used to make Westerns not on location but in the back lots, until his studio complained that all of his Indians, whom he recruited in Los Angeles, looked Jewish. (Among them was Jeff Chandler, né Ira Grossel, who was most famous for his impersonation of the Apache warrior Cochise.) So the compliant Hunter next went on location to Moab, Utah, hiring Ute Indians direct from the reservation for the filming of *Son of Cochise*. He recalled: "A few days after we sent the first rushes back to the studio, I got a wire saying, 'These Indians look even *more* Jewish than the ones in Hollywood.' After that I stayed home."[1] The point of that incident can be interpreted as follows. From its origins Hollywood has been stamped with a Jewish identity, but nobody else was supposed to know about it. But somehow, no matter how thorough the attempt to suppress or disguise it, Jewishness is going to bob to the surface anyway.

But that is only the beginning of an analytical enterprise that attempts to fathom American films as a form of Jewish creativity and self-expression. A casting director at Columbia Pictures named Max Arnow could christen an aspiring actor from Cleveland named Martin Fuss so that he would henceforth be known as Ross Hunter.[2] But neither could be without ambivalence in their effort to fancy themselves merely Americans and nothing else. The self-images of such

Jews were therefore bound to be more complicated than even the attitudes of gentiles toward Jews. Even in their struggle to conceal their ethnic origins, they could not help looking at their American reality (including Indians) differently. What the critic Robert Warshow ascribed to American Jewish fiction is applicable here. "The literary treatment of American Jewish life has always suffered from the psychological commitments of Jewish writers," he wrote in 1946. "Their motives are almost never pure: they must dignify the Jews, or plead for them, or take revenge upon them, and the picture they create is correspondingly distorted by romanticism or sentimentality or vulgarity."[3] The celluloid image of the Jew can therefore be understood as an index of how, in the twentieth century, some very influential Jews have handled these "psychological commitments." Hollywood may constitute the most formidable case of how American Jewish identity has been expressed and forged, because it is virtually impossible to disentangle how the movies have mirrored some version of reality from how they have revised that reality. Hollywood's Jews were instrumental in creating and contributing to the twentieth century's most impressive circulation, through technical means, of the vestiges of the primitive myths and the ancient symbols of our species. That is also why this particular subject—this strikingly modern mythopoesis—is so important.

Yet until recently, surprisingly little has been written on the subject of this chapter, which is how the depiction of Jews in American movies can be connected to the shifting status of Jews in the United States. My orientation is one that a couple of generations of filmmakers would have been eager to evade or ignore—and that is their own Jewish roots, a distinctive origin which was bound to affect how their brethren were presented and represented at twenty-four frames per second. No religious or communal organization ever elected these filmmakers as its spokesmen, or had the means in a relatively open and fluid society of holding them accountable; and most of the dominant figures in Hollywood would have been exceptionally uncomfortable in assuming the burden of helping to transform and articulate Jewish identity in America. That has nevertheless been among their roles, as they worked to form the mass culture from which their fellow Jews—among others—took their cues.

To be sure there has never exactly been silence on the subject of the Jewish role in Hollywood. In their major survey of American Jewish life in 1936, the editors of *Fortune* recognized "the great power of the movies in the influencing of modern society and the great influence of Jews in the movies." Nor was that role minimized in the frenzied imagination of the enemies of the Jews. In the 1930s the preposterous leader of the fascistic Silver Shirts, William Dudley Pelley, based part of his demagoguery upon his experience as a screenwriter in iniquitous Hollywood, where Jews served as "Oriental custodians of adolescent entertainment. . . . I've seen too many gentile maidens ravished and been unable to do anything about it. They have a concupiscent slogan in screendom: 'Don't hire until you see the whites of their thighs!' I know all about Jews." Colonel Lindbergh also warned that the Jews' "greatest danger to this country" included their large ownership and influence in movies.[4]

Yet it took nearly half a century for scholarly books to emerge that seriously explore how Jews have actually been depicted in American movies. Careful readers of Lester D. Friedman's *Hollywood's Image of the Jew* (1982) and Patricia Erens's *The Jew in American Cinema* (1985) will immediately realize how indebted I am to these two volumes in the observations that follow. If nothing else, Friedman and Erens have saved other scholars the trouble of viewing hundreds of films otherwise consigned to oblivion, since they lack what Vladimir Nabokov once called "the tender point of genius, the asparagus tip of art."[5] But anyone wishing to learn—or to contemplate—how Jewish characters and characteristics have been screened will find these two historical surveys, whatever their particular limitations, indispensable.

With regard to generalizations, advisory warnings must always be posted. The ambivalences and equivocations, the evasions and delusions, the defensiveness and tentativeness with which the filmmakers have projected their fellow Jews onto the screen have assumed distinctive patterns. But it is safe to generalize that, in the formation of an American Jewish screen memory, three phases can be traced.

The first pattern consisted of the ghetto films that characterized the silent era. Such works tended to be comedies, many of which lampooned the reputation clinging to Jews for their mercantile cleverness, for their adeptness in cutting corners as well as cloth. Such movies were also noteworthy for their theme of Jewish adjustment to the New World, as ancient rivalries, fears, and hatreds seemed to dissipate in the benign cauldron that Israel Zangwill called "the melting pot." The proof of such accommodation and acceptance was intermarriage.[6] This social phenomenon was the nexus for the most influential novel of the twentieth century, Joyce's *Ulysses*. But at the actual historical moment of Bloomsday, intermarriage occurred with almost freakish rarity. Before the Great War, a Jew in New York was statistically only slightly more likely to marry a gentile than a Negro would walk to the altar with a Caucasian.[7] But Hollywood has never been famous for its fidelity to historical truth. With drumbeat insistence it defined intermarriage as an ideal that should be encouraged, as the strongest possible evidence for the compatibility of Jewish birth and American citizenship. Intermarriage meant that the burden of an Old World past had been successfully jettisoned, that the immigrants and their descendants could no longer be confined to the dreary shadows of the *Judengasse*. Instead, they were entitled to reject the parochialism and marginality of the past and seize all the splendor and open promise of America itself.

The famous series that depicted the Cohens and the Kellys, as well as more forgettable films like *Clancy's Kosher Wedding* and *Private Izzy Murphy*, epitomized such dreams of assimilation. Although social reality was quite different, the Irish represented the ethnic group at whom the Jewish hunger for acceptance was most often directed. Several factors made the Irish suitable: they had spoken English from the beginning, derived prestige from having landed here ahead of virtually all the other immigrants in the nineteenth century, lived in cities, and as Catholics were still expected to appreciate what it meant to be outsiders. Also available was a show business tradition of the stage Irishman to provide ready-to-wear stereotypes. Hence the popularity of such films—especially when emblazoned with title cards such as the one for *Frisco Sally Levy* (1927): "The sun cannot shine in Ireland when it's raining in Jerusalem."[8]

The culmination of this first phase was *The Jazz Singer* (also 1927), which the author of the short story and play on which it was based, Samson Raphaelson, intended as a riposte to the more frivolous treatments of Jewish family life like *Abie's Irish Rose*. Like all such transitions of which historians are so fond, *The Jazz Singer* should also be considered the last important silent work (apart from Chaplin's), as well as the first "sound" film. Warner Brothers had not intended it to be a "talkie," for Al Jolson was simply supposed to croon into the newfangled Vitaphone sound-on-disc system; and apart from a few lines of dialogue that the ebullient Jolson speaks ("You ain't heard nothin' yet"), the bulk of *The Jazz Singer* transpires in complete silence.[9]

It is also the last within the category of ghetto films in its attempt to capture, however superficially, the restless energy and irrepressible talent that the boundaries of the immigrant neighborhoods could no longer contain. Shot partially on location around Hester Street, the film traces through one entertainer's career the parabola of a once-despised people toward fame and fortune and glory. For the audiences attending *The Jazz Singer*, Warner Brothers thoughtfully provided a program that included a glossary of Yiddish terms, such as *shickse*, a lexicon entry which *The Jazz Singer* probably introduced into the American cinema. But by then the concept was already familiar: she was the visible, romantic reward for "making it," the proof that all the barriers had been scaled. For that is certainly what the blonde character named Mary Dale means to Jack Robin (Al Jolson), who asserts with all the ferocious innocence of a star-spangled, newly-minted American that "tradition is all right but this is another day." Equally relevant is the observation of the protagonist's mother, who watches him perform before an enthusiastic audience in the Winter Garden that could scarcely have fathomed Jack Robin's cantorial and liturgical origins as Jakie Rabinowitz. Sara realizes that a birthright has been forsaken: "He's not my son any longer—he belongs to the whole world now."[10]

That should be regarded as an exit line for the sort of Jew whom Hollywood once depicted. For beginning early in the 1930s, the Jew who was shown on the screen belonged so much to the world that he no longer belonged to his own people, or finally to himself. At the very moment in Western history when an entire minority people was being designated for destruction, was being singled out as a fantastically powerful incarnation of evil, Jews were disappearing from the screen, their vulnerability unnoticed, their victimization unrecognized, their pain and grief unassuaged. In the service of the belief that the mounting anti-Semitism in America and abroad could be diminished were Jews to become less conspicuous, the endearing comic immigrants depicted in the silent era were replaced by crypto-Jews, or by "non-Jewish Jews," or by Jews who thought of themselves only as Americans, or by no Jews at all. Jolson himself, who died in 1950, never again assumed the role of a Jewish screen character. This phase, the Hollywood version of the Marrano, lasted until at least the end of the 1950s.

Such self-effacement is of course even more paradoxical because this era marked the perihelion of the studio system, whose brilliance was due almost entirely to Jewish personalities.[12] The entrepreneurial and artistic environment that the moguls created was—off the screen—heavily immigrant and second-generation. To do justice to these coarse, boorish, barely educated—but incredibly shrewd and audacious—characters has posed a challenge to novelists like F. Scott

Fitzgerald and Aldous Huxley and Norman Mailer; and sometimes these tycoons were given less than their due. The producer David O. Selznick preserved in his files a magazine clipping, in which *Time* alluded to "the crafty and extraordinary methods of one-time fur-peddlers, garment dealers and second-hand jewelers . . . Jews . . . who padded their payroll with relatives, settled their biggest deals over all-night poker games and . . . discussed the motion picture business in comic strip dialects."[13] When one of them once tried to admonish John Barrymore, the actor sniffed: "Put that finger down. I remember when it had a thimble on it."[14] Some, like Harry Cohn, were so crude and obscene that they would have brought a blush to the cheek of the Wife of Bath. Others, like the independent producer Sam Goldwyn, went regularly to the Metropolitan Opera and preferred to be around intellectuals rather than actors. Yet Goldwyn's motto was: "A producer shouldn't get ulcers; he should give them."[15] In general they were so vigorous and so tough in the pursuit of their objectives that Ronald Reagan later assured voters that he could stand up to the Soviets because, as head of the Screen Actors Guild, he had stood up to the moguls (though the studios caved in quickly at the onset of the HUAC investigations after the Second World War).

Their survival skills were often impressive; and some of their careers virtually spanned the history of Hollywood itself. Paramount's Adolph Zukor had been around so long, it was remarked during his one hundredth birthday party, that some of his friends had already been portrayed on the screen by Charlton Heston. Zukor's parents had intended him for the rabbinate, a destiny that a brother who remained in Hungary fulfilled instead. The moguls generally minimized or abandoned formal religious observance, and a pagan ethic of hedonism prevailed when they transplanted themselves to the West Coast. But they were instrumental in inventing a world that, off the set, was tinctured by their own ethnic background.[16] Louis B. Mayer placed so many of his relatives on the payroll that the initials of M-G-M were said to stand for "Mayer's *ganze mishpoche*." In the studio's commissary, both chicken soup and matzoh ball soup were served; and when one starlet ate matzoh balls for the first time, she inquired: "What do they do with the rest of the matzoh?"[17]

But this was also the era in which that atmosphere was not to be publicized or considered worthy of reflection. Two classic social scientific studies of Hollywood as a community do not even mention the Jewish character of the movie industry, though both authors—Leo Rosten and Hortense Powdermaker—were Jews. Rosten's book bends over backwards by noting how many figures in Hollywood, like Darryl F. Zanuck and Cecil B. DeMille, "are erroneously believed by many to be of the same faith as the mother of Christ";[18] Powdermaker's *Hollywood: The Dream Factory* (1950) is not even *that* oblique in omitting any mention of descendants of the mother of Christ in the film business. This was also the era of Sammy Glick, the slimy, cunning protagonist of *What Makes Sammy Run?* The narrator of Budd Schulberg's 1941 novel is a rabbi's son, an ex-newspaper columnist who urges Glick to assist an idealistic screenwriter, citing among other reasons "the need of Jews to help each other in self-defense." The response Glick gives is brutal: "What the hell did the Jews ever do for me?—except maybe get my head cracked open for me when I was a kid." As Glick seems to recall the harshness of the Lower East Side slum from which he had so furiously propelled himself, this coarse and ambitious egocentric mutters the word "Jews" with acrid hate.[19] Some of the moguls themselves felt very little need for Jews to help each other. It was in this second phase that Harry Cohn, the president and chief of production of Columbia Pictures, barked that the only Jewish actors who would play in his movies would play Indians, while Goldwyn commented that it wouldn't "work" on the screen if a Jewish actor portrayed a Jewish character.[20]

That meant that 1930s audiences often got their idea of what a Jew looked like from seeing George Arliss, but the consequences went well beyond casting. The Disraeli that Arliss played (twice) was a prime minister stripped of pride in his Jewish ancestry, a Disraeli who does not invoke the glories of Jewish history. When Arliss played Nathan Rothschild in *The House of Rothschild* (1934), he is shown forbidding his daughter (played by Loretta Young) to marry a gentile (played by Robert Young). The reason for the prohibition seems to be personal quirkiness rather than a compelling sense of peoplehood; and though the Rothschild family is shown battling for Jewish rights, again the motive appears to be personal honor rather than principles like *ahavath yisroel* (love of the Jewish people).[21]

The moguls' anxieties meant that, in *The Life of Emile Zola*, which won the Oscar for best picture of 1937, the novelist's valorous defense of Captain Dreyfus does not confront anti-Semitism. In depicting the most dramatic episode in Zola's life, this cinematic biography does not explain why Dreyfus might have been picked out as a scapegoat. The word "Jew" is never even heard in the film, though he is manifestly framed for that reason when the camera scans the general staff list.[22] Other examples could be multiplied. In *Confessions of a Nazi Spy*

(1939), a Warner Brothers exposé of German espionage activity in the United States, Jews are never mentioned by name; nor are Jewish characters represented on the screen. When Jewish characters could not be entirely avoided, as in Elmer Rice's adaptation of his own play, *Counsellor-at-Law* (1933), the role of the *arriviste* attorney, George Simon, was given to John Barrymore. Usually Jewish characters vanished from the screen even in minor roles. Thus, in the remakes of George S. Kaufman's *The Butter and Egg Man*, a Lehman becomes a Morgan and in a later version an Allen. In the Ben Hecht-Charles MacArthur play, *The Front Page*, the governor's assistant is named Irving Pincus; the remake, *His Girl Friday* (1940), calls him Joe Pettibone. In the Clifford Odets play, *Golden Boy*, the fight promoter is named Roxie Gottlieb; in the 1939 film, he is known as Roxie Lewis. Irwin Shaw's drama, *The Gentle People*, includes a Jewish tailor named Goodman; the movie version is confined to gentile people, when *Out of the Fog* (1941) converts him into an Irish tailor named Goodwin.[23] Charles Dickens describes Fagin as a Jew three hundred times in *Oliver Twist*; in David Lean's British film version (1948), Fagin (Alec Guinness) has a large beaked nose but is not described as a Jew at all, which did not prevent the New York Board of Rabbis from trying to keep the film out of the United States.[24] The point that Jewish distinctiveness was supposed to be bleached out need not be infinitely extended.

Of course, when the studio system was predominant, name changes for actors and actresses were de rigueur; and it is easy to forget that this process of homogenization was hardly restricted to Jews. After all, the quintessential American shooting star, John Wayne, came into the world as Marion Morrison. Or take Richard Wright's novel, *Native Son* (1940), which Hollywood nearly did. The almost unbearably intense subject of Wright's novel is the systematic racism that would provoke a ghetto black to kill a young white woman in her sleep. The sensation that *Native Son* created led one production company to write the author, mentioning plans for the working script. But when Wright read the proposed changes, he laughed until the tears became uncontrollable; the Harold Hecht Company wanted to make the character of Bigger Thomas into a white man.[25] Granted, the stars had their names altered long before Hollywood hunkered down in the 1930s and 1940s. Granted, the silent era had also ingeniously excised Jewish names (as when Theodosia Goodman, the daughter of a Cincinnati tailor, became a vamp named Theda Bara—an anagram for "Arab death"). But there was a special animus to the insurance policy that rendered Jews as inconspicuous as possible. This was the case even when actors and actresses were not involved. The producer Sam Spiegel was asked—for screen credit purposes—to split his surname to form a new identity, S. P. Eagle. The satisfaction of that request did not stop a subsequent Hollywood employer from suggesting further fission to disguise the producer's past: E. A. Gull.[26]

The evasions became so extreme that during the Second World War, when the scenarist Ben Hecht tried to drum up support for the Irgun in Palestine, David O. Selznick refused to sign a sponsoring telegram because the producer considered himself an American, not a Jew. The course of American history has subsequently confirmed how false this dichotomy is, since the doctrine of pluralism has been invoked and extended in ever-increasing ways. But in 1942 the status of the Jew was far less secure, and Hecht decided to clarify it. He challenged the maker of *Gone With the Wind* by offering to phone three of his gentile friends, to be named by Selznick himself, to ask whether they thought of the producer as an American or as a Jew. When all three picked the latter category, Selznick's name went on the telegram.[27]

But the anxieties and fears ran so deep that they affected the response, after the war and the Holocaust, that Hollywood gave to the problem of anti-Semitism. The studios' stabs at social conscience resulted in *Crossfire* and *Gentleman's Agreement* (both 1947). It was apt of the *Nation*'s film critic, James Agee, to complain how calculated the bravado of RKO and Twentieth Century-Fox actually was; but after the evasions of nearly two previous decades, the reminder that "movies about anti-Semitism aren't so desperately chancy" was a little churlish.[28] Fearing that a forthright assault on prejudice would backfire, the American Jewish Committee attempted in vain to stop the production of both films.[29]

The producer, the director, and the scriptwriter of *Crossfire* were all gentiles, although the final decision to make it must be credited to Dore Schary, the lone studio chief whose Jewish commitments could be deemed unambiguously affirmative. (He later served as national chairman of the Anti-Defamation League.) In following the spoor of a vicious bigot (played by Robert Ryan) who murders a decorated war hero named Joseph Samuels (Sam Levene), the film shows a villain so pathologically aberrant that viewers could scarcely have been expected to make any inductive generalizations about the phenomenon. Anti-Semitism is nevertheless condemned as undemocratic and un-American by the police detective; Robert Young calls it "always insane, always senseless."[30] *Crossfire* is not about Jews, which would have made it something of an anomaly in this second phase in the history of an ethnic image. It is instead about the antipathy toward Jews.

That also happens to be the theme of *Gentleman's Agreement*, which earned for Twentieth Century-Fox an Academy Award for best picture of 1947. One Jew, Laura Z. Hobson, wrote the novel; and another, Moss Hart, adapted it for the screen. But it was personally supervised by Zanuck, the only gentile to head production of a major studio; coincidentally he had earlier supervised the production of *The Jazz Singer*. Another gentile, Elia Kazan, won an Oscar for directing *Gentleman's Agreement*. Though its theme is supremely pertinent to the Jewish condition, its central character is not a Jew but a gentile pretending to be one (thus constituting a "switcheroo" on the screen Jews pretending to be gentiles, a Marrano in reverse). A "Jewish" movie whose pivotal figure is a pseudo-Jew therefore makes *Gentleman's Agreement* emblematic of the second phase, and worthy of a close look.

Hobson herself was the daughter of Michael Zametkin, the first editor of the *Jewish Daily Forward* (and later colleague of Abraham Cahan), and of Adella Kean Zametkin, a columnist for another Yiddish newspaper, the *Day*. Hobson herself became a staffer with *Time* magazine, later an unsuccessful screenwriter, and was enraged by the anti-Semitism that she discerned in Lindbergh's 1941 radio warning against Jewish influence. But her broadside, "Choice—for Gentiles," was never published. Then an item in *Time* reported that the Honorable John Rankin (D-Miss.) had called the gossip columnist Walter Winchell a "little kike" on the floor of Congress, without provoking a protest from any of his colleagues. That spurred Hobson to find the literary harpoon with which to strike at American anti-Semitism. The novel that she published in 1947 made no defense for Jewish particularity, nor did it attempt to legitimate a preference for religious continuity and *ahavath yisroel*. Indeed her autobiography has stressed her own inability to read the writings of her parents, whose agnosticism she shared. *Laura Z* revealed no interest in Judaic religion or values even as it chronicled her relationships with gentile men. In underscoring the arbitrariness of Jewish identity, in minimizing cultural and historical differences, Hobson's 1947 best-seller resembled Jean-Paul Sartre's *Réflexions sur la Question Juive*, published a year earlier. Both works can be compared to another assault on bigotry from a similar perspective: *Focus* (1945). Arthur Miller's only novel describes the major social consequences that follow when a shortsighted gentile wears eyeglasses that cause others to take him for a Jew.[31] These works, which appeared in the immediate aftermath of the greatest crime ever inflicted upon the Jews, shared not only a revulsion against the irrationality of prejudice, but also an unwillingness to consider the affirmative values that had kept the Jewish people so intact.

For those interested not only in how Jewish rights can be defended but also in how Jewish identity might be cultivated and strengthened, *Gentleman's Agreement* is not very helpful. At the beginning of the film, Philip Green (Gregory Peck) explains to his son at the breakfast table that Jews are as good or as bad as everyone else, that religion alone distinguishes Jews from Catholics and Protestants; they simply go to a different church, which is called a temple or synagogue. But that would make Jewish survival dependent upon a shatter-proof faith, and indeed the journalist's explanation for Jewish distinctiveness is sabotaged later in the movie (as in the novel), when the eminent physicist, Professor Lieberman (Sam Jaffe), announces: "I have no religion, so I am not Jewish by religion. I am a scientist, so I must rely on science which tells me I am not Jewish by race, since there's no such thing as a Jewish type. . . . I remain a Jew because the world makes it an advantage not to be one. So, for many of us, it becomes a matter of pride to call ourselves Jews."[32] *Gentleman's Agreement* offers no rationale for remaining Jewish because of the demands of faith, or because of reverence for a special heritage, or because of an imperishable sentiment of peoplehood. The film validates only a point of honor that operates so long as Jews are despised. Such orneriness might have made sense in terms of Philip Green's journalistic gambit, for a series entitled "I Was Jewish for Eight Weeks"; but so thin a rationale could hardly be expected to sustain a supposedly eternal people.

And even that rationale would disappear, in the post-World War II era, with the weakening of anti-Semitism, a decline to which films like *Gentleman's Agreement* and *Crossfire* may well have contributed. Indeed, when Moss Hart met a stagehand who claimed that the "wonderful moral" of *Gentleman's Agreement* had made his own association with it so enjoyable, the scenarist asked the stagehand how he interpreted the moral of the film. Hart was told: "Henceforth I'm always going to be good to Jewish people because you can never tell when they will turn out to be gentiles." A year after the Hobson novel and the Zanuck film appeared, the Supreme Court intervened in the real estate business by holding that the judicial enforcement of restrictive covenants (or "gentleman's agreements") violated the equal protection clause of the Fourteenth Amendment.[33] Other post-war symbols of tolerance could be cited, for just as a Jew could become Miss America (Bess Myerson, 1945), a black could become a major league baseball player (Jackie Robinson, 1947). Under Harry Truman the prestige of the federal government began to be committed more directly than ever against racial and religious discrimination. The Anti-Defamation League observed in 1949 that state fair practices acts had begun to reduce bigotry in the fields of employment, housing, and education; and it noted that less anti-Semitism had scarred the 1948 political campaigns than in 1940 and 1944. "The comparative absence of anti-Semitic activity" was attributed to "economic prosperity" and to the absence of "national and international problems which are sharply and deeply dividing Americans."[34]

The universalist ethos that captivated Hollywood resulted in a series of films through the 1950s devoid of the specificity of *Yiddishkeit*, as the distinctions between the children and grandchildren of the Eastern European immigrants and the rest of the populace seemed to dissolve. Removed from the particularity and immediacy of any specific social context, the Jew seemed a brother from another planet. In fairness to Hollywood, it must be conceded that, by the 1950s, its images were not spinning entirely out of orbit. Americans themselves were tending toward greater homogenization, seeking in many ways to model themselves after white Anglo-Saxon Protestants; and Jews too were becoming suburbanites. That, at any rate, is how they are depicted in the 1953 remake of *The Jazz Singer*; and their ascent into upper bourgeois comfort is traced in *Marjorie Morningstar* (1958). The Jolson of the ghetto film had become a gentile actor in the remake, Danny Thomas, just as a gentile named Natalie Wood was expected to give the definitive impersonation of the emerging American Jewish princess in the latter movie. The star of *Marjorie Morningstar* revealed her aptitude for the role in denying a newspaper report that she and her husband had their own "His" and "Hers" swimming pools: "We have one pool, just like everybody else."[35] With unparalleled well-being and comfort came more widespread social acceptance for minorities like Jews, and Hollywood films necessarily reflected a corresponding smugness and satisfaction.

By the 1960s, however, some Jews began to calculate the price of assimilation. In and out of Hollywood, some began to realize that the Jewish legacy was perhaps worth nurturing, if the alternative was the blurring of the differences between Jews and their neighbors, if the social contract contained a clause anticipating the end of a distinctive Jewish people. The renegotiation of the bargain can be demonstrated in what amounts to a third phase in the cinematic self-images of Jews. Often provisional in its affirmations, this cycle has not yet run its course, making conclusions treacherous. But the divergences from the two previous patterns were sometimes emphatic. Convenience dictates the inauguration of the third era in 1960, the year a Catholic was first elected to the presidency, the year that Israeli operatives landed in Argentina and brought Adolf Eichmann to Jerusalem, the year Elie Wiesel's memoir of Auschwitz, *Night*, was published in an English translation. It was also the year that Otto Preminger released *Exodus*. Based on the Leon Uris novel that was among the biggest best-sellers since *Gone With the Wind*, the film epitomizes the ethnic resurgence that has permeated films about Jews in the past three decades or so.

Like the 1927 version of *The Jazz Singer*, like *Gentleman's Agreement* two decades later, *Exodus* had its genesis not only in some independent social reality but in the formulaic cocoon of mass entertainment itself. Just as Samson Raphaelson got the idea for his short story, "Day of Atonement," from watching Jolson's kinetic vaudeville performance at Champaign, Illinois, just as Laura Z. Hobson worked on her fictional indictment of anti-Semitism while writing for movie sales, Uris knew that he had the blessing of Hollywood before he wrote his book. M-G-M had commissioned a novel about the birth of the Third Jewish Commonwealth because it expected that a best-seller would lengthen the lines at the box office, because Dore Schary (who had made *Crossfire* for RKO) figured that a facile adaptation could be made of such a novel. Of course that is not how Flaubert and Turgenev went about writing their masterpieces, nor did George Eliot need movie rights to inspire her to write fiction. But that is the way some novels get written in America; and by raising the specter of Arab boycotts of M-G-M theatres, Preminger bought up the film rights to Uris's 1958 blockbuster for a trifling $75,000.[36] He then compounded the *chutzpah* by hiring an ex-convict, Dalton Trumbo, to write the script under his own name. One of the gentiles included in the Hollywood 10 that had defied the House Committee on Un-American Activities, Trumbo jibed while working on the scenario that he had begun to "converse exclusively with shrugs, questions when statements are called for, and quaint Middle-European jokes."[37]

Despite his efforts, the novel itself may be better known than the screen adaptation, which is rather uncommon. The movie version is nevertheless important to the evolution of Hollywood's impression of the Jew, for *Exodus* seemed to echo earlier conventions, while in fact subverting them. Because the relationship between Ari Ben Canaan and Kitty Fremont is pivotal to the plot, *Exodus* bears a surface resemblance to all the earlier movies that had explored (and even exalted) intermarriage. The nurse is played by a blonde whose very surname, Saint, suggested the character ideal of Christianity. The star playing Ari happened to have the same given name as the founder of Christianity, as well as the same symbolic surname that Henry James gave to the protagonist of *The American* (1877), Christopher Newman. Yet though neither Paul Newman's mother nor his wife is Jewish, and though he practices no faith, he has considered himself a Jew "because it's more of a challenge."[38] After Danny Thomas and Natalie Wood, it had suddenly become acceptable for Jews to be playing Jews—and for their identity to be affirmed rather than concealed.

The movie itself heightens the surprise by reversing the usual Hollywood attitude toward intermarriage and universalism. When Eva Marie Saint, playing Kitty Fremont, announces that "people are the same no matter what they're called," a viewpoint usually expressed by movie-made Jews, Paul Newman rebuts her: "Don't believe it. People have a right to be different." Like most actual Israelis, Ari Ben Canaan doesn't seem to be much of a Jew; he is neither observant nor interested in religion, nor is he endowed with traits or gestures or sensitivities that Diaspora Jews would recognize as intimately their own. The heroism that he projects would earlier have been manifested in the multi-ethnic platoons—those rainbow coalitions—that fought Hollywood's version of the Second World War. But in *Exodus* Ari Ben Canaan battles not for the cause of democracy, nor for some cosmopolitan ideal of brotherhood, but as an unabashed Jewish nationalist. At the end of the film, it is not the Jew who struggles to find acceptance in the gentile world. It is Kitty Fremont who, wearing a khaki uniform and carrying a gun, stands next to Ari and then joins the other soldiers who will be repelling the Arab invaders, as the flames leap from the bottom of the screen.[39] Thus was signalled the extraordinary centrality that the fate of Israel was to exert in American Jewish life and culture.

In its aftermath came an almost exultant revelation in the fortuitous fact of Jewishness, with sprinklings of minor characters and occasional phrases soon overwhelmed by whole movies devoted to the residual mysteries of modern Jewish identity. The stars, for example, began to preserve their names. In the second phase, Julius Garfinkel had become John Garfield; in the third phase, Art Garfunkel kept his name. In the second phase Emanuel Goldenberg became Edward G. Robinson. In the third phase Jeff Goldblum kept his name; and a gentile, Caryn Johnson, actually changed hers to Whoopi Goldberg. In one spear-and-sandal epic, the ambitious Dino DeLaurentiis production of *The Bible* (1966), the part of God was originally assigned to Sir Laurence Olivier. (Asked whether they had seen this colossal film, many rabbis could only reply: "No, but I've read the book.") In the third phase, the deity was blasphemously played by George Burns, though the star of *Oh, God!* (1977) would undoubtedly insist that he had merely been typecast. Olivier himself descended from the heavens to play a cantor in what may well prove to be the last remake of *The Jazz Singer* (1980).

In the third phase the Indians not only bore odd resemblances to Hollywood Jews, but even began speaking Yiddish, as in Elliot Silverstein's *Cat Ballou* (1965). I once mentioned the emergence of such ethnic themes during the course of a lecture delivered to a lay audience in Florida, citing the case of Mel Brooks's *Blazing Saddles* (1974). In this parody Western, one of the most explosive gags occurs when Brooks, wearing full Indian regalia and sitting on a horse, suddenly starts speaking Yiddish. Afterwards one member of the audience mentioned to me her own experience of seeing the film in a neighborhood where few Jews resided. She too had roared uncontrollably at this gag—which seems to come out of nowhere; and when her own laughter died down, a woman who was seated a row ahead turned to her and said: "How lucky you are that you can understand the Indian language."

In the second phase of self-representation in Hollywood, films could be made about Captain Dreyfus that fudged or ignored his Jewish birth. In the current phase, the actor Richard Dreyfuss could tell an interviewer: "In a sense, everything I do has to do with my being Jewish."[40] Dreyfuss could portray a shady, pushy, sleazy entrepreneur in *The Apprenticeship of Duddy Kravitz* (1974); and his coreligionists felt so secure that not even the staff of the Anti-Defamation League was asked to put in overtime. In *The Big Fix* (1978), Dreyfuss could play a Jewish private detective named Moses Wine, just as George Segal had played one named Morris Brummel a decade earlier in *No Way to Treat a Lady*. Even after Gene Wilder played a sort-of Jewish cowboy in *The Frisco Kid* (1980), no one even bothered to give a decent burial to Leslie Fiedler's claim, in a discussion of

American Jewish fiction two decades earlier, that "the notion of the Jewish cowboy is utterly ridiculous, of a Jewish detective . . . nearly as anomalous."[41] For if Marilyn Monroe and Elizabeth Taylor could be Jews (by choice) off the screen, then Jews could be imagined as characters anywhere. When a black cabbie (in *Bye Bye Braverman*) and a Japanese career woman (in *Walk, Don't Run*) speak Yiddish, when Jewishness is introduced no matter how irrelevant the context, even moviegoers deprived of seeing Jewish roles for three decades earlier might have echoed the sentiment of the passenger who was standing at the liquor bar of the *Titanic*, just as the liner collided with fate: "I did ask for ice, but this is too much."

On or off the screen, to be a Jew rarely meant assuming the obligation to be a *good* Jew; for even the ethnic revival did not customarily provoke much piety or observance. The biographies and autobiographies of Hollywood figures rarely disclose any engagement with religious verities, if only because Jews—even more than other moderns—generally work without the safety net of faith. The only important exception is Sammy Davis, Jr., a movie actor since the age of seven, whose *Yes I Can* happens to boast a title which, in three monosyllables, encapsulates the national temperament itself. As in all such religious experiences, the author records the upward spiral of several stages in his struggle toward the light, from the *mezzuzah* that Eddie Cantor gave him for good luck, to the stigmata that a *mogen David* imprinted during the operation that saved only one of Davis's eyes, and finally to the formal conversion that he and his wife May Britt underwent. Although Frank Sinatra is arguably the moral hero of *Yes I Can*, its leading wisdom figure turns out to be Rabbi Max Nussbaum, the man most responsible for making Davis's "need for Judaism . . . permanent." It was fitting as well that a book also made him receptive to Judaism: Abram L. Sachar's *History of the Jews*, a classic survey of the subject, first published in 1930. This was also the book that the conscientious Carroll Baker read on the airplane that first took her to Hollywood, where the blonde starlet (*Baby Doll*) soon gave birth to a son with the striking name of Herschel David Garfein.[42]

Sammy Davis himself was astonished by his discoveries in Jewish history, by what Sachar summarized as "a will to live which no disaster could crush." The entertainer then wondered what religious message had enabled the Jews to survive millennia of catastrophes, and in an effort to find the answer kept an edition of the Talmud by his night table. Playing Sportin' Life in Goldwyn's *Porgy and Bess* (1959), Davis amazed the producer by his stubbornness in refusing to work on Yom

Kippur.[43] Yet very few other Hollywood Jews seemed willing to join in the religious inquiry that has helped make Sammy run, however wryly they might have noted the singular irony of an authentic jazz singer, without benefit of "blackface," testifying to the grandeur of the faith from which so many of them had fled.

Among the few who have shown signs of religious interest and return has been Dreyfuss, who has been attending a bimonthly Talmud class, along with director Jeremy Kagan (*The Chosen*), that the director of the UCLA Hillel Foundation has offered. Dustin Hoffman's second wife has also encouraged him "to do what I've been wanting to do for many years, which is to become more observant and pass that on to my kids. These are a few things that I really want to do before it's too late," the actor added. "I want to learn Hebrew. And I would love to be *bar mitzvahed*."[44] The recent *teshuvah* (religious return) of Hollywood is very easy to exaggerate, but even its faintest yearnings go beyond anything that had been expressed among earlier filmmakers and stars.

Although none of Steven Spielberg's films bears any particular traces of a Jewish sensibility, he is the sort of director-producer whose own apparently full comfort in his Jewish identity could only have clicked within the third phase. Without any of the apparent anxieties of the first- or second-generation Americans who founded and defined Hollywood, Spielberg has told an interviewer that his earliest memory from childhood—the imaginative source of nearly all of his most important movies—was of an Orthodox synagogue in Cincinnati, with old men wearing beards and black hats springing brightly out of a darkness akin to the onset of Creation or to a movie theater before the projection rolls. Beginning only two-and-a-half decades later, more earthlings have flocked to Spielberg's films than any other director's in history (four in the ten most lucrative of all time, plus another which he produced). Despite such unparalleled success, his mother still runs a kosher dairy restaurant in Los Angeles, and is able to expect her son and his family over for *shabbat* dinners. Spielberg has become a mogul in his own right, with his own production company and facilities. On many of the doorposts of Amblin Entertainment on the lot of Universal Studios are *mezzuzot*, symbols of religious identification that earlier generations of moguls would have shunned. In an oblique way he told their story, and that of his own grandparents, in the animated cartoon *An American Tail* (1986) that he produced. It starred a mouse named Fievel Mousekewitz; but otherwise Spielberg's work has been beamed almost entirely at a homogeneous Middle America.[45]

Let two films be enlisted in the service of a conclusion intended to disclose the force of Jewish assertiveness within a pluralistic society. One is *Hester Street* (1975), based on the 1896 novella by Abraham Cahan entitled *Yekl*. Admittedly it was not a major cinematic production. But the fact that it was done at all was something of a revelation, for much of its dialogue is in Yiddish, with English subtitles. While the native speakers of the language were expiring, its lexicon and syntax were being in part preserved at the behest of the director, Joan Micklin Silver, the daughter-in-law of Rabbi Abba Hillel Silver. Neither she nor most of the cast knew the tongue which, like nothing else, had once sealed Ashkenazic Jewry into a unit—from Minsk to Maxwell Street. But curiously enough, Cahan himself had written *Yekl* in English, a sign of the hunger of the first generation to cling to an America which they may have loved or feared more than they understood.[46] *Hester Street* is a parable of an immigrant milieu, poised so precariously between an Old World and a New. Suspended there is the assimilationist Jake, who has changed his name from Yekl, the individualistic husband who disdains "greenhorns" and already plays baseball. He is an unsympathetic boor. Bernstein, the impoverished scholar who cannot transform himself into an American, nevertheless merits the love of Gitl (Carol Kane). The suitable objects of marital—if not necessarily romantic—involvement are switched, and no viewer of this film could interpret it as a plea for acculturation or for the abandonment of tradition.

Finally attention should be paid to *Yentl* (1983). It was freely adapted from a short story by the most honored of all the contributors to Cahan's *Jewish Daily Forward*, the only one to make it all the way to Stockholm. It took Barbra Streisand fifteen years to film Isaac Bashevis Singer's "Yentl the Yeshiva Boy," and it is no secret that the Nobel laureate managed to restrain his enthusiasm for the result. But what counts here is not the short story writer's aggrieved reaction, nor even the star's taste or skill, but the career within which her intentions have been enmeshed. Even if Streisand had never done *Yentl*, her biography would have significance for this chronicle of the role of the Jew in American popular culture. For she has proven that "a nose with deviations" *isn't* "a crime against the nation," that standards of beauty should not be confined to the *shickse* and her imitators, that (in the critic Pauline Kael's terms) "talent is beauty."[47] Streisand could scarcely be imagined playing a character other than a

Jew, which is what she has done (with a few detours) ever since she cloned Fanny Brice in *Funny Girl* (1968). After 1930 or so, no Hollywood casting director would have dared to hire her; after 1964 or so, the resurgence of ethnic pride has helped give Streisand the power to hire or fire casting directors.

Yentl should not be dismissed as a transit to Narcissus but rather as the terminus of the path that one star has followed, a star who has given money openly to Jewish cultural causes (not anonymously, as the moguls were wont to do, to conventional Jewish philanthropies), a star who was reported to be studying the Talmud.[48] Nor did Streisand find anything odd about using as her vehicle a tale written in Yiddish enclosed entirely within a Jewish carapace. Like *Hester Street*, *Yentl* contains no gentile characters; nor are any imagined as suitable marriage partners, which—given the rush by a significant minority of Jews to do so in contemporary America—is a paradox. Like Jack Robin (and Al Jolson), Streisand "belongs to the whole world." But the film she directed, produced and helped to write does not assume that dialogue about brotherhood was needed to generate mass interest, nor that the Jewish characters in the film—played by Jews like Mandy Patinkin and Amy Irving—were supposed to uphold values as universal as the incest taboo.

To be sure, by having Yentl sail to America as her own declaration of independence, Streisand spun from the Singer original a very different ending.[49] But in that end is a beginning—from Yentl to Yekl and back again. One of the major ghetto films of the silent era, D. W. Griffith's *Romance of a Jewess* (1908), would have been an apt title for Streisand's movie—and not only because the plot hinges on sex role reversal, nor because it chooses to romanticize the *shtetl* rather than plead for the Jews or take revenge upon them. For in the larger sense *Yentl* suggests an attitude toward America itself, the nation which a leading Eastern European Orthodox rabbi, David Willowski, had condemned—while the film industry itself was coming into existence—as a "*trefe* land where even the stones are impure."[50]

Yet even Willowski, the Sluztker Rav, ended up in Chicago, in the heartland of this non-kosher country. It is a nation in which its Jewish minority has been more energetic in defending religious liberty than in using it, a minority that has generally been unwilling to subordinate its socioeconomic aspirations to the demands of religious tradition. For the factors that reduced synagogue attendance on Saturday mornings may have been the same that enlarged the audiences at Saturday matinees. Here in the United States no one's dreams were monitored or placed "under strict rabbinic supervision," or required to yield to the transcendent claims of corporate Jewish life. But even this abbreviated examination of Hollywood's impression of the Jew can suggest the indelible magic of those dreams, despite the oft-noted tension between commercial requirements and aesthetic imperatives in the social transmission of art. The objects of sublimity and enchantment that have flickered in the dark for nearly a century constitute only one sort of historical evidence; and the decline of piety cannot be blamed entirely on the fact that we lost it at the movies. But (to adopt André Malraux's sonorous credo) Hollywood has enabled us to fashion "from ourselves images sufficiently powerful to deny our nothingness."[51]

9

THE FUTURE AS HISTORY

Of all the extraordinary features associated with the Jews, not the least impressive has been longevity. So far back does their history twist, so striking is their endurance, and so intact is their sense of themselves as a historical unit, that they make virtually everyone else on the planet look like transients. From generation to generation they have managed to renew themselves. More than any other group, they have spanned what the late historian Fernand Braudel termed *la longue durée*. So venerable a people may even stir the suspicion that it is imperishable. But even if not, their lineage and heritage are bound to brush against questions about the meaning of history itself, about the rise and fall of societies and cultures, perhaps even about the purposes of a deity that would grant such protection and bestow such durability.

For the promises given at Mount Sinai, the everlasting link between the refugees fleeing bondage in Egypt and a supreme God, help to illuminate the singular Jewish response to history. Even American Jews in the 1980s are expected to identify so fully with their Israelite ancestors on Passover that the chasm of time is bridged and the Jewish people is made whole and one. The midrashic reminder that all Jews—past, present, and future—were supposed to have been standing and listening at Mount Sinai means that the distinction between time past and time present is erased.[1] It may therefore be pleasant to conjecture that when co-religionists can be recognized in a strange community, the explanation may not be a definable Jewish physiognomy or "type." The faces appear vaguely familiar because all had met once before: at the foot of Mount Sinai.

That is the traditional view—that there is only one story to be lived and retold until the end of days, even when the locales have shifted to Shaker Heights and Beverly Hills. The remarkable length of that story is really a sign of exemption from the cycles of splendor and decay to which the various empires and nations all around the Jews have been subjected. Sanctioned by a special relationship to God and bound to a special set of laws and rules, the Jews have not thought of themselves as confined within the ephemera of time but as an *am olam* (an eternal people). They have persisted outside of history, beyond the writ of merely temporal power and vainglory.

But scholars who examine the annals of temporal power also know that different visions of Jewish destiny have also been expounded. The doom of the Jewish people has also been prophesied. These eschatological expectations have sometimes been uttered by those who have feared the end of this people, more often by those who have desired such an end. Such views have sometimes come from Jews, often from their adversaries. Even though the Jews tell themselves that their particular story can be concluded only with the advent of a messianic age, hatred and tyranny have often intervened, threatening to extinguish a people that has dreamed of universal harmony. The belief that such dreams and such history had been— or would soon be—short-circuited is the subject of this concluding chapter.

The first notice that any other people took, in a form that has survived, already announces a final destruction. In the museum of antiquities in Cairo is a granite stele that celebrates the victory circa 1220 B.C.E. of the Egyptians in Gezer, Ashkelon, and elsewhere. The inscription reads: "Israel is defeated and shall never rise again."[2] This boast of Merneptah seemed premature thirteen centuries later when, at the dawn of the common era, Judea held out for four years against the most powerful empire on earth. The Arch of Titus in Rome commemorates yet another annihilation; and in the wake of the defeat of the Bar Kochba uprising in the following century, the Jewish people scattered and was dispersed into exile. And yet in 1913, when Freud visited the Italian capital for the first time, he scribbled on the back of a post card depicting the Arch of Titus this assurance to a psychoanalytic colleague: "The Jew survives it!" The Forum that was once central to "the Eternal City" was in ruins, and Latin had become a "dead" language. But when Freud wrote the preface to the Hebrew edition of *Totem and Taboo*, he testified to the irreducible Jewishness that formed the marrow of his own identity and which he refused to alter.[3]

Though the Jews had indeed survived both the rise and the fall of empires such as Rome's, their history can be partly told as expectations of extinction. From the experience of the Diaspora in Europe, it is possible to tabulate five different visions of imminent doom. A sixth has its origins in Western Europe, especially Germany, but has flourished in an American setting. It is the most recent, and therefore the most uncertain. It is also the only version of Jewish doom that is generated from within the Jewish community itself, that is not a reflection of hostility or contempt but voices an internal fear that the Jews themselves will prove unwilling to perpetuate their history.

That tradition has been punctuated by outbursts of fury described in the *Haggadah*: "In every age they rise up to destroy us." Jewish life from the fall of Rome until the Enlightenment was separatist and corporate, and it was pierced by almost every imaginable tragedy that religious anti-Semitism could devise. Baffled that the divinity of Jesus was not acknowledged and the sanctity of the New Testament was not accepted, revolted by customs and rituals that diverged dramatically from the "one true faith," Christian Europe inflicted segregation and expulsion, discrimination and confiscation, pogrom and slaughter upon the "perfidious" Jews. To burn the Talmud, to bathe entire communities in bloodshed could sometimes be construed as devotion to Christ and credentials for sainthood.

But medieval Catholicism could not be characterized only in terms of violence and destructiveness, however intense. A strong ideological undercurrent blocked the systematic annihilation of the Jewish people. Catholic leaders and thinkers formulated a reason to preserve the remnant of Jewry, if only as a reminder of the debasement and degradation of those who spurned the redemption that the Trinity promised. Their wretchedness and misery vindicated the truthfulness of Christianity, to whose origins the exiled Jews provided a grotesque but living link. Their lineage all the way to Galilee and Mount Sinai conferred upon them some right to live because Christendom could behold a reminder of the sources of its own piety. The Jews, Pope Innocent III wrote, "are doomed to wander about the earth as fugitives and vagabonds, and their faces must be covered in shame.

They are under no circumstances to be protected by Christian princes."[4]

The violence of medieval Judeophobia therefore did not demand the physical extermination of the descendants of Jesus. But Christianity was predicated on the expectation that all human beings would embrace the Savior—and that meant the eventual disappearance of Jews as well as Judaism. The various prophecies of the Second Coming, the various means of conversion—from the persuasive to the coercive—were based on the assumption that the Jews would, like everyone else, recognize that Christ had risen and would return. The people and the religion of Jesus himself were therefore consigned eventually to oblivion. Such predictions were not detached and neutral, but were often propelled forward by a fanaticism intended to fulfill such prophecies. What was foreseen was desired; what was desired was often enacted. Relapsed *conversos* who were considered heretics were still being burned at the stake as late as the eighteenth century.

Such persecutions were becoming an anachronism in the age of Enlightenment, however. The forceful solution to the historical anomaly of the Jewish people—accept Christ or die—was becoming discredited. Even though religious bigotry waned discernibly, even as reason was expected to subvert the foundations of revelation and authority among Christians, notions of tolerance were slow to spread; and the champions of Enlightenment themselves balked at encouraging the diversity that Jewry represented. The earlier erratic policies of kings and princes to expel the Jews from their midst had not succeeded. But could the only conspicuous group of non-Christians in Europe be absorbed into the new nation-states that were emerging?

Voltaire seemed to answer in the negative, largely because the Jewish religion was only the manifestation of deeper, innate traits. Intrinsic to this people, he argued, was its "raging fanaticism . . . I would not be in the least surprised were these people someday to become deadly to the human race." A late metaphysical essay directly addressed the Jews, whom this rationalist luminary condemned for "surpass[ing] all nations in impertinent fables, in bad conduct, and in barbarism. You deserve to be punished, for this is your destiny." Having resisted the Greek and Roman influences which the *philosophe* believed had enhanced Christianity, the Jews could not easily be assimilated into the larger community. Even if Judaism were to be abolished, something ineradicable and fundamentally subversive in the Jewish character might well endure.[5]

Despite a credo of opposition to obscurantism, Voltaire's politics were therefore corrupted with a form of racial anti-Semitism that was an augury of the late nineteenth century. But for all of his influence, he was hardly synonymous with the Enlightenment itself; and the revolutionaries who built upon and transformed the legacy of the *philosophes* reached a different conclusion. The revolution of 1789 accelerated the conviction that, once superstition and intolerance were banished, human affairs could be drastically improved and a new society molded according to the laws of reason. The minimal expectation was that the Jews would occupy an equal status in the performance of civic duties. The maximal expectation was that Jews enjoyed the same potential as other Frenchmen to be regenerated into new beings. Separation was eroded as Jews emerged from the shadows of the *Judengassen* and into civil society. In the first debate in the French revolutionary assembly on the subject of the Jews, a liberal Parisian deputy, Clermont-Tonnerre, proposed that France give "to Jews as individuals, everything; to Jews as a distinct community, nothing." This was the bargain that was struck. By forfeiting the separate corporate existence which had harbored Jews from some external dangers throughout the Middle Ages and thereafter, the Jews were supposed to merge as individuals into the nation-state. In abandoning communal cohesion devoid of rights, the Jews would become citizens distinguishable from others only in the practice of their religious faith.[6]

"Normalization" meant that the ties of peoplehood would be loosened, if not necessarily severed; and the result was one of the greatest explosions of talent in all of Western history. As individuals or as families, Jews swept through advancing sectors of the economy, through the counting-houses and the stock exchanges and the liberal professions, through the mercantile palaces and the press galleries, the concert halls and the exhibition rooms, and sometimes the legislatures and cabinet offices as well. Many new loyalties became national, an intensification of the medieval dictum of *dina de-malkhuta dina* ("the law of the kingdom is the law"). Living in Paris, Heine felt himself in exile—not from Palestine but from Germany, against whose proclivity for irrational frenzy the poet nevertheless sounded an early warning. Amid the horror that struck little more than a century later, one of the victims was the historian Marc Bloch, whom the Germans executed for his role in the Resistance. Though he may well have been the most influential historian of his era and was far from a parochial figure, Bloch personified the supremacy of nationalist allegiances which were adumbrated in 1789. His testament affirmed his Jewish origins. Yet he also considered himself "a stranger to all creedal dogmas, as to all pretended community of life and spirit based on race. I have, through life, felt that I was above all, and quite simply, a Frenchman."[7] But at the dawn of the nineteenth century, no one could have foreseen how high a price the Jews would pay for their emancipation, for receiving "everything" as individuals.

It could not have been anticipated how abruptly the centuries of corporate continuity could come to a halt, how within a lifetime or two the complicated and intricate traditions of learning and piety seemed to wither and even vanish. "You really had brought some traces of Judaism with you from the ghetto-like village community," Kafka wrote in his undelivered *Letter to His Father* in 1919. "It was not much and it dwindled a little more in the city. . . . But still, the impressions and memories of your youth did just about suffice for some sort of Jewish life." But then, as many besides Franz Kafka were to discover, "it was too little to be handed on to the child; it all dribbled away while you were passing it on."[8] Nor was it realized how imperfectly the civil societies of Europe would keep their side of the bargain. Anti-Semitism was often tenacious. Because discrimination and prejudice remained significant impediments in the lives of Jews, some took refuge in universalistic creeds and movements that offered the hope of transcending the barriers of nation and race and religion and class. In the Europe of the nineteenth and early twentieth centuries, the most consequential of the efforts to eliminate such divisions was socialism. It represents the third of the visions of the end of the Jewish people.

Despite the attraction of socialism for many Jews, some of the leading ideologues of the movement were themselves deeply infected by antagonism toward Jews. For the socialists denounced as intrinsically cruel and exploitative a capitalist economy within which many Jews appeared so active and so successful. This animus against the Jew as capitalist was especially true of Marx, the baptized descendant of rabbis, though he acknowledged no ties binding him to the Jewish people or its past. Before founding "scientific" socialism, he advocated not only the complete emancipation of the Jews but also the complete emancipation of society from "judaization," the commercial spirit which he considered central to the actual ethos of Jewry. Other socialist tribunes transferred onto the Jews themselves their objections to capitalism, and could not disentangle the pecuniary achievements of some Jews from a general indictment of the Jewish people. The founder of the libertarian variety of socialism, Pierre-Joseph Proudhon, called "the Jew . . . the enemy of mankind. It is necessary to send this race back to Asia, or exterminate it."[9]

But even if Jews had been financial failures within the system of capitalism, their status in the historical dialectic would have been insecure and the attitudes of socialist theorists equivocal, if not hostile. For in the equation of material progress, the Jews signified a surd, an irrational number that simply did not add up. Because socialism at its most noble expressed a dream of human brotherhood, it could not easily legitimate the otherhood that Judaism has required of its adherents. A future which would expunge class conflict and national rivalries could not grant any enclave to a people believing itself to be eternally yoked to the Torah and bound by a covenant. In the visions of human perfectability stemming from the French revolutionary tradition were no provisions for a distinctive people like the Jews. Implicit in the philosophical systems and ersatz religions that the "prophets of Paris" created was the disappearance of the Jewish people; the messianic role in such schemes of historical progress was offered instead to scientists, engineers, and administrators. Recognizably Jewish inhabitants are absent from the utopias of socialist novelists.[10]

The Jewish question became especially sticky for the Marxist version of socialism. Karl Kautsky was a sharp critic of racism and of anti-Semitism; and, as the *völkisch* ideology became ascendant in the late nineteenth-century Hohenzollern and Hapsburg empires, he forthrightly championed Jewish rights. But Kautsky was also trapped within the belief system that posited a classless, cosmopolitan, rational society of the future. He therefore wrote that "the Jews have become an eminently revolutionary factor, while Judaism has become a reactionary factor. . . . We have [not] completely emerged from the Middle Ages, as long as Judaism still exists among us. The sooner it disappears, the better it will be, not only for society, but also for the Jews themselves . . ." The historical determinism that Marxism was so confidently tracing would not ensure "a transition from Orthodox Judaism to ecclesiastical Christianity, but the creation of a new and higher type of man." Kautsky therefore opposed the Zionist movement as well as the impulse to transmit the Jewish heritage to the next generation; he believed that such efforts ran counter to the grain of history.[11]

How to define the Jews continued to bedevil Marxist theory and practice, and in Russia their fate unfolded with special poignancy and anguish. By the time Czar Alexander III died in 1894, 40% of his Jewish subjects had been reduced to pauperism under the brutal impact of economic discrimination and other forms of persecution. Four years later the Chief Procurator of the Holy Synod, Constantin Pobedonostsev, could no longer disguise the aim of Romanov policy: "One third [of Russian Jewry] will die out, one third will leave the country, and one third will be completely dissolved in the surrounding population." The radical response of czarist autocracy and obscurantism was aptly summarized by Joseph Conrad as "senseless desperation provoked by senseless tyranny."[12] Unfortunately, the Bolsheviks who eventually succeeded the Romanovs have not rescinded the death sentence that had been passed on a millennium of Jewish life in Russia. Without establishing a policy of intentionally killing Jews, the Soviet regime has largely succeeded in killing Judaism, as well as other manifestations of a particular historical culture such as Zionism and *Yiddishkeit*. Succeeding generations of Jews have been systematically prevented from discovering their origins and exploring their identity. By sabotaging the perpetuation of Jewish learning and piety, by murdering the creative leaders of Yiddish culture and by making the teaching of Hebrew a crime, the Soviet regime has gone far toward annihilating Jewish life in the second largest community in the Diaspora, even though the recent reforms of the Gorbachev regime have made that process appear more humane. This most imposing peril to Jewish survival is the most extreme extension of the secular challenge that the Enlightenment delivered to the Jewish community and that socialist doctrine posed to the Jewish religion and sense of peoplehood.

But however fatally Soviet history has distorted the premises of universalism, the most extreme image of Jewish doom was, paradoxically, a repudiation of the Enlightenment itself. This ideology was grounded in a denial of the essential unity of the human species. Instead of dreaming of the moment when the mass of individual Jews might merge into a collective humanity, the racists who reversed the faith of the Enlightenment insisted upon the innate malevolence and danger to others that the *Untermenschen* exhibited. Racial differences became the hinge upon which history turned, and Nazism became the enactment of a century of racist thought. The *völkisch* writer Paul de Lagarde anticipated Hitler in his scorn for those whose sentimentality and humanitarianism interfered with the historical destiny of some races to triumph, others to die. Lagarde fulminated against Aryans who were "too cowardly to trample this usurious vermin [, the

Jews,] to death. With trichinae and bacilli one does not negotiate, nor are trichinae and bacilli to be educated; they are exterminated as quickly and thoroughly as possible."[13] From such prescriptions of what the *Volk* ought to do, the line can be drawn to the Final Solution, which its perpetrators compared to scientific, prophylactic "de-lousing," to be performed without the irrational fury that characterized earlier enactments of anti-Semitism. The novelty of this conception has been put into perspective by the historian of the Holocaust, Raul Hilberg: "The missionaries of Christianity had said in effect: You have no right to live among us as Jews. The secular rulers who followed had proclaimed: You have no right to live among us. The German Nazis at last decreed: You have no right to live."[14]

This is not the place to record the incalculable and irreplaceable losses inflicted upon the Jewish people. But it should be noted how explicit Nazi ideology was on the subject of Jewish destiny. *Mein Kampf* warned in 1924 that "if . . . the Jew conquers the nations of this world, his crown will become the funeral wreath of humanity, and once again this planet, empty of mankind, will move through the ether as it did thousands of years ago." It was therefore necessary to crush the people which, fortified with Marxist ideology, had become the enemy of mankind and especially of the Aryan race. On January 30, 1939, the *Fuehrer* asserted before the Reichstag: "Today I shall act the prophet once again. If international financial Jewry inside and outside of Europe should succeed in thrusting the nations into a world war once again, then the result will not be the Bolshevization of the earth and with it the victory of Jewry, it will be the annihilation of the Jewish race in Europe." (At this point, the minutes record "long and vigorous applause.") In his New Year's message almost three years later, the prophecy was reiterated: "The Jew will . . . not exterminate the people of Europe; he will be the victim of his own machinations instead." On four other occasions in 1942, the *Fuehrer* repeated such predictions to the Reichstag, and ensured that genocide came horribly close to full realization.[15]

The hostile ideology of Nazism, like medieval Catholicism and the revolutionary Enlightenment and Soviet Marxism, had corollaries in policy and action. All four visions of a world without Jews were also creeds that could be made operational through an exercise of power. All four visions involved the making not only of prognostications but also of policies, and not only depicted the future but sought to hasten its arrival. In such instances it is not easy to disengage the desire from the deed, the prediction from the compulsion to make that prediction come true.

But a fifth vision can be uncoupled from any of its potential consequences, for it underscores the singularity of the Jewish people without posing any direct danger to its posterity. This perspective has not affected the freedom of the Jews to pursue their own course, and may even inadvertently arouse a sense of wonder and mystery. This is the mentality that might be termed meta-history. Its most famous practitioners in the twentieth century have been Oswald Spengler (1880–1936) and Arnold J. Toynbee (1889–1975).

The Decline of the West, which enjoyed an exceptional vogue upon its publication at the end of the First World War, presented the deterministic view that cultures are organisms resembling the ages of man, whose destination is decay and death. With an assurance more appropriate to a headwaiter than a historian, Spengler claimed that the "Magian" Jews, who were among the first nations to be born, reached vigorous maturity just as the "Faustian" Occident was inaugurating its own life cycle. Judaic culture in the modern era was therefore losing its grip on its own adherents even as it was losing its own sense of purpose, its own warrant for sustaining itself. The business skills that had given the Jews such an early advantage were increasingly diffused throughout the West. Spengler therefore believed that the Jewish people had fulfilled its historical mission and was "faced with dissolution." It had ceased to grow: "The Jewish Consensus ceased to have a history at all. Its problems were solved, its inner form was complete, conclusive, and unalterable. . . . Epochs succeeded to epochs, every century witnessed fundamental human changes, but in the ghetto and in the souls of its denizens all stood still." Here the special attitude toward the past, as reflected in the *Haggadah* and the *Mishnah*, had become a symptom of sterility and ossification, a prelude to decay. Losing its internal cohesion, Jewish life could no longer persevere.[16]

Toynbee also gave readers of the ten volumes of *A Study of History*, plus his *Reconsiderations*, the same impression. That corpus generated an enormous literature of controversy and made him perhaps the most famous historian of his time. Indeed *Time* put Toynbee on its cover (the story was written by Whittaker Chambers), and reviewers hailed it as "an immortal masterpiece" and "probably the greatest historical work ever written." Allan Nevins's blurb situated Toynbee on Olympus, where civilizations were considered the only useful units of scrutiny, and the rise and fall of almost two dozen of them were traced. The astonishing scope and range of *A Study of History* required that the Jews, who have been found on every inhabited continent and formed communities in so many civilizations, had to be scrutinized; and Toynbee's attitude was ambivalent. He credited the Hebrews "with an unparalleled spiritual insight," and with "a mighty feat of spiritual intuition to perceive in the lineaments of a primitive volcano-demon of the Arabian Wilderness the epiphany of a God who was omnipresent and omnipotent." Other references in his magnum opus are by no means uniformly critical. But Toynbee seemed to disparage the Jews as a "fossilized relic" of "Syriac Civilization." At least on the subject of Jewish history, his interpretation is systematically flawed— in its manipulation of evidence, in its obscurity, in its condescension and hostility, and in its blindness to the resilience and vitality of a people that has defied the "laws" of history itself.

These flaws were devastatingly exposed in Maurice Samuel's *The Professor and the Fossil*, which emphasizes Toynbee's obfuscation of the enduring dynamism of this "fossilized relic" from a "Syriac Civilization" (which incidentally never existed). When it came to the Hebrews and their descendants, Toynbee switched to paleontology. He saw mostly sterility and desuetude—but not powers of regeneration. He saw only an overwhelming tendency in the modern era toward assimilation—not the struggle to maintain a distinctive identity. On this matter Samuel deserves the last word: "The assimilatory proclivity of the Jewish people is as ancient as the people itself, which entered history as it were trying to assimilate; the Israelites . . . worshipped the molten calf at the very foot of Sinai. . . . This ordinary, this universal tendency to yield to the lures and pressures of the human environment, this ordinary and universal reluctance to maintain an identity, develop a gift, accept a destiny," Samuel concluded, "makes the survival of the Jew all the more extraordinary, [and] adds a touch of spice to his singular history."[17]

Nor was such continuity to be ruptured in North America either, where a Jewish presence has been maintained for over three centuries. Its influence and comfort, its well-being and efflorescence are reminiscent of the Weimar Republic, of the Golden Age of Spain, of Alexandria, and Babylonia. The United States never confronted a "Jewish question" because the emancipation from British rule did not precede the emancipation of the Jews. Like other Caucasians, they were, with minor exceptions, born free—or could become citizens through a process of naturalization that the liberal state did not complicate. Despite the predominance of the white, Anglo-Saxon Protestant culture, the United States conceived of itself as an asylum for those seeking freedom from religious and political oppression, as a frontier society in which labor was scarce and economic opportunities beckoned, as a melting pot that would produce what an early nationalist, St. John Crèvecoeur, deemed "a new man."[18]

No wonder then that those who have envisioned the end to Jewish life in America do not ascribe its likely causes to religious persecution or to racial discrimination; danger has not lurked outside the perimeter of the community. What has been calibrated instead is the impact of benign assimilation, the overpowering influence of the civil society in making Jews feel so much at home that their will to remain Jews is sapped. It is the sixth and final *eschaton* that merits discussion here.

Unlike the previous predictions, this one is voiced primarily within the community itself. Unlike most of the previous predictions, the vanishing of the Jews is not generally welcomed or encouraged; and no policy is designed to implement it. American Jews who have sought assimilation have rarely been programmatic about it, have not wished to call attention to their own origins by advocacy or ideology. Those who have regarded Jewishness as a birth defect have been eager to conceal it rather than ruminate on the fate of their erstwhile brethren. No American of consequence has echoed the plea of the Romantic intellectual Rahel Varnhagen, at the dawn of German emancipation: "The Jew in us must be rooted out; that is a sacred truth, even if life itself is sacrificed in the process." No American has publicly agreed with Arthur Koestler's argument that, with the birth of Israel, religious Jews should return to the Zion for which they have prayed, while non-religious Jews, for the sake of their progeny, should feel guiltless in merging into the general population. Having worked within the Zionist movement, Koestler wished the new state well; but he believed that only with the disappearance of the Jews would Christendom cure itself of the sickness of anti-Semitism.[19]

Such direct appeals for assimilation have been extremely rare in the United States, though they have not been unknown. Felix Adler, for example, took the case so seriously that he resigned from the pulpit of the flagship Reform synagogue, New York's Temple Emanuel, and then in 1876 withdrew from Judaism altogether. Forming the Ethical Culture Society as a universalist sect, he dreamed of a religion of humanity and, anticipating Koestler, predicted that anti-Semitism would vanish only when Jews did. In any event, the future that Ethical Culture anticipated has receded from view; and its own limited constituency is so parochial, so heavily Jewish that it probably spawned the definition of an assimilationist as one who associates only with Jews who do not associate with Jews.

Norman Podhoretz's essay, "My Negro Problem—And Ours," made a more tentative argument for assimilation, for the racial crisis of the 1960s provoked the editor of *Commentary* into endorsing miscegenation: "The wholesale merger of the two races is the most desirable alternative [to bigotry] for everyone concerned. I am not claiming that this alternative can be pursued programmatically or that it is immediately feasible . . . [But] the Negro problem can be solved in this country in no other way." Interestingly enough, Podhoretz made no exception for the Jews, who were the group of whites most actively involved in civil rights and most sympathetic to the ideal of racial equality. He also wondered why contemporary Jews wished to preserve their distinctiveness, especially since the Holocaust had demonstrated the lethal consequences of Jewish birth. So that the color question in the United States could be resolved, Podhoretz did not in 1963 call explicitly for the termination of Jewish life; nor did Podhoretz expect that termination. But however delicately formulated, "My Negro Problem—And Ours" remains the closest that a responsible American Jew has come publicly to an unabashedly assimilationist position.[20]

Usually those who predict the complete absorption of American Jewry into the wider national community are anguished that it may happen. It is often as much an alarm as an effort at foresight, a fear far more than a prediction. Putting history on fast-forward, Herman Wouk warned in 1959 that "the threat of Jewish oblivion in America . . . is the threat of pleasantly vanishing down a broad highway at the wheel of a high-powered station wagon, with the golf clubs piled in the back . . ." *This is My God* imagines what happens next: "Mr. Abramson left his home in the morning after a hearty breakfast, apparently in the best of health, and was not seen again." The novelist, an Orthodox Jew, explained that "of course Mr. Abramson will not die. When his amnesia clears, he will be Mr. Adamson, and his wife and children will join him, and all will be well. But the Jewish question will be over in the United States."[21]

Support for this adumbration has mounted, with demographers and other sociologists supplying most of the evidence. Some Zionists, journalists, and rabbis have also contributed to a sense of pessimism about the Jewish predicament in America.

As early as 1964 Thomas B. Morgan published an article in *Look* magazine entitled "The Vanishing American Jew." Over two decades ago the vital signs already seemed to be flickering: low birth rates, increasing rates of intermarriage.[22] Since then, if anything, the erstwhile marathon man may have begun to resemble the incredible shrinking man. Even if the Jewish population may not be getting smaller in absolute numbers, it is certainly declining relative to the rest of the country. No demographer really knows the exact figures. But it may be hovering around 5,775,000, and the average age of American Jewry is higher than any other major ethnic group. The average black in the United States is 22 years old; the average Hispanic is 18. As though befitting an ancient lineage, the average American Jew is more than double their ages: 46.[23]

It also appears that one Jew out of every three (or four) who marries does so outside the faith. Moreover, Jews who do marry other Jews may not be producing enough children to reach the replacement level (about 2.1 per family). Only one Jew in two is affiliated in any way with the organized community. Perhaps only one Jewish child in three is receiving a Jewish education.[24] One notorious set of straight-line projections, based on current or likely intermarriage rates, with 60% of the offspring raised as Jews, yielded for the American Tricentennial in 2076 a Jewish minority as numerous as 944,000 or as depleted as 10,420. That particular study was subsequently discredited, however, though not before its conclusions were widely disseminated.[25]

These are among the statistics that have been presented, sometimes quite luridly, that project a dead end for American Jewry. But neither Jeremiah nor Isaiah needed spread sheets to buttress his prophecies, and qualitative evidence has also been marshalled to depict the twilight. Take the synagogue. Without at least some sensitivity to the religious vocation, it may be impossible to sustain a rationale or incentive to remain Jewish. But over two centuries of skepticism, anticlericalism and materialism, from Voltaire to Marx to Freud, seem to have affected Jews more markedly than others; for they are much less likely to worship regularly than their Protestant or Catholic neighbors. As Jews become de-tribalized, religion has nevertheless been expected to bear the large, if not entire, burden of Jewishness. The temple has assumed the responsibility of explaining and symbolizing what was once appreciated in the home, and the learning and social welfare once entrusted to a gamut of institutions have been largely confined to rabbis and other synagogue personnel. The strain is too heavy. Participation of Jewish young people in religious cults appears higher than their proportion of the general population; the president of Rev. Sun Myung Moon's Unification Church is an apostate Jew named Moses Durst. The candid diary of one Long Island rabbi has recorded the effects of "the Judaism franchise business," with his co-religionists "all over the United States . . . building monuments to themselves with roughly the same speed and taste as Colonel Sanders putting up his fried-chicken stands." The shallowness of much of what has passed for Judaism has therefore led to warnings that American Jews "are enjoying the powers with which their tradition has endowed them, but they are not renewing these powers. American Jewry is 'spending its capital,' using up its resource without replacing it."[26]

Other depletions have robbed the community of sources of renewal. Despite some heroic efforts, the language of the Eastern European immigrants is almost entirely lost. Neither the incorporation of some of its choicest cuts into the argot of other Americans, nor a Nobel Prize to a Yiddish fabulist, nor publication of anthologies of Yiddish verse has deflected the threat of silence. The *Jewish Daily Forward* has become a weekly, as are the two newspapers aimed at Hasidim.[27] The deprivation of a shared tongue means the thinning of a distinctive identity. Even the success of Jews has been blamed for accelerating communal disintegration. Defense agencies struggled for decades to abolish discrimination in higher education. They won. But by a historical irony, those Jews with the highest achievements in education are the most likely to separate themselves from a community whose values encouraged them to study so ambitiously in the first place. As more Jews became professionals rather than business people, the implications for communal vitality have been interpreted as ominous too, since physicians, attorneys, academicians, scientists, and engineers tend to be less philanthropic (and often less wealthy) than the successfully self-employed. So far, however, that particular occupational shift seems not to have occurred.[28]

But perhaps the most striking sign of an endangered community has been the end of endogamy. Jay Gatsby once dismissed the love that Tom Buchanan felt toward his wife as "just personal." But that is the main determinant of marriage for Jews as for other Americans; and as the Jewish generations become ever more distant from their immigrant and Old World origins, love between Jews and gentiles becomes more plausible, and concern for the perpetuation of the Jewish people has seemed more eccentric. The very stereotypes that have made Jewish partners so attractive (sobriety, security, responsibility) may be diminishing, as the community and its families try to reconcile the ideals of integration and survival in the most private and emotional, poignant and intimate of issues.[29]

The very latitudinarianism and amiability of American life have lowered—though not eliminated—the defense mechanisms that once promoted the instincts of survival. A sensibility once permeated with uncertainty and suspicion has been softened. To be sure, Jews remain too obstinate to kneel at the foot of the cross. They continue to resist a Christianity which can no longer be vindicated by pointing to the wretchedness of the pariahs whose existence the Church barely tolerated. To be sure, the Jews have been elusive enough to circumvent the fate that historical pressures, demographic weakness, the sovereignty of nation-states, and the waning of religious impulses seem to have decreed. But it is undeniable that very many American Jews have grown slack in their commitment to their faith and people and have neglected to transmit even the vestiges of their heritage to their children. As one discriminatory barrier after another is shattered, as one pinnacle after another is scaled, the community that had nourished such talents and ambitions has seemed, according to some observers, to shrivel.

Cogent analyses like Charles S. Liebman's *The Ambivalent American Jew* and Hillel Halkin's *Letters to an American Jewish Friend* have therefore expressed the gravest of reservations about the future of the largest community in the Diaspora. Both authors are Americans of Orthodox backgrounds who made *aliyah*. In 1973 Liebman argued that "if the Jewish community is to survive, it must become more explicit and conscious about the incompatibility of integration and survival." He did not doubt that "some nominal form of Judaism will persist in the United States. However, the fact that some group, no matter how small, will continue to call itself Jewish . . . offers me little consolation." Liebman therefore concluded that "if Judaism as I understand it is to perpetuate itself in America, it must, at least to some extent, reject the value of integration, which I see as sapping its very essence." Four years later, Halkin was more certain that the classical Zionist argument had been correct, that "the Jews *as a people* had a future in the modern world only as an autonomous community living in a land of their own and organized, if possible, in the form of a nation-state." For the social forces that were imperiling life in the Diaspora since Emancipation are irreversible, Halkin asserted; and even the most prosperous and populous of Diaspora communities are doomed.[30]

The laws of historical development, the data of sociology, the astuteness of Zionist ideology have been invoked in the direction of one conclusion. And these predictions are so often encased in such certainty, uttered with such confidence, that the mere historian—who knows that not even hindsight can be 20/20—must sometimes feel like Toots Shor, the affable but uneducated restaurateur who once found himself attending a Broadway production of *Hamlet*. Looking around the animated crowd in the lobby during the first intermission, Shor blurted out: "I'm the only son of a bitch here who doesn't know how this god-damn thing is gonna come out."[31] Perhaps the American Jewish community will someday be reduced to ruins, to a ghost town, with the wind blowing tumbleweeds through deserted streets that once teemed with life. But since knowledge of the future is never vouchsafed to us, skepticism is a reliable starting principle.

The ultimate fate of individuals can be dependably known. "All stories, if continued far enough, end in death," Hemingway proclaimed, "and he is no true storyteller who would keep that from you."[32] But how the story of the Jewish people will end is unclear, for it has continuously broken the rules that have applied to others. Eschatology cannot be an exact science; and from a survivalist perspective, pessimism may be unwarranted.

Oblivion has commonly been the fate of those who foolishly announced that oblivion was to be the fate of the Jewish people. Merneptah, the victor in Gezer and Ashkelon, is not exactly a household name. Had his boast been accurate, it would have been redundant for one of his successors, Gamal Abdel Nasser, to report at the outset of the Six-Day War that 75% of the Israeli Air Force had been destroyed and that Egyptian armored units had cut deep into Israeli territory, or for Radio Cairo to broadcast that Tel Aviv was in flames and Haifa's oil refinery demolished. Asked at the beginning of the 1967 war what would be the fate of the Jews of Israel, the head of the P.L.O., Ahmed Shukeiry, replied: "Those who survive will remain in Palestine. I estimate that none of them will survive."[33] The Roman Empire that Titus served is no more; and while fears for the military destruction of Israel itself have not been repressed, its defense forces are widely acknowledged to be dominant in the region that Roman legions had once conquered.

The effort that began in early Christianity to eliminate the Jewish people through conversion has not been entirely abandoned. But its scope has been drastically reduced, and the hopes of proselytizers have proven vain. The meta-historical volumes that disparaged Jewish survival go unassigned on college campuses and largely unread.

Fascination with *The Decline of the West* has itself declined; and neither professionals nor amateurs bother much to study the history in *A Study of History*, though college courses in Jewish studies have expanded prodigiously. "The Vanishing American Jew" that *Look* once tried to trace is very much around; the magazine itself has vanished.

Some consoling sense of continuity can be salvaged even from the desolation of the Holocaust, for not even the Final Solution was completely successful. Before her murder at the age of fifteen, Anne Frank exclaimed: "I want to go on living even after my death!" She has. Her *Het Achterhuis* has been translated into forty languages and dialects; and well over sixty million people have read it, or attended the play or saw the film based on her diary in the Secret Annexe. "Her voice was preserved out of the millions that were silenced, this voice no louder than a child's whisper," her biographer has written. "It has outlasted the shouts of the murderers and has soared above the voice of time."[34]

One child who was spared was David Weiss, who was fourteen when the Germans arrived in the Roumanian-Hungarian town of Sighet. When the boxcar doors opened at Auschwitz, his aunt exhorted him: "May the Torah that you have studied protect you!" She was gassed that first day, as were his mother and his grandparents. His father was torn apart by the dogs of the S.S., and his sister died at Bergen-Belsen at the age of twenty. But at the age of fifteen, David Weiss saw an S.S. auxiliary about to eat a sandwich wrapped in a page of the Code of Jewish Law. Weiss fell to his knees and begged to be given the wrapping. He read it and passed it on to other prisoners, the last of whom collapsed and died during forced labor; the fragment was on him when he was dragged into the crematorium. But Weiss survived, and has been teaching Talmud at the Jewish Theological Seminary and at Columbia University, while writing a mammoth interpretation of the Talmud. On the eve of the Second World War, 43,000 young European men had been studying in 420 *yeshivot*. According to one recent survey, 55,000 young Israeli men are studying in almost 700 *yeshivot* (plus women, plus those refusing state assistance).[35] Some justification remains for the notion of an *am olam*.

Nor are the final returns in yet on American Jewry. It cannot and should not be held to the standards of the *shtetl*, which surpassed in the dense texture of its *Yiddishkeit* several earlier Diaspora communities as well. Even though American Jewry cannot count on further waves of immigration to replenish it, it has managed to renew itself, as enough of its members still believe that they have promises to keep.

Not even a dramatic rise in marriages in which the spouse does not convert to Judaism seems to have crippled communal resilience—at least not yet. For intermarriage does not appear to signify on any consistent basis disaffiliation with the organized community, nor erasure of Jewish identity. So long as approximately half of intermarried couples raise children who identify themselves as Jews, the actual Jewish population is not depleted, which means that the choice may not be as stark as endogamy or end game. Despite inhibitions against proselytization, there are probably more conversions to Judaism than the reverse.

With grisly black humor the commissar whom Greta Garbo played in *Ninotchka* (1939) justifies the purges of the 1930s for producing "fewer but better Russians." That may be happening in the United States too. Many of those who have chosen to remain within the fold of the community have become more pious or engaged with Jewish culture than were their parents, so that a possibly shrinking Jewish population may include many who are more dedicated and knowledgeable than an earlier generation. After a visit to American synagogues and communal institutions in 1984, the Israeli editor-in-chief of the *Encyclopedia Judaica* was especially struck by the impact of converts and of women in American Jewish life, and concluded: "These are not the symptoms of a disappearing Jewry."[36]

This upbeat stance is expanded in Charles Silberman's *A Certain People*, the most powerful and provocative overview of the state of American Jewry. The main themes of the 1985 best-seller are undoubtedly familiar enough to exclude their repetition here, but it should be noted that Silberman has attempted to shatter the conventional wisdom that holds that insecurity and oppression have helped to cement Jewish history into a community of fate. In no environment was such a rationale ever desirable; in the American environment it is no longer possible, for the sense of exile has largely evaporated. Nevertheless, *A Certain People* has presented a formidable array of statistics to demonstrate vibrancy and promise, buttressing a sense of optimism as well as singularity. For Silberman's evidence also suggests how resistant American Jewry has been to the classical categories of Zionist thought. Despite the realization of a Jewish state, the largest community in the Diaspora has not been drained of those who have wished to participate in the destiny of the Jewish people. Nearly a century after Herzl envisioned the state of Israel, American Jewry consists mostly of those who wish neither to make *aliyah* nor to disappear. For history tends to frustrate the prescience of even the most acute thinkers; and within the constraints of numbers and of circumstance, the will to survive and to thrive may prove decisive.

Perhaps the reader will permit a concluding unscientific postscript. One of the constants of Jewish history is the fear that surfaces in every generation that it may be the last, the final link in the chain that bound it to its ancestors. Knowledge and piety were supposedly so weakened, the threads of community were so frayed, and the fidelity to the Covenant had so palpably lapsed, that no more Jews could be imagined. Elijah (!) was already complaining to the Lord that "the children of Israel have forsaken Thy covenant . . . and slain Thy prophets with a sword; and I, even I only, am left" (First Kings 19:14). Many a sage thereafter has feared that he was *aharon ha-aharonim*, the last of the last, as Simon Rawidowicz (1896–1957) pointed out in a brilliant essay that was first published in Hebrew in 1948. When Maimonides completed his *Guide to the Perplexed*, he told scholars in southern France that only they and their neighbors were truly devoted to the Torah and the Talmud, that the future depended upon them alone. Even as he worried that his generation of Jews might be terminal, new settlements were springing up across the Rhine; and Maimonides could not have known that for centuries thereafter, not only elsewhere in Europe but also in future cities like New York, scholars would sometimes specialize in philosophical problems that his own writings posed.[37]

Of the seven young Jewish intellectuals who met in Berlin in 1819 to form the *Wissenschaft des Judentums*, devoting their lives to the study of a culture to which they could no longer subscribe, all but one converted to Christianity. Even the lone scholar who resisted, Leopold Zunz, doubted that Judaism would remain viable. Indeed, when late in his life he met Judah Leib Gordon, Zunz asked the Hebrew poet of the *Haskalah* (enlightenment): "And when did you live?" (Not knowing that other gifted poets were only then reaching maturity, Gordon himself wondered in 1880: "For whom do I labor? Who will . . . tell me that I am not the last poet of Zion, and you my last readers?" And yet the first wave of emigrants to Palestine was about to arrive.)[38] One of Zunz's own disciples was the learned Moritz Steinschneider, who was so certain that Judaism would be consigned to the museum of reliquaries in the twentieth century that he once pointed to his bulging bookshelves and announced: "We have only one task left—to give the remains of Judaism a decent burial."[39] The indirect source of this funeral announcement was the scholar whose own studies of mysticism were to enliven and transform the understanding of the Jewish tradition, Gershom Scholem.

Professor Rawidowicz himself suspected that the fear of finality helped Jews to master the crises that beset them, "as if Israel's incessant preparation for the end made this very end . . . impossible." In warding off the inevitable, at least for another generation, this psychological mechanism may have facilitated the triumph over time. His conclusion merits quotation: "A nation dying for thousands of years means a living nation. Our incessant dying means uninterrupted living, rising, standing up, beginning anew. . . . If we are the last," he pleaded, "let us be the last as our fathers and forefathers were. Let us prepare the ground for the last Jews who will come after us, and for the last Jews who will rise after them, and so on until the end of days."[40]

Each of those generations is enjoined to feel a responsibility toward those who came before and to those who will come after, and to study the past as a way of apprehending the purposes of the God of the Covenant. It may be consolation that even the greatest American man of letters in this century, Edmund Wilson, a writer of intimidating erudition and curiosity, once wrote that he had gotten lost in the labyrinth of four millennia of Jewish history and simply could not get out. For those whom it has enriched, and who do not want that story to be interrupted or finished, comfort can also be derived from the words that are inscribed in Hebrew letters on Wilson's tombstone on Cape Cod. Part of the liturgy, the words are recited after reading each of the books of the Pentateuch: *Hazak Hazak Venithazek*. "Be strong, be strong, and let us strengthen one another!"[41]

NOTES

Acknowledgments

1. Quoted in Yosef Hayim Yerushalmi, *Zakhor: Jewish History and Jewish Memory* (Seattle: University of Washington Press, 1982), p. 35.

1. Introduction

1. James Madison to Jacob de la Motta, August 20, 1820, James Madison Papers, Library of Congress, quoted in Allon Schoener, *The American Jewish Album: 1654 to the Present* (New York: Rizzoli, 1983), p. 48.

2. Quoted in Oscar Handlin, *Al Smith and His America* (Boston: Little, Brown, 1958), p. 85.

3. Henry L. Feingold, *A Midrash on American Jewish History* (Albany: State University of New York Press, 1982), pp. x–xiv; Benny Kraut, "Living in Two Civilizations: Hope and Confrontation," *Modern Judaism*, 4 (February 1984), 327–30.

4. Michael E. Parrish, *Felix Frankfurter and His Times: The Reform Years* (New York: Free Press, 1982), p. 276.

5. Ted Morgan, *On Becoming American* (Boston: Houghton Mifflin, 1978), p. 110; Theodore Draper, *Present History: On Nuclear War, Détente, and Other Controversies* (New York: Random House, 1983), p. 424.

6. Steven M. Cohen, "What We Think: Results of This Year's National Survey of American Jews," *Moment*, 10 (January-February, 1985), 36–37.

7. Steven M. Cohen, *American Modernity and Jewish Identity* (New York: Tavistock, 1983), pp. 56–57, 61–63.

8. Gary A. Tobin, "We Are Many, We Are One," Maurice and Marilyn Cohen Center for Modern Jewish Studies, Brandeis University (1987), p. 14.

9. Marshall Sklare, *America's Jews* (New York: Random House, 1971), p. 44.

10. *Ibid.*, p. 60.

11. Stephan Thernstrom, *The Other Bostonians: Poverty and Progress in the American Metropolis, 1880–1970* (Cambridge: Harvard University Press, 1973), pp. 149–53, 173–75.

12. Thomas Sowell, *Ethnic America: A History* (New York: Basic Books, 1981), p. 98.

13. Edward S. Shapiro, "Jews with Money," *Judaism*, 36 (Winter 1987), 7–8, 10.

14. Nietzsche quoted in Walter Kaufmann, *Nietzsche: Philosopher, Psychologist, Antichrist* (Princeton, N.J.: Princeton University Press, 1968), p. 289; Mark Twain, "Concerning the Jews" (1899), in *The Complete Essays of Mark Twain*, edited by Charles Neider (Garden City, N.Y.: Doubleday, 1963), p. 249; Milton Himmelfarb, *The Jews of Modernity* (New York: Basic Books, 1973) p. 96.

15. Sklare, *America's Jews*, p. 58.

16. Charles E. Silberman, *A Certain People: American Jews and Their Lives Today* (New York: Summit, 1985), p. 53n.

17. Everett Carll Ladd, Jr. and Seymour Martin Lipset, *The Divided Academy* (New York: McGraw-Hill, 1975), pp. 150–53, 161.

18. Dan A. Oren, *Joining the Club: A History of Jews and Yale* (New Haven, Conn.: Yale University Press, 1985), pp. 62–63, 88–89; Marcia Graham Synnott, *The Half-Opened Door: Discrimination and Admissions at Harvard, Yale, and Princeton, 1900–1970* (Westport, Conn.: Greenwood Press, 1979), pp. 17, 141.

19. Dvora Ben Shaul, "Big Bangs and Whimpers," *Jerusalem Post*, January 6, 1984, p. 6; Harry Anderson, "Tracking the Faculty Stars," *Newsweek on Campus* (September 1987), 11.

20. Burton Bernstein, *Family Matters: Sam, Jennie, and the Kids* (New York: Summit, 1982), pp. 112, 113, 115, 116–17, 134, 151.

21. Edward Rothstein, "Fanfares for Aaron Copland at 80," *New York Times*, November 9, 1980, section 2, p. 21.

22. Philip Roth, *Portnoy's Complaint* (New York: Bantam, 1970), p. 171.

23. Quoted in Arnold Beichman, *Herman Wouk: The Novelist as Social Historian* (New Brunswick, N.J.: Transaction Books, 1984), p. 58, n. 3.

24. Quoted in Howard Morley Sachar, *The Course of Modern Jewish History* (New York: Dell, 1963), p. 406.

25. Silberman, *A Certain People*, pp. 360–66.

26. "More Come to be Buried than to Live," *Moment*, 12 (September 1987), 13.

27. Quoted in Silberman, *A Certain People*, pp. 183–84.

28. Doron P. Levin, "Jewish Charities Raise Huge Sums in the U.S., But Resistance Grows," *Wall Street Journal*, March 31, 1983, pp. 1, 14; Marc Lee Raphael, *A History of the United Jewish Appeal, 1939–1982*, Brown Judaic Studies 34 (Chico, Cal.: Scholars Press, 1982), pp. 113–15; Silberman, *A Certain People*, pp. 184–99.

29. Quoted in *American Jewish Biographies*, edited by Murray Polner (New York: Lakeville Press, 1982), p. 111.

30. Carol Kur, "The Hadassah Way," *Moment*, 3 (March 1978), 19.

31. Dan V. Segre, "Is Anti-Zionism a New Form of Antisemitism?," in *Antisemitism in the Contemporary World*, edited by Michael Curtis (Boulder, Colo.: Westview, 1986), pp. 145–54; Nathan Glazer, "Anti-Zionism—a Global Phenomenon," in ibid., pp. 155–63; Arthur Hertzberg, "Zionism as Racism: A Semantic Analysis," in ibid., pp. 164–71; Robert S. Wistrich, "The 'Jewish Question': Left-Wing Anti-Zionism in Western Societies," in ibid., pp. 51–57.

32. Feingold, *Midrash on American Jewish History*, p. 226.

33. Guy de Rothschild, *The Whims of Fortune* (New York: Random House, 1985), pp. 314–25; Murray J. Rossant, "Baron Guy de Rothschild: Starting Over in America," *New York Times Magazine*, December 5, 1982, pp. 42–45, 110–11.

34. Himmelfarb, *Jews of Modernity*, pp. 119–24; Cohen, *American Modernity and Jewish Identity*, p. 118.

35. Ibid., pp. 122–23.

36. Arthur A. Goren, *The American Jews* (Cambridge: Harvard University Press, 1982), pp. 106–7; David Singer, "Living with Intermarriage," in *American Jews: A Reader*, edited by Marshall Sklare (New York: Behrman House, 1983), pp. 397–99; Silberman, *A Certain People*, pp. 287–97.

37. Ibid., p. 123.

38. Arthur Hertzberg, *Being Jewish in America* (New York: Schocken, 1979), pp. 82, 85; Silberman, *A Certain People*, p. 166.

39. Letter to the Hebrew Congregation in Newport, 1790, in *A Documentary History of Jews in the United States*, edited by Morris U. Schappes (New York: Schocken, 1971), p. 80.

2.   The Past as Prologue

1. John Keegan, "The Brave," *New York Review of Books*, 28 (April 16, 1981), 17.

2. Quoted in Otto Friedrich, "Of Words That Ravage, Pillage, Spoil," *Time*, 123 (January 9, 1984), 48.

3. Daniel J. Boorstin, *America and the Image of Europe: Reflections on American Thought* (Cleveland: World, 1960), pp. 167–75.

4. Douglas MacArthur, *Reminiscences* (New York: McGraw-Hill, 1964), p.

14; Henry L. Stimson and McGeorge Bundy, *On Active Service in Peace and War* (New York: Harper and Brothers, 1948), p. xii.

5. Boorstin, *America and the Image of Europe*, pp. 175–82.

6. Lionel Kochan, *The Jew and His History* (New York: Schocken, 1977), p. 3; Clement Greenberg, "The Jewishness of Franz Kafka," *Commentary*, 19 (April 1955), 321–22; Hanoch Bartov, "A Sermon at Southampton," *Forum*, 40 (Winter 1980/81), v–vi, 19–20.

7. Hannah Arendt, *Men in Dark Times* (New York: Harcourt, Brace and World, 1968), p. 13; idem., *The Jew as Pariah: Jewish Identity and Politics in the Modern Age*, edited by Ron H. Feldman (New York: Grove Press, 1978), pp. 96–97, 105.

8. Isaiah Berlin, *Personal Impressions* (New York: Viking, 1980), p. 72.

9. Lucy S. Dawidowicz, *The Holocaust and the Historians* (Cambridge, Mass.: Harvard University Press, 1981), pp. 28–29.

10. Israel Shenker, *Coat of Many Colors: Pages from Jewish Life* (Garden City, N.Y.: Doubleday, 1985), pp. 184–88.

11. *Franz Rosenzweig: His Life and Thought*, edited by Nahum N. Glatzer (New York: Schocken, 1961), pp. 292–302; Kochan, *The Jew and His History*, pp. 99–114; Alexander Altmann, "Franz Rosenzweig on History," in *Studies in Religious Philosophy and Mysticism* (Ithaca, N.Y.: Cornell University Press, 1969), pp. 275–76, 281–91.

12. Salo W. Baron, "World Dimensions of Jewish History," in *History and Jewish Historians* (Philadelphia: Jewish Publication Society of America, 1964), pp. 23–42.

13. Hess quoted in Kochan, *The Jew and His History*, pp. 3–4; Isaiah Berlin, "The Life and Opinions of Moses Hess," in *On Intellectuals: Theoretical Studies/ Case Studies*, edited by Philip Rieff (Garden City, N.Y.: Doubleday Anchor, 1970), pp. 137–81.

14. Gershom Scholem, *The Messianic Idea in Judaism and Other Essays in Jewish Spirituality* (New York: Schocken, 1971), p. viii.

15. Yerushalmi, *Zakhor*, pp. 9, 11, 44–45, passim; Leon Wieseltier, "Culture and Collective Memory," *New York Times Book Review*, January 15, 1984, p. 10.

16. Yerushalmi, *Zakhor*, pp. 16–18.

17. Ibid., pp. 20–22, 26, 33, 52, 66–67, 69, 81.

18. Ibid., pp. xiv, 86, 88, 91; Kochan, *The Jew and His History*, pp. 67–68.

19. Yerushalmi, *Zakhor*, pp. xiv, 94–95.

20. Simon Dubnow, *Nationalism and History: Essays on Old and New Judaism*, edited by Koppel S. Pinson (Cleveland: World, 1961), p. 338.

21. Kochan, *The Jew and His History*, pp. 88–98; Robert Seltzer, "From Graetz to Dubnow: The Impact of the East European Milieu on the Writing of Jewish History," in *The Legacy of Jewish Migration: 1881 and Its Impact*, edited by David Berger (New York: Brooklyn College Press, 1983), pp. 49–58.

22. Arendt, *The Jew as Pariah*, pp. 96–105; Harold Bloom, *Kabbalah and*

Criticism (New York: Seabury Press, 1975), pp. 17–18; François Furet, "Gershom Scholem and Jewish History," in *In the Workshop of History*, translated by Jonathan Mandelbaum (Chicago: University of Chicago Press, 1984), pp. 225–29.

23. Cynthia Ozick, "The Mystic Explorer," *New York Times Book Review*, September 21, 1980, p. 33; George Steiner, "Inner Light," *New Yorker*, 49 (October 22, 1973), 152, 174.

24. Ozick, "The Mystic Explorer," p. 1.

25. Richard Kostelanetz, "Gershom Scholem: The Mystics' Medium," *Present Tense*, 4 (Spring 1977), 33.

26. Gershom Scholem, "Toward an Understanding of the Messianic Idea in Judaism," in *The Messianic Idea in Judaism*, pp. 1, 31, 35.

27. Archibald MacLeish, "America was Promises," in *Collected Poems, 1917–1952* (Boston: Houghton Mifflin, 1952), pp. 333–41.

28. William Faulkner, *Requiem for a Nun* (New York: Random House, 1951), p. 92.

29. William James, "Is Radical Empiricism Solipsistic?," in *Essays in Radical Empiricism* (London: Longmans, Green, 1912), p. 238.

30. Quoted in Berlin, "Life and Opinions of Moses Hess," p. 154.

31. Quoted in R. W. B. Lewis, *The American Adam: Innocence, Tragedy and Tradition in the Nineteenth Century* (Chicago: University of Chicago Press, 1955), pp. 23–24.

32. George Santayana, *The Life of Reason, or The Phases of Human Progress* (New York: Scribner's, 1905), I, p. 284.

33. Henry Adams, *The Education of Henry Adams*, edited by Ernest Samuels (Boston: Houghton Mifflin, 1973), p. 3.

34. B. F. Skinner, *Walden Two* (New York: Macmillan, 1962), pp. 115, 235–39.

35. Mark Twain, *Adventures of Huckleberry Finn* (Berkeley: University of California Press, 1985), p. 2; Vladimir Nabokov, *The Annotated Lolita*, edited by Alfred Appel, Jr. (New York: McGraw-Hill, 1970), pp. 150, 274, 299.

36. Keith Sward, *The Legend of Henry Ford* (New York: Atheneum, 1968), pp. 100–5.

37. Quoted in William R. Brown, *Imagemaker: Will Rogers and the American Dream* (Columbia: University of Missouri Press, 1970), p. 38.

38. Thomas Jefferson to James Madison, September 6, 1789, in *The Portable Thomas Jefferson*, edited by Merrill D. Peterson (New York: Viking, 1975), p. 449; "Report of the Commissioners for the University of Virginia," in ibid., pp. 332–39.

39. Diane Ravitch, "Decline and Fall of Teaching History," *New York Times Magazine*, November 17, 1985, p. 117.

40. Raul Hilberg, "Bitburg as Symbol," in *Bitburg in Moral and Political Perspective*, edited by Geoffrey H. Hartman (Bloomington: Indiana University Press, 1986), p. 19.

41. John Milton Cooper, Jr., "Theodore Roosevelt: On Clio's Active Service," *Virginia Quarterly Review*, 62 (Winter 1986), 22–37.

42. Arthur M. Schlesinger, Jr., "John Fitzgerald Kennedy," *Proceedings of the Massachusetts Historical Society*, 75 (1964), 113–14.

43. Garry Wills, *The Kennedy Imprisonment: A Meditation on Power* (Boston: Atlantic-Little, Brown, 1982), pp. 134–39; Arthur M. Schlesinger, Jr., *A Thousand Days: John F. Kennedy in the White House* (New York: Fawcett Crest, 1967), p. 586.

44. Quoted in Lewis, *American Adam*, p. 22.

45. Lincoln Steffens, *The Autobiography of Lincoln Steffens* (New York: Harcourt, Brace, 1931), p. 799.

46. Quoted in Richard H. Pells, *Radical Visions and American Dreams: Culture and Social Thought in the Depression Years* (New York: Harper & Row, 1973), p. 98.

47. Quoted in Solomon Liptzin, *Germany's Stepchildren* (Philadelphia: Jewish Publication Society of America, 1944), p. 81.

48. Quoted in Meryle Secrest, *Being Bernard Berenson: A Biography* (New York: Holt, Rinehart and Winston, 1979), p. 395.

49. Norman Podhoretz, *Making It* (New York: Random House, 1967), p. 123.

50. Saul Bellow, *The Victim* (New York: Vanguard, 1947), p. 145.

51. Carl Bridenbaugh, "The Great Mutation," *American Historical Review*, 68 (January 1963), 322–23.

52. Gertrude Stein, "The Making of Americans," in *Selected Writings of Gertrude Stein*, edited by Carl W. Van Vechten (New York: Vintage, 1972), pp. 73, 264–65.

3. Culture

1. Brooks Atkinson (editor), *The Selected Writings of Ralph Waldo Emerson* (New York: Modern Library, 1950), pp. 45, 62.

2. Quoted in F. O. Matthiessen, *American Renaissance: Art and Expression in the Age of Emerson and Whitman* (New York: Oxford University Press, 1941), p. 526.

3. Robert Clark, "More than Good Friends," *New York Times Higher Education Supplement*, June 14, 1985, p. 15.

4. Evelyn Waugh in *Writers at Work: The Paris Review Interviews*, Third Series, edited by George Plimpton (New York: Viking, 1967), pp. 103, 113.

5. *New York Times Book Review*, March 17, 1985, p. 40.

6. June Sochen, "Fanny Brice and Sophie Tucker: Blending the Particular with the Universal," in *From Hester Street to Hollywood: The Jewish-American Stage and Screen*, edited by Sarah Blacher Cohen (Bloomington: Indiana University Press, 1983), pp. 45–46.

7. Kenneth Aaron Kanter, "The Jews on Tin Pan Alley, 1910–1940," *American Jewish Archives*, 34 (April 1982), 7, 23–24.

8. Ronald Sanders, "The American Popular Song," in *Next Year in Jerusalem: Portraits of the Jew in the Twentieth Century*, edited by Douglas Villiers (New York: Viking, 1976), pp. 197–202, 214; Ronald Sanders, *The Days Grow Short: The Life and Music of Kurt Weill* (New York: Holt, Rinehart and Winston, 1980), pp. 378, 380, 385.

9. Alec Robertson, *Dvorak* (London: J. M. Dent, 1964), p. 70.

10. Milton Mezzrow and Bernard Wolfe, *Really the Blues* (Garden City, N.Y.: Doubleday Anchor, 1972), pp. 11–12, 14–15, 42, 79–80, 96, 176, 177, 181, 186, 198, 257–58, 261, 282, 285, 290.

11. Quoted in Van Vechten (editor), *Selected Writings of Gertrude Stein*, p. 338.

12. Hasia R. Diner, *In the Almost Promised Land: American Jews and Blacks, 1915–1935* (Westport, Conn.: Greenwood Press, 1977), pp. 118–63.

13. Kanter, "The Jews on Tin Pan Alley," 31.

14. Greil Marcus, *Mystery Train: Images of America in Rock 'n' Roll Music* (New York: Dutton, 1976), pp. 179–80; John Lahr, *Automatic Vaudeville: Essays on Star Turns* (London: Methuen, 1984), p. 48–56.

15. Otto Preminger, *Preminger: An Autobiography* (New York: Bantam, 1978), pp. 159–62; Deems Taylor, *Some Enchanted Evenings: The Story of Rodgers and Hammerstein* (New York: Harper and Brothers, 1953), p. 100.

16. John Rockwell, "The Genius of Gershwin Still Inspires Composers," *New York Times*, March 8, 1987, section 2, p. 23.

17. Edward Rothstein, " 'Heav'nly Lan'," *New Republic*, 192 (March 18, 1985), 28.

18. Edward Jablonski, "The Making of 'Porgy and Bess,' " *New York Times Magazine*, October 19, 1980, pp. 88–100; Wilfrid Sheed, *The Good Word and Other Words* (New York: Penguin, 1980), p. 156; Rockwell, "The Genius of Gershwin," pp. 23, 36.

19. Quoted in *American Jewish Biographies*, edited by Murray Polner (New York: Lakeville Press, 1982), p. 73; Edward Rothstein, "Fanfares for Aaron Copland at 80," *New York Times*, November 9, 1980, section 2, pp. 21, 24.

20. Jonathan Lieberson, "The Unimportance of Being Oscar," *New York Review of Books*, 33 (November 20, 1986), 36–37.

21. Joe Goldberg, "André Previn Back in L.A.," *New York Times Magazine*, May 4, 1986, pp. 38, 42, 48.

22. Bernstein, *Family Matters*, p. 141.

23. Michael Walsh, "*West Side Story*, Gentrified," *Time*, 125 (April 1, 1985), 85.

24. William A. Henry III, "More Than Song and Dance," *Time*, 127 (June 16, 1986), 90; Charles Michener, "Words and Music—by Sondheim," *Newsweek*, 81 (April 25, 1973), 54–56, 61, 64; Samuel G. Freedman, "Sondheim's 'Follies' Revisited," *New York Times*, September 1, 1985, section 2, pp. 1–2;

Samuel G. Freedman, "The Words and Music of Stephen Sondheim," *New York Times Magazine*, April 1, 1984, pp. 25, 26.

25. Sanders, *The Days Grow Short*, pp. 6, 389.

26. John Rockwell, "The Enigma of Kurt Weill," *New York Times*, September 13, 1987, pp. E35–36.

27. *New York Times*, February 23, 1986, section 2, 1, 5.

28. Stephen Holden, "Barbra Streisand: 'This is the Music I Love. It is my Roots,' " *New York Times*, November 10, 1985, section 2, pp. 1, 23.

29. Ibid., p. 23.

30. Glenn Gould, "Streisand as Schwarzkopf," in *The Glenn Gould Reader*, edited by Tim Page (New York: Knopf, 1984), pp. 308–12.

31. E. Anthony Rotundo, "Jews and Rock and Roll: A Study in Cultural Contrast," *American Jewish History*, 72 (September 1982), 82–107.

32. Quoted in Anthony Scaduto, *Dylan* (New York: Signet, 1973), pp. 255–56.

33. Aron Hirt-Manheimer, "The Art of Art Spiegelman," *Reform Judaism*, 15 (Spring 1987), 22–23; Ken Tucker, "Cats, Mice and History—The Avant-Garde of the Comic Strip," *New York Times Book Review*, May 26, 1985, p. 3.

34. Harold Rosenberg, *Saul Steinberg* (New York: Knopf, 1978), p. 10; Hilton Kramer, "Getting a Line on Steinberg," *New York Times Magazine*, April 16, 1978, p. 40.

35. Selma G. Lanes, *The Art of Maurice Sendak* (New York: Harry N. Abrams, 1980), pp. 25–26, 104, 185, 235, 253, 269; *New York Times*, November 8, 1987, p. H27; Michael Walsh, "Mastering the Wild Things," *Time*, 126 (October 14, 1985), 108; Maurice Sendak, "Where the Wild Things Began," *New York Times Book Review*, May 17, 1987, p. 48.

36. Barbara Gelb, "Mike Nichols: The Special Risks and Rewards of the Director's Art," *New York Times Magazine*, May 27, 1984, p. 41.

37. Robert Brustein, *Seasons of Discontent: Dramatic Opinions, 1959–1965* (New York: Simon and Schuster, 1965), pp. 170–71.

38. Philip Roth, *The Counterlife* (New York: Penguin, 1988), p. 149; *New York Times Book Review*, December 7, 1986, p. 46.

39. "Under Forty: A Symposium on American Literature and the Younger Generation of American Jews," *Contemporary Jewish Record*, 7 (February 1944), 10, 11, 16, 17.

40. Harold Bloom, "The Masks of the Normative," *Orim*, 1 (Autumn 1985), 10; idem., *Agon: Towards a Theory of Revisionism* (New York: Oxford University Press, 1982), pp. 318–29; Robert Alter, "The Jew Who Didn't Get Away: On the Possibility of an American Jewish Culture," in *The American Jewish Experience*, edited by Jonathan D. Sarna (New York: Holmes and Meier, 1986), pp. 269–81.

41. "A Conversation with Amos Oz," *Reform Judaism*, 15 (Summer 1987), 8; Albert S. Axelrad, *Meditations of a Maverick Rabbi*, edited by Stephen J. Whitfield (Chappaqua, N.Y.: Rossel Books, 1985), pp. 128–35.

42. Abram L. Sachar, *A Host at Last* (Boston: Little, Brown, 1976), pp. 79, 81–83.

43. Shenker, *Coat of Many Colors*, pp. 174–83; Leo W. Schwarz, *Wolfson of Harvard: Portrait of a Scholar* (Philadelphia: Jewish Publication Society of America, 1978), pp. 133, 154–55, 180.

44. Saul Bellow, "I Took Myself as I Was . . . ," *ADL Bulletin*, 33 (December 1976), 3.

4. Humor

1. Concurring opinion in *Jacobellis v. Ohio*, 378 U.S. 197 (1963).

2. Theodor Reik, *Jewish Wit* (New York: Gamut Press, 1962), pp. 86–87.

3. Roth, *Portnoy's Complaint*, p. 299.

4. Albert Goldman, "Laughtermakers," in Villiers (editor), *Next Year in Jerusalem*, p. 229.

5. Avner Ziv, "Psycho-Social Aspects of Jewish Humor in Israel and in the Diaspora," in *Jewish Humor* (Tel Aviv: Papyrus, 1986), pp. 48–49.

6. Henri Bergson, *Laughter: An Essay on the Meaning of the Comic* (New York: Macmillan, 1911), pp. 136, 197.

7. Lawrence Levine, *Black Culture and Black Consciousness: Afro-American Folk Thought from Slavery to Freedom* (New York: Oxford University Press, 1977), p. 306; Alex Haley, *The Autobiography of Malcolm X* (New York: Grove Press, 1966), pp. 192–93.

8. Chaim Bermant, *What's the Joke?: A Study of Jewish Humour Through the Ages* (London: Weidenfeld and Nicolson, 1986), p. 200; Brooks quoted in Goldman, "Laughtermakers," p. 229.

9. William Novak and Moshe Waldoks (editors), *The Big Book of Jewish Humor* (New York: Harper and Row, 1981), p. xx.

10. Emmanuel Le Roy Ladourie, *Carnival in Romans* (New York: George Braziller, 1979), pp. 305–24; Peter Burke, *Popular Culture in Early Modern Europe* (New York: Harper and Row, 1978), pp. 178–204; Scholem, *The Messianic Idea in Judaism*, p. 55; Bermant, *What's the Joke?*, pp. 37–45.

11. William Novak and Moshe Waldoks, "On the Cutting Edge of Jewish Laughter," *Jewish Exponent* Centennial Edition (1987), 186–88.

12. Taylor Stoehr, "Paul Goodman and the New York Jews," *Salmagundi*, No. 66 (Winter-Spring 1985), 53.

13. Irving Howe, *Steady Work: Essays in the Politics of Democratic Radicalism, 1953–1966* (New York: Harcourt, Brace and World, 1966), p. iv.

14. Isaac Rosenfeld, *Alpha and Omega* (New York: Viking, 1966), pp. 263–79; Paul Gray, "The 3,000-Year-Old Man," *Time*, 124 (September 24, 1984), 74; Enoch Brater, "Ethnics and Ethnicity in the Plays of Arthur Miller," in Cohen (editor), *From Hester Street to Hollywood*, pp. 133–34.

15. Quoted in Lothar Kahn, "Heine's Jewish Writer Friends: Dilemmas of

a Generation, 1817–33," in *The Jewish Response to German Culture: From the Enlightenment to the Second World War*, edited by Jehuda Reinharz and Walter Schatzberg (Hanover, N.H.: University Press of New England, 1986), p. 133.

16. Novak and Waldoks, *Big Book of Jewish Humor*, p. 96; Joseph Boskin, "Beyond *Kvetching* and *Jiving:* The Thrust of Jewish and Black Folkhumor," in *Jewish Wry: Essays on Jewish Humor*, edited by Sarah Blacher Cohen (Bloomington: Indiana University Press, 1987), pp. 60, 63–65.

17. Quoted in Albert Goldman, *Freakshow* (New York: Atheneum, 1971), p. 248.

18. Roth, *Portnoy's Complaint*, pp. 161–62.

19. Bruno Bettelheim, "Portnoy Psychoanalyzed," *Midstream*, 15 (June–July, 1969), 3–10.

20. John Cohen (editor), *The Essential Lenny Bruce* (New York: Ballantine, 1967), pp, 40–41.

21. Mark L. Levine, George C. McNamee, and Daniel Greenberg (editors), *The Tales of Hoffman* (New York: Bantam, 1970), p. 129.

22. Howard Teichmann, *George S. Kaufman: An Intimate Portrait* (New York: Dell, 1973), pp. 279–81.

23. Novak and Waldoks, *Big Book of Jewish Humor*, p. 95; Silberman, *A Certain People*, pp. 69–70.

24. "Analyzing Jewish Comics," *Time*, 112 (October 2, 1978), 76.

25. Max Weber, *Ancient Judaism*, translated by Hans H. Gerth and Don Martindale (Glencoe, Ill.: Free Press, 1952), pp. 194–201, 205–6, 218.

26. Quoted in Gershom Scholem, *Sabbatai Sevi: The Mystical Messiah, 1616–1676* (Princeton, N.J.: Princeton University Press, 1973), pp. 12–13.

27. Abodah Zarah 3b (Babylonian Talmud).

28. Leo Rosten, *The Joys of Yiddish* (New York: Pocket Books, 1970), p. 235.

29. Novak and Waldoks, *Big Book of Jewish Humor*, p. 92; Mason quoted in Stefan Kanfer, "Rabbi's Son Makes Good," *Time*, 130 (November 23, 1987), 99.

30. Roth, *Portnoy's Complaint*, p. 228.

31. Mark Shechner, "Woody Allen: The Failure of the Therapeutic," in Cohen (editor), *Hester Street to Hollywood*, p. 236.

32. Quoted in Joanne Kaufman, "Back in the Big Time: Comedian Jackie Mason," *Wall Street Journal*, February 17, 1987, 32; Robert Brustein, "The Hit of the Building," *New Republic*, 197 (October 19, 1987), 27–30.

33. Review of Irving Howe, *World of Our Fathers*, in *New Boston Review*, 3 (January 1977), 7.

34. S. J. Perelman, *Don't Tread on Me: The Selected Letters of S. J. Perelman*, edited by Prudence Crowther (New York: Viking, 1987), pp. xii, 163–64; idem., *The Most of S. J. Perelman* (New York: Simon and Schuster, 1958), pp. 68–70.

35. Quoted in "Blazing Brooks," *Time*, 105 (January 13, 1975), 56.

36. Richard J. Anobile (editor), *Woody Allen's Play It Again, Sam* (New York: Grosset and Dunlap), p. 89.

37. Woody Allen, *Four Films of Woody Allen* (New York: Random House, 1982), pp. 267–68.

38. Caryn James, "Auteur! Auteur!: The Creative Mind of Woody Allen," *New York Times Magazine*, January 19, 1986, p. 22.

39. John Lahr, *Notes on a Cowardly Lion* (New York: Knopf, 1969), pp. 253–82; Martin Esslin, *The Theatre of the Absurd* (Garden City, N.Y.: Doubleday Anchor, 1961), pp. 10, 236–37.

40. Quoted in Richard Hofstadter, *Anti-intellectualism in American Life* (New York: Knopf, 1970), pp. 160n–61n.

41. Ted Sennett, *Your Show of Shows* (New York: Collier, 1977), pp. 47–55.

42. Kenneth Tynan, *Show People: Profiles in Entertainment* (New York: Simon and Schuster, 1979), pp. 97–99.

43. Philip Roth, *The Great American Novel* (New York: Holt, Rinehart and Winston, 1973), p. 27.

44. Quoted in Ben H. Bagdikian, *The Media Monopoly* (Boston: Beacon, 1983), p. 114.

45. Karl Kraus, *Half-Truths and One-and-a-Half-Truths: Selected Aphorisms*, edited and translated by Harry Zohn (Montreal: Engendra Press, 1976), p. 45.

46. Sy Kleinman, "Jewish Humor is No Laughing Matter," in *The 1986 Jewish Directory and Almanac*, edited by Ivan L. Tillem (New York: Pacific Press, 1985), p. 436.

5. Liberalism

1. James Joyce, *Ulysses* (New York: Modern Library, 1961), pp. 331–33.

2. Alan M. Fisher, "Realignment of the Jewish Vote?," *Political Science Quarterly*, 94 (Spring 1979), 106.

3. Quoted in Brustein, "The Hit of the Building," 29.

4. Ben Halpern, *Jews and Blacks: The Classic American Minorities* (New York: Herder and Herder, 1971), pp. 75–84.

5. Quoted in "Voices," *Life*, 7 (January 1984), 178.

6. Sklare, *America's Jews*, pp. 114–17.

7. Michael Walzer, "Is Liberalism (Still) Good for the Jews?," *Moment*, 11 (March 1986), 14–15; idem., *Exodus and Revolution* (New York: Basic Books, 1985), pp. 6, 149.

8. Maurras quoted in Michael Sutton, *Nationalism, Positivism and Catholicism: The Politics of Charles Maurras and French Catholics, 1890–1914* (Cambridge, England: Cambridge University Press, 1982), p. 56; Brandeis quoted in Allon Gal, *Brandeis of Boston* (Cambridge, Mass.: Harvard University Press, 1980), p. 206.

9. Allen, *Four Films of Woody Allen*, p. 265.

10. Feingold, *Midrash on American History*, pp. 203–4.

11. Quoted in H. R. Trevor-Roper, "Master of the New Learning," *Times Literary Supplement*, February 10, 1984, p. 127.

12. Richard Valeriani, *Travels with Henry* (Boston: Houghton Mifflin, 1979), pp. 196–97.

13. Quoted in Herbert Block, *Herblock's State of the Union* (New York: Viking, 1974), p. 153.

14. *New York Times*, November 4, 1928, p. 28; Stephen S. Wise to Henry I. Moskowitz, October 19, 1928, in *Stephen S. Wise: Servant of the People: Selected Letters*, edited by Carl Hermann Voss (Philadelphia: Jewish Publication Society of America, 1970), p. 160; Melvin I. Urofsky, *A Voice That Spoke for Justice: The Life and Times of Stephen S. Wise* (Albany: State University of New York Press, 1982), p. 240.

15. David Singer, "American Jews as Voters: The 1986 Elections," American Jewish Committee (December 1986), p. 4.

16. Milton Himmelfarb, "Are Jews Becoming Republicans?," *Commentary*, 72 (August 1981), 27.

17. Quoted in Leonard Dinnerstein, *Uneasy at Home: Antisemitism and the American Jewish Experience* (New York: Columbia University Press, 1987), pp. 64–65.

18. Leonard Dinnerstein, "Jews and the New Deal," *American Jewish History*, 72 (June 1983), 474.

19. Singer, "American Jews as Voters: The 1986 Elections," p. 3.

20. Robert H. Abzug, *Inside the Vicious Heart: Americans and the Liberation of Nazi Concentration Camps* (New York: Oxford University Press, 1985), pp. 27–30.

21. Himmelfarb, *Jews of Modernity*, pp. 66, 91.

22. Fisher, "Realignment of the Jewish Vote?," 106, 112.

23. Ibid., 109.

24. Morton Kondracke, "Scaring Up Votes," *New Republic*, 191 (October 1, 1984), 12; Himmelfarb, "Are Jews Becoming Republicans?," 27.

25. Quoted in Justin Kaplan, *Mr. Clemens and Mark Twain: A Biography* (New York: Simon and Schuster, 1966), pp. 363–64.

26. David Harris, "Understanding Mondale," *New York Times Magazine*, June 19, 1983, p. 29.

27. Cohen, "What We Think," *Moment*, 36–37.

28. Quoted in Kanfer, "Rabbi's Son Makes Good," 99.

29. Kondracke, "Scaring Up Votes," 14–15.

30. Elliott Abrams, Letter to the Editor, *New Republic*, 191 (December 31, 1984), 6; Nathan Glazer in symposium on "Jews and American Politics—1984 . . . and After," *This World*, No. 10 (Winter 1985), 18; Seymour Martin Lipset, "Jews Are Still Liberals and Proud of It," *Washington Post*, December 30, 1984, p. C2.

31. Michael Kinsley, "Still Chosen," in *Curse of the Giant Muffins and Other Washington Maladies* (New York: Summit, 1987), p. 80; Arthur Hertzberg,

"Reagan and the Jews," *New York Review of Books*, 32 (January 31, 1985), 11–14.

32. Cohen, "What We Think," *Moment*, 35.

33. Alan Fisher, "Continuity and Erosion of Jewish Liberalism," *American Jewish Historical Quarterly*, 66 (December 1976), 348; Lipset, "Jews Are Still Liberals and Proud of It," *Washington Post*, p. C1.

34. Edward S. Shapiro, "Jews and American Politics," *Midstream*, 31 (March 1985), 12.

35. Singer, "American Jews as Voters," pp. 4–7.

36. Himmelfarb, "Are Jews Becoming Republican?," 28.

37. Quoted in Paul Slansky, "It's All Over Now," *Soho News*, November 5, 1980, p. 6.

38. Finley Peter Dunne, *Mr. Dooley on Ivrything and Ivrybody*, edited by Robert Hutchinson (New York: Dover, 1963), p. 153.

39. *Olmstead v. United States*, 277 U.S. 438, 469, 471 (1928).

40. *United States v. Macintosh*, 283 U.S. 605, 625 (1931).

41. Quoted in Jack W. Germond and Jules Witcover, *Wake Us When It's Over: Presidential Politics of 1984* (New York: Macmillan, 1985), pp. 423–25.

42. *New York Times*, November 23, 1980, p. 29, December 14, 1980, p. 32, and April 22, 1981, p. A19.

43. Quoted in Joyce Purnick, "Moral Majority Establishes Beachhead in New York," *New York Times*, February 5, 1981, p. B4.

44. Jonathan D. Sarna, "Jews, the Moral Majority, and American Tradition," *Journal of Reform Judaism*, 29 (Spring 1982), 1–8; Lipset, "Jews Are Still Liberals and Proud of It," *Washington Post*, p. C2; William Schneider, "The Jewish Vote in 1984: Elements in a Controversy," *Public Opinion*, 7 (December-January, 1985), 19–20.

45. Jefferson to Danbury Baptist Association, January 1, 1802, in Peterson (editor), *Portable Thomas Jefferson*, pp. 303–4; Leonard W. Levy, *The Establishment Clause: Religion and the First Amendment* (New York: Macmillan, 1986), pp. 181–84.

46. David Biale, *Power and Powerlessness in Jewish History* (New York: Schocken, 1986), pp. 184–91.

47. Quoted in Lewis Browne, *That Man Heine: A Biography* (New York: Literary Guild, 1927), p. 126.

48. Nathan Perlmutter and Ruth Ann Perlmutter, *The Real Anti-Semitism in America* (New York: Arbor House, 1982), pp. 166, 175.

49. Irving Howe, "A Time for Compassion and Commitment," in idem. et al., *American Jews and Liberalism* (New York: Foundation for the Study of Independent Social Ideas, 1986), p. 12.

50. Kinsley, *Curse of the Giant Muffins*, pp. 78–82.

6. Radicalism

1. Henry Kissinger, *Years of Upheaval* (Boston: Little, Brown, 1982), pp. 661, 975.

2. Peter Grose, *Israel in the Mind of America* (New York: Knopf, 1983), pp. 72, 82, 118.

3. *New York Times*, April 4, 1974, p. 7; April 5, 1974, p. 18; April 6, 1974, p. 13; April 7, 1974, IV, p. 3; April 10, 1974, p. 20.

4. Lewis S. Feuer, *Spinoza and the Rise of Liberalism* (Boston: Beacon, 1958), p. 48.

5. Michael Walzer, *The Revolution of the Saints: A Study in the Origins of Radical Politics* (New York: Atheneum, 1968), p. 47.

6. Steven E. Aschheim, *Brothers and Strangers: The East European Jew in German and German Jewish Consciousness, 1800–1923* (Madison: University of Wisconsin Press, 1982), p. 33.

7. Daniel Bell, *Marxian Socialism in the United States* (Princeton, N. J.: Princeton University Press, 1967), p. 98; John Higham, *Send These to Me: Jews and Other Immigrants in Urban America* (New York: Atheneum, 1975), p. 89.

8. John Laslett, *Labor and the Left: A Study of Socialist and Radical Influences in the American Labor Movement. 1881–1924* (New York: Basic Books, 1970), pp. 99–100, 117, 119, 120–23, 129, 133–35.

9. Daniel Aaron, *Writers on the Left* (New York: Avon, 1965), pp. 213–15, 343, 376, 437, 464; Alan M. Wald, *The New York Intellectuals: The Rise and Decline of the Anti-Stalinist Left from the 1930s to the 1980s* (Chapel Hill: University of North Carolina Press, 1987), pp. 3–4; Earl Latham, *The Communist Controversy in Washington: From the New Deal to McCarthy* (New York: Atheneum, 1969), p. 107.

10. Testimony of Daniel J. Boorstin in *Thirty Years of Treason*, edited by Eric F. Bentley (New York: Viking, 1971), pp. 602, 604, 605, 608.

11. Kwame Nkrumah, *Autobiography* (London: Panaf, 1973), pp. 36–37; Peter Goldman, *The Death and Life of Malcolm X* (New York: Harper and Row, 1974), pp. 175n–76n, 254–55.

12. Robert S. Wistrich, *Revolutionary Jews from Marx to Trotsky* (London: Harrap, 1976), p. 187.

13. Leonard B. Rosenberg, "The 'Failure' of the Socialist Party of America," *Review of Politics,* 31 (July 1969), 329–52.

14. Aileen S. Kraditor, *The Radical Persuasion, 1890–1917: Aspects of the Intellectual History and the Historiography of Three American Radical Organizations* (Baton Rouge: Louisiana State University Press, 1981), pp. 217–18.

15. Samuel Gompers, *Seventy Years of Life and Labor,* revised and edited by Philip Taft and John A. Sessions (New York: E. P. Dutton, 1957), pp. 74–81, 213–15; Morton Keller, *Affairs of State* (Cambridge, Mass.: Harvard University Press, 1977), p. 397.

16. Higham, *Send These to Me,* p. 98.

17. *New York Times*, June 2, 1969, p. 45; Joseph Freeman, *An American Testament: A Narrative of Rebels and Romantics* (New York: Holt, Rinehart, 1936), pp. 58–60.

18. Victor S. Navasky, *Kennedy Justice* (New York: Atheneum, 1971), pp.

141–50; Eric Breindel, "King's Communist Associates," *New Republic*, 190 (January 30, 1984), 14.

19. Jacques E. Levy, *Cesar Chavez; Autobiography of La Causa* (New York: W. W. Norton, 1975), pp. 100, 117, 125–26, 146–47; Joan Baez, *Daybreak* (New York: Dial, 1968), pp. 56–67; Jeremy Larner, "The Negro in the South: 'Half a Loaf Is Ashes,' " *New Leader*, 43 (September 12, 1960), 11.

20. Jack Newfield, *A Prophetic Minority* (New York: Signet, 1967), pp. 78, 79; Schlesinger, *A Thousand Days*, pp. 710–11.

21. Mark I. Pinsky, "Red, White and Jew," *Moment*, 5 (November 1980), 19; William Bradford Huie, *Three Lives for Mississippi* (New York: WCC Books, 1965), pp. 106, 135–36, 157, 171, 174.

22. Stanley Rothman and S. Robert Lichter, *Roots of Radicalism: Jews, Christians, and the New Left* (New York: Oxford University Press, 1982), pp. 81–82.

23. Nora Sayre, *Sixties Going on Seventies* (New York: Arbor House, 1973), pp. 78–92.

24. Roger L. Simon, *The Big Fix* (New York: Pocket Books, 1974), p. 19; "From Jews to Jaws: A Chat with Richard Dreyfuss," *Davka*, 5 (Fall 1975), 34–35; Alan Lelchuk, *American Mischief* (New York: Farrar, Straus and Giroux, 1973), pp. 3, 280–281, 286–93.

25. Biale, *Power and Powerlessness in Jewish History*, pp. 196–97.

26. Albert Einstein, *Ideas and Opinions* (New York: Crown, 1954), pp. 185–87.

27. Charles Liebman, *The Ambivalent American Jew* (Philadelphia: Jewish Publication Society of America, 1973), pp. 143–44; Arthur Liebman, *Jews and the Left* (New York: John Wiley, 1979), pp. 7–11.

28. Scholem, *Sabbatai Sevi*, p. xi; David Biale, *Gershom Scholem: Kabbalah and Counter-History* (Cambridge, Mass.: Harvard University Press, 1979), pp. 111–13.

29. Marc Karson, "Catholic Anti-Socialism," in *Failure of a Dream?: Essays in the History of American Socialism*, edited by John H. M. Laslett and Seymour Martin Lipset (Garden City, N. Y.: Doubleday, 1974), pp. 164–66, 179–80; Laslett, *Labor and the Left*, p. 136, n. 5.

30. Werner Cohn, "The Politics of American Jews," in *The Jews: Social Patterns of an American Group*, edited by Marshall Sklare (New York: Free Press, 1958), pp. 614–26; W. D. Rubinstein, *The Left, the Right and the Jews* (New York: Universe, 1982), pp. 9, 227, 230; Nathan Glazer, *Remembering the Answers: Essays on the American Student Revolt* (New York: Basic Books, 1970), p. 243.

31. Quoted in J. L. Talmon, *Israel Among the Nations* (New York: Macmillan, 1971), pp. 24–25.

32. "Interview: Saul Alinsky," *Playboy*, 19 (March 1972), 64.

33. Glazer, *Remembering the Answers*, pp. 232, 236; Mordecai Richler, *The Apprenticeship of Duddy Kravitz* (New York: Ballantine, 1974), pp. 49–50.

34. Dennis McNally, *Desolate Angel: Jack Kerouac, the Beat Generation and America* (New York: Random House, 1979), pp. 156, 185–86, 221, 280, 293–94; Allen Ginsberg, *Kaddish and Other Poems, 1958–1960* (San Francisco: City Lights, 1961), p. 31; Morgan, *On Becoming American*, p. 224.

35. Robert and Michael Meeropol, *We Are Your Sons: The Legacy of Ethel and Julius Rosenberg* (Boston: Houghton Mifflin, 1975), pp. 276–81, 285–93, 296–335; *New York Times*, May 19, 1968, p. 1.

36. Lewis S. Feuer, *Marx and the Intellectuals: A Set of Post-Ideological Essays* (Garden City, N. Y.: Doubleday Anchor, 1969), p. 34.

37. Howe, *World of Our Fathers*, p. 352.

38. Clifford Odets, *Six Plays* (New York: Modern Library, 1939), p. 55.

39. Kenneth Keniston, *Youth and Dissent: The Rise of a New Opposition* (New York: Harcourt, Brace, Jovanovich, 1971), pp. 273–77.

40. Lewis S. Feuer, *The Conflict of Generations: The Character and Significance of Student Movements* (New York: Basic Books, 1969), pp. 154–61, 423–31.

41. Abbie Hoffman, *Soon To Be a Major Motion Picture* (New York: G. P. Putnam's Sons), pp. 3–4, 15.

42. See Jack Nusan Porter and Peter Dreier (editors), *Jewish Radicalism: A Selected Anthology* (New York: Grove Press, 1973); Alan Mintz and James A. Sleeper (editors), *The New Jews* (New York: Vintage, 1971); Arthur Waskow, *The Bush Is Burning!: Radical Judaism Faces the Pharoahs of the Modern Superstate* (New York: Macmillan, 1971); and *Response* Magazine (1967–).

43. Lawrence H. Fuchs, *The Political Behavior of American Jews* (Glencoe, Ill.: Free Press, 1956), pp. 178–80, 185, 189; Glazer, *Remembering the Answers*, pp. 236–38; Talcott Parsons, "The Sociology of Anti-Semitism," in *Jews in a Gentile World: The Problem of Anti-Semitism*, edited by Isacque Graeber and S. H. Britt (New York: Macmillan, 1942), p. 106.

44. Nikos Kazantzakis, *Journeying: Travels in Italy, Egypt, Sinai, Jerusalem and Cyprus* (Boston: Little, Brown, 1975), pp. 179–80.

45. Howe, *World of Our Fathers*, p. 319; T. S. Eliot, *After Strange Gods: A Primer of Modern Heresy* (New York: Harcourt, Brace, 1934), p. 20.

46. Laslett, *Labor and the Left*, pp. 99–100; Moses Rischin, *The Promised City: New York's Jews, 1870–1914* (New York: Harper and Row, 1970), pp. 175–76; Chomsky quoted in Polner (editor), *American Jewish Biographies*, p. 64.

47. Quoted in Edwin R. Bayley, *Joe McCarthy and the Press* (New York: Pantheon, 1982), p. 3.

48. Glazer, *Remembering the Answers*, pp. 236–38; Leonard Dinnerstein and Gene Koppel, *Nathan Glazer: A Different Kind of Liberal* (Tucson: University of Arizona, 1973), pp. 53–54.

49. Joseph Conrad, *Under Western Eyes* (Garden City, N. Y.: Doubleday, Page, 1924), p. 353.

7. Journalism

1. Norman Cohn, *Warrant for Genocide: The Myth of the Jewish World Conspiracy and the Protocols of the Elders of Zion* (New York: Harper and Row, 1967), p. 273.

2. Treitschke quoted in Aschheim, *Brothers and Strangers*, pp. 42–43, 68; Burckhardt quoted in George L. Mosse, *Germans and Jews: The Right, the Left, and the Search for a "Third Force" in Pre-Nazi Germany* (New York: H. Fertig, 1970), p. 58.

3. Adolf Hitler, *Mein Kampf* (Boston: Houghton Mifflin, 1943), pp. vii, 57–59, 61.

4. Hay quoted in Higham, *Send These to Me*, p. 183.

5. Cohn, *Warrant for Genocide*, p. 159; Morton Rosenstock, *Louis Marshall: Defender of Jewish Rights* (Detroit: Wayne State University Press, 1965), pp. 128–29, 130; Leo P. Ribuffo, "Henry Ford and *The International Jew*," *American Jewish History*, 69 (June 1980), 444–46, 453, 461, 469–70.

6. H. L. Mencken, *Prejudices: A Selection*, edited by James T. Farrell (New York: Vintage, 1958), pp. 107–8.

7. Conor Cruise O'Brien, "Israel in Embryo," *New York Review of Books*, 21 (March 15, 1984), 36.

8. Selig Adler, *The Isolationist Impulse: Its Twentieth Century Reaction* (New York: Collier, 1961), p. 279.

9. Stephen D. Isaacs, *Jews and American Politics* (Garden City, N. Y.: Doubleday, 1974), pp. 50–52; Stephen Birmingham, "Does a Zionist Conspiracy Control the Media?", *More*, 6 (July–August 1976), 17.

10. "Jackson and the Jews," *New Republic*, 190 (March 19, 1984), 9.

11. Jonathan D. Sarna, *Jacksonian Jew: The Two Worlds of Mordecai Noah* (New York: Holmes and Meier, 1981), p. 164, n. 16.

12. Stephen J. Whitfield, "From Publick Occurrences to Pseudo-Events: Journalists and Their Critics," *American Jewish History*, 72 (September 1982), 52–81, reprinted in idem., *Voices of Jacob, Hands of Esau: Jews in American Life and Thought* (Hamden, Conn.: Archon, 1984), pp. 180–207.

13. [Kalman Seigel,] "Journalism," *Encyclopedia Judaica* (Jerusalem: Macmillan, 1971), X, p. 307; Isaacs, *Jews and American Politics*, p. 49.

14. Bagdikian, *The Media Monopoly*, p. xv; John W. C. Johnstone, Edward J. Slawski and William W. Bowman, *The News People: A Sociological Portrait of American Journalists and Their Work* (Urbana: University of Illinois Press, 1976), pp. ix, 9, 26, 198, 225.

15. Rothman and Lichter, *Roots of Radicalism*, p. 97; Marcus Arkin, *Aspects of Jewish Economic History* (Philadelphia: Jewish Publication Society of America, 1975), pp. 212–13.

16. Donald L. Niewyk, *The Jews in Weimar Germany* (Baton Rouge: Louisiana State University Press, 1980), p. 15; Amos Elon, *Herzl* (New York: Holt, Rinehart and Winston, 1975), p. 99.

17. Stephen Hess, *The Washington Reporters* (Washington, D. C.: Brookings Institution Press, 1981), p. 90.

18. Rothman and Lichter, *Roots of Radicalism*, p. 97; Edward J. Epstein, *News from Nowhere: Television and the News* (New York: Vintage, 1973), pp. 222–23.

19. Carl Bernstein and Bob Woodward, *All the President's Men* (New York: Simon and Schuster, 1974), p. 51.

20. "The Kingdom and the Cabbage," *Time*, 110 (August 15, 1977), 73–74, 80.

21. Introduction to *The Essential Lippmann: A Political Philosophy for Liberal Democracy*, edited by Clinton Rossiter and James Lare (New York, 1965), p. xi; William L. Rivers, *The Opinion-makers* (Boston: Beacon, 1965), pp. 59, 60; Ronald Steel, *Walter Lippmann and the American Century* (New York: Random House, 1980), pp. 462–63, 526–27.

22. E. J. Kahn, Jr., *The World of Swope* (New York: Simon and Schuster, 1965), pp. 33, 133n, 182–84, 240–41, 260–63; Eric F. Goldman, *The Crucial Decade—and After: America, 1945–1960* (New York: Vintage, 1960), p. 60.

23. Kahn, *The World of Swope*, pp. 7, 16, 26, 30–31, 41, 55n, 226–28, 360; Rosemarian V. Staudacher, "Herbert Bayard Swope," in *American Newspaper Journalists, 1900–1925*, edited by Perry J. Ashley (Detroit: Gale, 1984), pp. 280–90.

24. Ben Hecht, *A Child of the Century* (New York: Signet, 1955), pp. 108, 112–13, 180–81, 364–65; Doug Fetherling, *The Five Lives of Ben Hecht* (Toronto: Lester and Orpen, 1977), pp. 18–41, 71–86.

25. Tynan, *Show People*, p. 116; Anthony Heilbut, *Exiled in Paradise: German Refugee Artists and Intellectuals in America from the 1930's to the Present* (New York: Viking, 1983), p. 254; Maurice Zolotow, *Billy Wilder in Hollywood* (New York: G. P Putnam's Sons, 1977), p. 273.

26. *Encyclopedia Judaica*, X, pp. 303–4; Ruppin quoted in Raphael Patai, *The Jewish Mind* (New York: Scribner's, 1977), pp. 377–79.

27. A. J. Liebling, *The Wayward Pressman* (Garden City, N. Y.: Doubleday, 1947), pp. 103–4.

28. W. A. Swanberg, *Pulitzer* (New York: Scribner's, 1967), pp. 8, 38–39, 42, 136, 377; Michael Schudson, *Discovering the News: A Social History of American Newspapers* (New York: Basic Books, 1978), pp. 95–105.

29. Harrison E. Salisbury, *Without Fear or Favor: The New York Times and Its Times* (New York: Times Books, 1980), pp. 28–30; Gay Talese, *The Kingdom and the Power* (Cleveland: World, 1969), pp. 59, 91–94, 168–69; Birmingham, "Zionist Conspiracy," 14, 15.

30. Salisbury, *Without Fear or Favor*, pp. 28–29, 401; Isaacs, *Jews and American Politics*, pp. 47–48.

31. Talese, *The Kingdom and the Power*, pp. 59, 60, 91–93, 109–16, 168; Salisbury, *Without Fear or Favor*, p. 403; Birmingham, "Zionist Conspiracy," 15.

32. Richard H. Meeker, *Newspaperman: S. I. Newhouse and the Business of News* (New Haven, Conn.: Ticknor and Fields, 1983), pp. 2–3, 23, 158, 165, 166; *Time*, 114 (September 10, 1979), 68.

33. John E. Cooney, *The Annenbergs* (New York: Simon and Schuster, 1982), pp. 56, 66–67, 126, 160–61, 184–86, 380; A. James Reichley, "Moe's

Boy Walter at the Court of St. James," *Fortune*, 81 (June 1970), 88, 90–93, 134, 136, 139.

34. Dorothy Schiff quoted in Jeffrey Potter, *Men. Money and Magic: The Story of Dorothy Schiff* (New York: Signet, 1977), p. 123; Jack Newfield, *Bread and Roses Too: Reporting About America* (New York: E. P. Dutton, 1971), pp. 237–44; Nora Ephron, *Scribble Scribble: Notes on the Media* (New York: Bantam, 1979), pp. 1–9.

35. Isaacs, *Jews and American Politics*, pp. 43–44.

36. Ibid., p. 45.

37. Elon, *Herzl*, pp. 114–17.

38. David McLellan, *Karl Marx: His Life and Thought* (New York: Harper and Row, 1973), pp. 285–89; Feuer, *Marx and the Intellectuals*, p. 38.

39. Walter Lippmann, "Public Opinion and the American Jew," *American Hebrew*, 110 (April 14, 1922), 575; Steel, *Walter Lippmann*, pp. 188–95.

40. Anthony Lewis, "The Mysteries of Mr. Lippmann," *New York Review of Books*, 27 (October 9, 1980), 5; Steel, *Walter Lippmann*, pp. 195–96, 330–33, 373–76, 446; David Halberstam, *The Powers That Be* (New York: Knopf, 1979), p. 370; Walter Lippmann, *The Stakes of Diplomacy* (New York: Henry Holt, 1915), pp. 62–63; D. Steven Blum, *Walter Lippmann: Cosmopolitanism in the Century of Total War* (Ithaca, N. Y.: Cornell University Press, 1984), pp. 36–39, 43–44.

41. Raymond Sokolov, *Wayward Reporter: The Life of A. J. Liebling* (New York: Harper and Row, 1980), pp. 1, 9, 14, 21, 25, 30, 42, 98–99, 135, 151–52, 232, 262–63, 305, 310.

42. Sarna, *Jacksonian Jew*, p. 152.

43. Hecht, *Child of the Century*, pp. 84, 482–586; Fetherling, *Five Lives of Ben Hecht*, pp. 119–39; Kahn, *World of Swope*, pp. 433–39.

44. Robert Leiter, "Renaissance Man," *Present Tense*, 11 (Winter 1984), 18–23; William A. Henry III, "Breaking the Liberal Pattern," *Time*, 124 (October 1, 1984), 78.

45. Fred W. Friendly, *The Good Guys, the Bad Guys and the First Amendment* (New York: Random House, 1976), p. 34; Donald Paneth, *The Encyclopedia of American Journalism* (New York: Facts on File, 1983), p. 511.

46. Edwin Emery and Michael Emery, *The Press and America: An Interpretative History of the Mass Media*, 4th ed. (Englewood Cliffs, N. J.: Prentice-Hall, 1978), pp. 312, 314.

47. Victor S. Navasky, "Safire Appraised," *Esquire*, 97 (January 1982), 44–50; Jordan A. Schwarz, *The Speculator: Bernard M. Baruch in Washington, 1917–1965* (Chapel Hill: University of North Carolina Press, 1981), pp. 201–6.

48. Sarna, *Jacksonian Jew*, pp. 5–6.

49. Graham Storey, *Reuters: The Story of a Century of News-Gathering* (Westport, Conn.: Greenwood Press, 1969), pp. 3–31, 87; *Encyclopedia Judaica*, XIV, pp. 111–12.

50. *Encyclopedia Judaica*, IV, pp. 1134–35; Ernst Kahn, "The Frankfurter Zeitung," *Leo Baeck Yearbook* (London: Secker and Warburg, 1957), II, p. 229.

51. *The Times* (London), *The History of The Times: The Tradition Established, 1841–1884* (London: Macmillan, 1939), pp. 294–96; *Encyclopedia Judaica*, X, pp. 1489–90.

52. Sokolov, *Wayward Reporter*, p. 320.

53. Halberstam, *Powers That Be*, pp. 549–51; Nathan Glazer, "The Immigrant Groups and American Culture," *Yale Review*, 48 (Spring 1959), 395–97.

54. Letter to Edward Carrington, January 16, 1787, in Peterson (editor), *Portable Thomas Jefferson*, p. 415.

55. Paneth, *Encyclopedia of American Journalism*, p. 288.

56. Pauline Kael, "Raising Kane," in Kael, Herman J. Mankiewicz and Orson Welles, *The Citizen Kane Book* (Boston: Atlantic-Little, Brown, 1971), pp. 29, 57; Schlesinger, *A Thousand Days*, p. 928.

8. Movies

1. Bill Davidson, "Ross Hunter: The Last Dream Merchant," *Show*, 2 (August 1962), 74.

2. Ibid., 75.

3. Robert Warshow, *The Immediate Experience: Movies, Comics, Theatre, and Other Aspects of Popular Culture* (Garden City, N. Y.: Doubleday Anchor, 1964), p. 22.

4. Silberman *A Certain People*, p. 150; Leo P. Ribuffo, *The Old Christian Right: The Protestant Far Right from the Great Depression to the Cold War* (Philadelphia: Temple University Press, 1983), pp. 43–63; Adler, *The Isolationist Impulse*, pp. 277–80.

5. Simon Karlinsky (editor), *The Wilson-Nabokov Letters, 1940–1971* (New York: Harper and Row, 1979), p. 270.

6. Lester D. Friedman, *Hollywood's Image of the Jew* (New York: Frederick Ungar, 1982), pp. 24–26, 31; Patricia Erens, *The Jew in American Cinema* (Bloomington: Indiana University Press, 1985), pp. 47, 61, 86, 97.

7. Sklare, *America's Jews*, p. 184.

8. Stuart Samuels, "The Evolutionary Image of the Jew in American Films," in *Ethnic Images in American Film and Television*, edited by Randall M. Miller (Philadelphia: The Balch Institute, 1978), pp. 25–26; Erens, *Jew in American Cinema*, pp. 33, 37–38, 81–96; Friedman, *Hollywood's Image of the Jew*, pp. 28–33, 43.

9. Robert L. Carringer, Introduction to *The Jazz Singer* (Madison: University of Wisconsin Press, 1979), pp. 11–25; Leonard Mosley, *Zanuck: The Rise and Fall of Hollywood's Last Tycoon* (Boston: Little, Brown, 1984), pp. 99–104.

10. Carringer, Introduction to *The Jazz Singer*, pp. 11–32; Alfred A. Cohn, scenario of *The Jazz Singer*, pp. 10, 79; Whitfield, *Voices of Jacob, Hands of Esau*, pp. 159–71.

11. Erens, *Jews in American Cinema*, p. 185.

12. Lary L. May and Elaine Tyler May, "Why Jewish Movie Moguls: An Exploration in American Culture," *American Jewish History*, 72 (September 1982), 6–25; Howe, *World of Our Fathers*, pp. 164–66; Kevin Starr, *Inventing the Dream: California Through the Progressive Era* (New York: Oxford University Press, 1985), pp. 311–16; Carlos Clarens, "Moguls—That's a Jewish Word," *Film Comment*, 17 (July–August, 1981), 34–36.

13. Ronald Haver, *David O. Selznick's Hollywood* (New York: Knopf, 1980), p. 73.

14. Starr, *Inventing the Dream*, p. 315.

15. David Aberbach, "The Mogul Who Loved Art," *Commentary*, 72 (September 1981), 70–71.

16. Lary May, *Screening Out the Past: The Birth of Mass Culture and the Motion Picture Industry* (New York: Oxford University Press, 1980), pp. 167–78; Norman L. Friedman, "Hollywood, the Jewish Experience, and Popular Culture," *Judaism*, 19 (Fall 1970), 482, 483–84, 487; Budd Schulberg, *Moving Pictures: Memories of a Hollywood Prince* (New York: Stein and Day, 1981), pp. 191, 232; Dore Schary, *Heyday: An Autobiography* (Boston: Little, Brown, 1979), pp. 152–53.

17. Gore Vidal, *Matters of Fact and Fiction: Essays, 1973–1976* (New York: Random House, 1977), p. 4.

18. Leo C. Rosten, *Hollywood: The Movie Colony, the Movie Makers* (New York: Harcourt, Brace, 1941), p. 178.

19. Budd Schulberg, *What Makes Sammy Run?* (New York: Modern Library, 1941, 1952), pp. 133–34.

20. Friedman, *Hollywood's Image of the Jew*, pp. 64, 74.

21. Erens, *Jew in American Cinema*, pp. 159–61.

22. Ibid., pp. 162–63; K. R. M. Short, "Hollywood Fights Anti-Semitism, 1940–45," in idem. (editor), *Film and Radio Propaganda in World War II* (Knoxville: University of Tennessee Press, 1983), pp. 148–49.

23. Henry Popkin, "The Vanishing Jew of Our Popular Culture," *Commentary*, 14 (July 1952), 50–55; Friedman, *Hollywood's Image of the Jew*, pp. 57, 84–85; Erens, *Jew in American Cinema*, pp. 135–36, 147, 149–52, 163.

24. Michael A. Anderegg, *David Lean* (Boston: Twayne, 1984), pp. 58–60.

25. Constance Webb, *Richard Wright: A Biography* (New York: G. P. Putnam's Sons, 1968), pp. 292–93.

26. Norman Zierold, *The Moguls* (New York: Avon, 1972), p. 198.

27. Hecht, *Child of the Century*, pp. 504–6.

28. James Agee, *Agee on Film* (New York: McDowell, Obolensky, 1958), pp. 269–70.

29. Erens, *Jew in American Cinema*, pp. 175–76, 178.

30. Schary, *Heyday*, pp. 152—53; Friedman, *Hollywood's Image of the Jew*, pp. 122–25; Erens, *Jew in American Cinema*, pp. 173–76; Peter Roffman and Jim Purdy, *The Hollywood Social Problem Film: Madness, Despair, and Politics from the Depression to the Fifties* (Bloomington: Indiana University Press, 1981), pp. 238–39.

31. Laura Z. Hobson, *Laura Z: A Life* (New York: Arbor House, 1983), pp. 10–12, 279–83, 317, 328–31, 335, 383–84, 395–96; Ruth R. Wisse, "Reading About Jews," *Commentary*, 69 (March 1980), 44.

32. Laura Z. Hobson, *Gentleman's Agreement* (New York: Simon and Schuster, 1947), pp. 212–13; Friedman, *Hollywood's Image of the Jew*, p. 128; Roffman and Purdy, *Hollywood Social Problem Film*, pp. 239–41.

33. John Mason Brown, "Seeing Things," *Saturday Review*, 30 (December 6, 1947), 71; *Shelley v. Kraemer*, 334 U. S. 1 (1948).

34. Dinnerstein, *Uneasy at Home*, pp. 187, 190, 192, 193–94.

35. Murray Kempton, "Natalie Wood: Is *This* the Girl Next Door?," *Show*, 2 (March 1962), 51.

36. Friedman, *Hollywood's Image of the Jew*, pp. 190–92; Erens, *Jew in American Cinema*, pp. 217–20; Otto Preminger, *Preminger: An Autobiography* (New York: Bantam, 1978), pp. 196–98, 200–1.

37. Dalton Trumbo to Ingo Preminger, January 2, 1960, in *Additional Dialogue: Letters of Dalton Trumbo, 1942–1962*, edited by Helen Manfull (New York: M. Evans, 1970), 529; Preminger, *Autobiography*, pp. 144–45, 199.

38. Quoted in John Skow, "Verdict on a Superstar," *Time*, 120 (December 6, 1982), 71.

39. Erens, *Jew in American Cinema*, pp. 217–20; Friedman, *Hollywood's Image of the Jew*, pp. 190–92; Alan Spiegel, "The Vanishing Act: A Typology of the Jew in Contemporary American Film," in Cohen (editor), *From Hester Street to Hollywood*, pp. 263–64.

40. Hirt-Manheimer, "From Jews to *Jaws:* A Chat with Richard Dreyfuss," 35.

41. Leslie A. Fiedler, *To the Gentiles* (New York: Stein and Day, 1972), p. 102; Spiegel, "The Vanishing Act," pp. 257–58.

42. Carroll Baker, *Baby Doll: An Autobiography* (New York: Arbor House, 1983), pp. 94–95.

43. Sammy Davis, Jr., and Jane and Burt Boyar, *Yes I Can* (New York: Farrar, Straus and Giroux, 1965), pp. 148–49, 194, 204–5, 209–13, 237–38, 246, 280–85, 314–15, 346, 380, 431–34, 457–58, 463, 545, 567, 591–92.

44. Michael Elkin, "A Jewish Renaissance Among Hollywood Stars?," *Baltimore Jewish Times*, November 20, 1987, pp. 64–65, 67.

45. Richard Corliss, "I Dream for a Living," *Time*, 126 (July 15, 1985), 54, 63; Fred A. Bernstein, *The Jewish Mothers' Hall of Fame* (Garden City, N. Y.: Doubleday, 1986), pp. 1–7; "Maker of Hit after Hit, Steven Spielberg is Also a Conglomerate," *Wall Street Journal*, February 9, 1987, pp. 1, 10.

46. Abraham Cahan, *Yekl and The Imported Bridegroom and Other Stories of the New York Ghetto* (New York: Dover, 1970), pp. 1–89.

47. Pauline Kael, *Going Steady* (New York: Bantam, 1971), p. 161; Barry Gross, "No Victim, She: Barbra Streisand and the Movie Jew," *Journal of Ethnic Studies*, 3 (Spring, 1975), 34–39.

48. Chaim Potok, "Barbra Streisand and Chaim Potok," *Esquire*, 98 (October 1982), 117–18, 120–21, 124, 126–27.

49. Isaac Bashevis Singer, *Short Friday and Other Stories* (New York: Farrar, Straus and Giroux, 1964), pp. 131–59.

50. Quoted in Jeffrey S. Gurock, "From Exception to Role Model: Bernard Drachman and the Evolution of Jewish Religious Life in America, 1880–1920," *American Jewish History*, 76 (June 1987), 463.

51. André Malraux, *Anti-Memoirs*, translated by Terence Kilmartin (New York: Holt, Rinehart and Winston, 1968), p. 24.

9. The Future as History

1. Wieseltier, "Culture and Collective Memory," *New York Times Book Review*, p. 9; Louis Ginzberg, *The Legends of the Jews* (Philadelphia: Jewish Publication Society of America, 1947), III, p. 97; Howard R. Greenstein, *Judaism—An Eternal Covenant* (Philadelphia: Fortress Press, 1983), pp. xiii–xv, 9–10, 107–8.

2. James B. Pritchard, *Ancient Near Eastern Texts* (Princeton, N. J.: Princeton University Press, 1955), pp. 376, 378; Simon Rawidowicz, "Israel: The Ever-Dying People," in *Studies in Jewish Thought*, edited by Nahum N. Glatzer (Philadelphia: Jewish Publication Society of America, 1974), p. 221.

3. Elliott Oring, *The Jokes of Sigmund Freud: A Study in Humor and Jewish Identity* (Philadelphia: University of Pennsylvania Press, 1984), pp. 63–64; Sigmund Freud, *The Standard Edition of Freud's Complete Psychological Works*, translated and edited by James Strachey (London: Hogarth Press, 1955), XIII, p. xv.

4. Quoted in Abram Leon Sachar, *A History of the Jews* (New York: Knopf, 1935), p. 193.

5. Arthur Hertzberg, *The French Enlightenment and the Jews* (New York: Columbia University Press, 1968), pp. 300–2, 306–7, 312, 363–64.

6. Hertzberg, *Being Jewish in America*, pp. 39–40.

7. Marc Bloch, "Testamentary Instructions," in *Strange Defeat: A Statement of Evidence Written in 1940* (New York: W. W. Norton, 1968), pp. 177–78; H. Stuart Hughes, *The Obstructed Path: French Social Thought in the Years of Desperation, 1930–1960* (New York: Harper and Row, 1968), pp. 48–52.

8. Franz Kafka, *Letter to His Father*, translated by Ernst Kaiser and Eithne Wilkins (New York: Schocken, 1966), pp. 79–81.

9. Quoted in Lewis S. Feuer, *Ideology and the Ideologists* (New York: Harper and Row, 1976), pp. 140–48.

10. Werner L. Gundesheimer, "Genocide and Utopia," *Jerusalem Quarterly*, 26 (Winter 1982), 31.

11. Quoted in Jacob B. Agus, *Jewish Identity in an Age of Ideologies* (New York: Frederick Ungar, 1978), pp. 167–68.

12. Quoted in Sachar, *Course of Modern Jewish History*, p. 246; Conrad, *Under Western Eyes*, p. viii.

13. Lucy S. Dawidowicz, *The War Against the Jews, 1933–1945* (New York: Bantam, 1976), pp. 40–41; Lagarde quoted in Fritz Stern, *The Politics of Cultural Despair: A Study in the Rise of the Germanic Ideology* (Berkeley: University of California Press, 1961), p. 63n.

14. Raul Hilberg, *The Destruction of the European Jews* (Chicago: Quadrangle, 1961), pp. 3–4.

15. Quoted in Eberhard Jäckel, *Hitler's Weltanschauung: A Blueprint for Power*, translated by Herbert Arnold (Middletown, Conn.: Wesleyan University Press, 1972), pp. 54, 60–65; Robert G. L. Waite, *The Psychopathic God: Adolf Hitler* (New York: Basic Books, 1977), pp. 370–72.

16. Oswald Spengler, *The Decline of the West,* translated by Charles Francis Atkinson (New York: Knopf, 1928), II, pp. 316–23; Liptzin, *Germany's Stepchildren,* pp. 162–64; H. Stuart Hughes, *Oswald Spengler: A Critical Estimate* (New York: Scribner's 1962), pp. 125–26.

17. Arnold J. Toynbee, *A Study of History* (New York: Oxford University Press, 1939), IV, p. 262; Walter Kaufmann, *From Shakespeare to Existentialism* (Garden City, N. Y.: Doubleday Anchor, 1960), pp. 392–95, 400–2, 404, 413–14; Maurice Samuel, *The Professor and the Fossil* (New York: Knopf, 1956), pp. 18–22, 68–71, 74, 107–8, 148–50.

18. Ben Halpern, *The American Jew: A Zionist Analysis* (New York: Schocken, 1983), pp. 12–30; Yehoshua Arieli, *Individualism and Nationalism in American Ideology* (Baltimore: Penguin, 1966), pp. 71–75.

19. Varnhagen quoted in S. S. Prawer, *Heine's Jewish Comedy* (New York: Oxford University Press, 1983), p. 401; Arthur Koestler, "The Vital Choice," in Villiers (editor), *Next Year in Jerusalem,* pp. 98–105.

20. Norman Podhoretz, *Doings and Undoings: The Fifties and After in American Writing* (New York: Farrar, Straus, 1964), pp. 369–70; idem, *Breaking Ranks: A Political Memoir* (New York: Harper and Row, 1979), pp. 130–34.

21. Herman Wouk, *This is My God* (Garden City, N. Y.: Doubleday, 1959), pp. 251–57, 281–82.

22. Thomas B. Morgan, "The Vanishing American Jew," *Look,* 28 (May 5, 1964), 42–46.

23. Thomas Sowell, *Markets and Minorities* (New York: Basic Books, 1981), pp. 10–11.

24. Chaim I. Waxman, *America's Jews in Transition* (Philadelphia: Temple University Press, 1983), pp. 136–37, 139–40, 166–78, 187–88; Calvin Goldscheider and Alan S. Zuckerman, *The Transformation of the Jews* (Chicago: University of Chicago Press, 1984), pp. 173–74, 176–81.

25. Elihu Bergman, "The American Jewish Population Erosion," *Midstream,* 23 (October 1977), 9–19.

26. Martin Siegel, *Amen: The Diary of Rabbi Martin Siegel,* edited by Mel Ziegler (New York: World, 1971), p. 15; Leon A. Jick, *In Search of a Way* (Mount Vernon, N. Y.: Temple Books, 1966), p. 84.

27. Joseph Berger, "For Yiddish, a New but Smaller Domain," *New York Times,* October 11, 1987, p. E9.

28. Tobin, "We Are Many, We Are One," p. 18.

29. Sklare, *America's Jews,* pp. 180–209; Singer, "Living with Intermarriage," in Sklare (editor), *American Jews: A Reader,* pp. 395–409.

30. Liebman, *The Ambivalent American Jew,* p. viii; Hillel Halkin, *Letters to an American Jewish Friend* (Philadelphia: Jewish Publication Society of America, 1977), pp. 32–37, 41–42, 112.

31. Quoted in Morgan, *On Becoming American,* pp. 263–64.

32. Ernest Hemingway, *Death in the Afternoon* (New York: Scribner's 1932), p. 122.

33. Quoted in Howard M. Sachar, *A History of Israel* (New York: Knopf, 1982), pp. 633–34, 642–43; Waxman, *America's Jews in Transition,* p. 112.

34. Anne Frank, *The Diary of a Young Girl,* translated by B. M. Mooyaart (Garden City, N. Y.: Doubleday, 1967), p. 217; R. Peter Straus, "His Daughter's Father: Otto Frank," *Moment,* 3 (December 1977), 28; Ernst Schnabel, *Anne Frank: A Portrait in Courage* (New York: Harcourt, Brace, 1958), p. 192.

35. Shenker, *Coat of Many Colors,* pp. 41–43; Moshe Kohn, "The Yeshiva Books," *Jerusalem Post Magazine,* February 3, 1984, p. 4.

36. Silberman, *A Certain People,* pp. 299, 318; Geoffrey Wigoder, "An Optimistic Approach," *Jerusalem Post Magazine,* May 4, 1984, p. 17.

37. Rawidowicz, *Studies in Jewish Thought,* pp. 210–17.

38. Ibid., pp. 217–18; Lucy S. Dawidowicz, *The Jewish Presence* (New York: Harcourt Brace Jovanovich, 1978), pp. 29–30; Judah Leib Gordon, "For Whom Do I Toil?," in *The Jew in the Modern World: A Documentary History,* edited by Paul R. Mendes-Flohr and Jehuda Reinharz (New York: Oxford University Press, 1980), p. 315.

39. Scholem, *The Messianic Idea in Judaism,* pp. 305–7.

40. Rawidowicz, *Studies in Jewish Thought,* pp. 219–23.

41. Alfred Kazin, *New York Jew* (New York: Knopf, 1978), p. 290.

Index of Names